WOMEN AND MINISTRY

CROSSWAY BOOKS BY DAN DORIANI

The Life of a God-Made Man
Women and Ministry

WOMEN AND MINISTRY

What The Bible Teaches

DAN DORIANI

CROSSWAY BOOKS

A DIVISION OF
GOOD NEWS PUBLISHERS
WHEATON, ILLINOIS

Women and Ministry

Copyright © 2003 by Dan Doriani

Published by Crossway Books
        a division of Good News Publishers
        1300 Crescent Street
        Wheaton, Illinois 60187

Cover design: David LaPlaca

Cover photo: Getty Images

First printing 2003

Printed in the United States of America

Library of Congress Cataloging-in-Publication Data
Doriani, Daniel M., 1953-
    Women and ministry : what the Bible teaches / Dan Doriani.
        p. cm.
    Includes bibliographical references.
    ISBN 1-58134-385-X
    1. Women clergy—Biblical teaching. 2. Pastoral theology—Biblical teaching. 3. Bible—Criticism, interpretation, etc. I. Title.
BV676.D67   2003
262'.14'082—dc21   2002152754

ML		13	12	11	10	09	08	07	06	05	04	03
15	14	13	12	11	10	9	8	7	6	5	4	3	2	1

CONTENTS

PREFACE

EXPERIENCES AND CONVICTIONS

With this preface I invite my readers to enter a controversy. Readers will naturally want to judge if they can trust the author who hopes to guide them through complex, emotionally charged issues. Is he a polemicist or a peacemaker? What are his formative experiences? What are his biases and convictions? Are these biases and convictions likely to lead to truth or to confusion? These questions deserve answers.

First then, I hope to make peace not war. Indeed, I am a reluctant combatant in this campaign. My doctoral dissertation lightly touched upon the gender debate; that touch has led to a series of invitations to speak and write on the topic over the years. I did not choose this topic; it chose me.

Now that the gender debate has chosen me, I engage it hoping to bless the spiritually gifted women in my life. My female students at Covenant Seminary are the most obvious group. Gifted and energetic, they seek to serve where God appoints. But I cannot forget the women in my family: my wife, my mother, and my daughters. My wife does not aspire to teach or to lead, but with her musical gifts and her hospitality, she has much to offer the church. My mother, whom I love and admire, is a seminary graduate. Ordained in midlife in 1974, she is the semi-retired pastor of a small semi-rural church. My daughters are twenty, eighteen, and fourteen years old as I write. Each bears signs of leadership and speaking gifts, making me acutely aware that I advance views that affect them.

As for my theological convictions, I leave you, gentle reader, to judge if they will lead you toward the truth or away from it. As an evangelical and a Presbyterian, I am committed to the authority of Scripture and to Reformed theology. I generally call church leaders "elders" and "deacons" rather than bishops, boards, trustees, or consistories. My goal is not to promote the Presbyterian system but to reflect the language of the New Testament, which typically calls church leaders "elders," "overseers," and "deacons." Readers can adjust my language to fit their church's organization.

Finally, while I ascribe supreme authority to the Bible, I believe history, reason, science, and human experience can play a subsidiary role in illumining our discussions. Specifically, while I affirm that men and women have equal value and dignity, scientific studies progressively uncover gender differences that go beyond reproduction. Evidence keeps accumulating that, as feminist scholar Carol Gilligan said, women speak "in a different voice." Historical and cultural studies also illumine our work. Such studies show that our culture treasures freedom more than order. So when I say God establishes an order that puts men in charge of some strategic tasks, I know I both violate the sensibilities of the dominant culture and quench the aspirations of certain women.

It tests our faith when biblical injunctions clash with our inclinations. The Lord says he gives his commands for our good. The benefits are often obvious. When God prohibits murder, adultery, theft, and falsehood, he protects us from sin's self-inflicted wounds. Yet some laws offend us—especially laws that snuff out secret hopes. When that happens, the question is not, "Do we like this command?" but "Is it God's will?" Without shelving our will and reason, there are times when we must simply listen to God's Word and obey it.

OVERVIEW

I will argue that God decreed that kings, priests, judges, and elders should lead Israel and that apostles, elders, and deacons should lead the church. Pure democracy, where everyone is a candidate for every office and the majority rules, does not appear to be God's plan. Chapter 1 sets the tone for the study. Chapter 2 seeks patterns in the ministries of women in biblical history. Chapter 3 examines the roles of women in Jesus' ministry. Chapter 4 considers foundational texts for male-female relations from Genesis and Ephesians. Chapters 5 and 6 study central passages on women and ministry, 1 Corinthians

11 and 1 Timothy 2. This plan does not cover every issue or text, but it says enough to support the practical chapters. Chapter 7 presents a theology of gifts and calling, and chapter 8 offers concrete advice for the ministries of women. To keep the book as readable as possible, I limited my comments on the complexities of the gender debate to the footnotes for chapters 1 to 8 and to the advanced studies found in Part Two. Chapter 9 explains how and why Christians disagree about this topic, comparing the methods of feminists and traditionalists. Chapter 10 presents a brief history of women in ministry. The appendices present some technical studies.

THANKS AND DEDICATION

I thank my colleagues on the faculty of Covenant Theological Seminary for reviewing chapter drafts. Student questions, criticisms, and suggestions also greatly strengthened this book. I thank the board of Covenant for granting me a sabbatical in the spring of 2002 to complete this project, which began as a series of lectures sponsored by the Francis Schaeffer Institute. David Speakman deserves special commendation for his faithful research assistance.

I bless my wife, Debbie, who models excellence both in traditional female tasks of feeding the hungry and visiting the sick, and in the public work of teaching music. I dedicate this book to my three wonderful daughters—Abigail, Sarah, and Beth—who play as hard and reason as analytically as any boy but who know a woman need not be mannish to be great.

Part One

1

INTRODUCTION TO
THE CALLINGS OF WOMEN

As THE SPEAKER STROLLED to the podium, my friend leaned over and whispered, "You know he and his wife do conferences together sometimes; they say her sections are better attended when people have a choice." So it goes. Some wives are better speakers than their husbands, some pastors beget daughters who are more talented than their sons, and some female secretaries seem to hold whole churches together. Do these facts prove that God has gifted women to teach and lead?

That is a question traditional churches need to answer even if they would rather avoid it. To be candid, I would prefer to avoid it, too. I never meant to write this book. But the topic has pursued me since a tangent from my dissertation led to a talk or two, then an article or two, and then an invitation from the Francis Schaeffer Institute to deliver lectures presenting a biblical theology of women's ministry.

While I drifted toward academic expertise on the subject, my mother became an ordained minister, and my wife and I became the parents of three daughters and no sons. Experience informs this book, but it owes more to the Schaeffer lectures where women and men of every conviction, race, and educational background listened, laughed, and respected each other through potentially contentious lectures and discussions. It is no easier to capture the spirit of a lecture on a page than it is to capture the spirit of a book on film, but we felt we stumbled onto one thing at least: the need for a short, sweet case for a version of the traditional view of women's roles in the church. That is what this book aims to be.

This book, therefore, is for women who have heard that the Bible appoints men to lead the church; now these women have a few questions. Does the Bible really say that? If so, why? Does the prohibition belong to the class of rules that no longer applies today, like laws about animal sacrifices and head coverings? If Scripture does forbid women to preach, does that devalue them? If so, how can contemporary people, who know women have the same value and abilities as men, accept the Bible as true?

This book is for women in ministry, for female seminary students, for businesswomen, for secretaries, doctors, teachers, psychologists, administrators, wives, and mothers who know their worth and wonder how the Bible can say no to women's spiritual ambitions. It is for my teenage daughters and their friends who will soon face these questions. It is for strong women who have great aspirations but wonder if greatness means doing everything a man does. And it is for men who want to respect women and encourage the best use of their gifts.

This book is for leaders of traditional churches who struggle with their official position and think their denomination stuck them with a stance they don't fully understand or accept. They wish the issue would go away. They let women do almost anything if it doesn't cause trouble with the hierarchy. This book is also for congregations that view themselves as the last bastions of conservative orthodoxy and restrict women's service to a tiny knot of activities centered on kitchen and nursery. It is for churches that hardly notice the range of women's ministries in Scripture.

God loves women enough to send his Son to live and die and live again for them, but what does that mean for the ministries of women? I believe God ordained men to preach, to teach doctrine with authority, and to oversee the church. I also believe the Spirit has gifted women for ministry and wants women to serve in many spheres, whether alone or beside men, as peers. Some people say this puts women in a box, but let me modify the metaphor and say it puts them in a car.

Cars are like boxes in some ways. While driving, we must remain within the confinement of their doors. But cars can be roomy and comfortable, with gadgets and hidden compartments to explore. More important, they have wheels and take people places. The church is a roomy vehicle, filled with a family on a journey. The doors and speed limits set boundaries, but the family accepts these restrictions because these make the trip possible and safe. On the journey, father may do most of the driving, but mother drives too, and both parents navigate, tell stories, and help the children have a good time.

The church is like a car. Safe travel occurs within the parameters set by our nature and God's Word. We are going somewhere, and the relationships built during travel can be as sweet as the destination. Pastors must steer a large car and keep an oft-contentious family unified as they travel. I hope to help pastors in two ways. First, I have kept the heart of the book short enough that readers may complete it before the binding rots off. Second, to help women enter the ministries God appoints, I propose various ministries for women, while affirming that God calls men to preach and oversee the church.

The controversial nature of the issue leaves me a reluctant writer. This topic is broad and complicated enough that sincere people disagree sharply even when they share similar mind-sets. The biblical data are complicated, demanding sophisticated interpretive skills. The issues also stir strong emotions. I will never forget the public debate where an accuser declared that I cannot legitimately claim to love my wife, daughters, or female friends since my views oppress women.

To promote calm, let me note that I use the term "feminist" descriptively, not pejoratively. "Egalitarian" and "feminist" both describe those who believe women and men should have identical roles in the church. "Traditionalist" and "complementarian" both describe those who believe women and men should have complementary roles.

But even if we stayed calm and agreed on every biblical and theological question, challenges would remain. We would need Solomonic wisdom to put our principles into practice. Consider a point as trivial as church ushers.

USHERS, RULES, AND RELATIONSHIPS

A few years ago, I noticed something odd. Most conservative churches have female greeters, but almost none have female ushers.

This seemed amazing, for I could not imagine why the possession of a Y chromosome was a prerequisite for handing out bulletins and taking collections. An argument for male ushers might go like this: 1) Ushers facilitate worship, which is a task of spiritual leadership; 2) Ushers' high visibility gives the appearance that they are church leaders; 3) Ushering is one of a few tasks where men can perform small but meaningful service at church.

But the arguments for female ushers are stronger: 1) To prohibit women from ushering is gratuitous legalism. Whatever the appearance may be, ushers perform no spiritually sensitive duties. The post should be open to all. 2) Ushers offer a welcome, and female visitors may feel more welcome if women are visible among the church's ushers. Imagine a recently divorced woman visiting a church and seeing a phalanx of large men in dark suits at the door with nary a woman in sight. To ban female ushers is to erect needless barriers.

If I were a pastor again, I would want to use both men and women as ushers. Yet if the church were already dealing with several controversies, I might keep it to myself. In my opinion, the belief that males must usher is almost silly. But changes of custom can cause controversy, and pastors must pursue peace. If the cost of controversy outweighed the benefit of a better welcome for female visitors, the wise pastor would wait for a better time to change the policy. In church leadership, wisdom and sensitivity are nearly as important as doctrinal rectitude.

Not everyone grasps this point. Occasionally someone calls or writes to me seeking ecclesiastical rulings about women's ministries. "Just tell me," they say, "are the following acts legal or illegal: May a woman preach? May women teach men in Sunday school? May women pray or read Scripture in worship? May they serve on the boards of churches and Christian schools?" We need biblical data, but the "just tell me" mentality is misguided. It forgets two things.

First, good relationships ease all processes. When people love and respect each other, they clear misunderstandings and solve problems more rapidly. If we think only of rules that permit this and forbid that, we forget that we can get every rule right and still see church life go wrong. Indeed, if we think knowledge of the rules can thwart all errors, we have already erred. If we master the rules for gender roles but apply them in loveless, legalistic ways, we mistreat people. On the other hand, if we misconstrue a minor rule but listen, serve, love, and encourage women and men, the church will probably remain quite healthy. To apply the Bible successfully, we need a good heart, not just good answers.

Second, since every church has its own history and level of maturity, the application of biblical principles for women in ministry will vary from place to place. No one knows enough to dictate details of organization for unfamiliar churches. Local leaders should not depend on distant experts to set every ministry structure. Local leaders must know their people and their times. Rulings can become outdated, not because biblical truth changes, but because cultures change. As a culture moves, people ask new questions and challenge biblical teaching in novel ways. The truth does not change, but what we say to our culture does, since we must correct the errors of our generation, not generations past. When people rely on others to tell them exactly what to do, the faculty of discernment atrophies. Therefore, this book presents biblical teachings and general principles for church life. It illustrates those principles with some concrete ideas. But it avoids detailed rulings.

THE IMPORTANCE OF THE TASK

The controversy over gender roles makes me an uneasy writer, but the importance of the topic makes me willing. Many feminists, from university professors to government officials, ascribe gender differences, beyond reproduction and lactation, to social influences. They say patriarchal cultures pressure women to achieve less and to nurture rather than compete. Even if women say they want to bear children and stay at home to care for them, some feminists will not take the statement at face value, since they believe society taught the women to say such things. In fact, radicals say, the more men and women are alike, the better off women are. If women achieve and compete as men do, they will be free and fulfilled.

But even secular analysts debate these points. Beth Bailey recounts the shift toward egalitarianism in dating and sex in *From*

Front Porch to Back Seat: Courtship in Twentieth-Century America.
Wendy Shalit argues that the results have been disastrous for women
in *Return to Modesty.* In the natural sciences, the evidence accumulates that the neurobiology and biochemistry—the brains and the
hormones—of men and women, boys and girls, are quite different.
Michael Gurian's twin books, *The Wonder of Girls* and *The Wonder of
Boys,* written to help parents raise girls and boys, shows that the differences between boys and girls have a basis in nature or biology.
Neurological and hormonal forces lie behind the male drive to work,
achieve, compete, and gain independence. The same forces lie behind
the "intimacy imperative," the female quest for a web of safe, inti-
mate, long-lasting relationships. It is dangerous to generalize, but it
seems that intimacy is more likely to be a woman's highest goal,
whereas achievement is more likely to be a man's.[1]

Anyone who has coached male and female athletes can testify to
these differences. In boys' teams, losing causes tension and winning
heals rifts. Girls compete vigorously, but on girls' teams, a string of
defeats may hardly be upsetting if everyone is working together and
encouraging one another.

These are generalizations, of course. Particular women are more
competitive, independent, and analytical than particular men. But if
we compare men and women globally, the differences are clear. Yet we
must not exaggerate, because men and women are more similar than
dissimilar. We are not from different planets—Venus and Mars. We
are not different species. Both men and women bear God's image. He
created us together to crown creation and govern it for him. Further,
some male-female differences may be a result of sin, not God's design.
God made both men and women for relationships and for accountable dominion over his world.

But God designed women, not men, to bear and nurse children. He
implanted in women a stronger biological response to the tears of
infants and children. And, I believe, the Lord is wise and loving enough
to shape the minds and hearts of women so they would take pleasure
in the role of giving and organizing life. At the age of twenty-two, Anna
Grigoryevna married a forty-two-year-old who was a convict, an epilep-
tic, a pathological gambler, and perhaps the greatest novelist who ever

lived, Fyodor Dostoyevsky. She was his stenographer, financial manager, and protector. She persuaded him to stop gambling. She gave him and herself happiness. Is that not a good life, too?[2]

There might be a hint that women are more relational than men in Genesis 2 when God creates Eve to be Adam's companion. There seems to be another hint after the Fall when the punishment on man and woman diverges. Each feels God's displeasure in what is dearest. The man faces it at work as God curses the ground so that it bears thorns and thistles. The woman faces it in relationships as she has a desire for her husband, but he rules over her.

THE CHURCH'S RESPONSIBILITY

Some deny that the Bible teaches such things. Others agree that it does and reject what it says. But that is hardly new. People have always taken offense at biblical teachings; Scripture always provokes reactions. No person or culture perfectly conforms to biblical truth. Therefore, the Bible confronts every person and society. Few like correction, especially when it challenges what is familiar. Most understand gender according to the customs of their day. Their customs seem obvious, even sacred. The tenets of commonsense feminism are old and widespread enough that they seem beyond question in our culture. And many people would rather condemn the Bible than entertain the idea that their culture is in error.[3]

But Christian leaders must hold fast to the truth precisely when it is least popular, when it most violates the sensibility of the age. If we call ourselves God's servants, we must follow his Word, as we understand it, however difficult that may be.

The prophets and apostles knew this. Isaiah decried the Israelites who "say to the seers, 'See no more visions,' and to the prophets, 'Give us no more visions of what is right. Tell us pleasant things. Prophecy illusions. . . . Stop confronting us with the Holy One of Israel'" (Isa. 30:10-11). People want a comfortable religion. But God chooses to make people feel uncomfortable, temporarily, so they can find genuine comfort, permanently.

The apostle John experienced the same thing in a vision recorded in Revelation 10:9-11. An angel gave John a small scroll and told him,

"Take it and eat it. It will turn your stomach sour but in your mouth it will be as sweet as honey." Indeed, the scroll was sweet in his mouth but sour in his stomach. Then the angel said, "You must prophesy again about many peoples, nations, languages and kings." The vision suggests that the Word of God always tastes sweet to believers. Even a prophecy of judgment has a certain sweetness because our Lord is just, and we rejoice when he displays his justice, even in judging evil. Yet, when the time comes to prophesy against the nations, the Word becomes sour if they resist the message. John and Isaiah understood that it would be a cruel kindness to hide the truth that mankind is liable to judgment. Therefore, they described God's judgment and the way of escape from it.

Christian leaders sometimes fail to see this. When asked to address a difficult question, we try to avoid it. We say the issue is complicated, that it is unimportant, that it would take too long to explain, that we are still studying it. We may justify our silence by telling ourselves we don't want to upset anyone and drive them away from the church over a trivial point.

Maybe. But what should we say about leaders who detect a spiritual problem and refuse to state the diagnosis or offer the cure? My colleague Jerram Barrs once observed that if a woman with feminist sympathies visits a church with male leaders, she will naturally ask the pastor about his view of women teaching and leading. Pastors often avoid the question, saying, "This is our denomination's view," and little more. This approach fails both pastorally and pragmatically.

Pastorally, the decision to pass the buck to the denomination may have three sources: weak faith, spiritual cowardice, or culpable ignorance. "Weak faith" means a pastor knows the reasons for male leadership but lacks confidence in their persuasive power, and so he keeps them to himself. "Spiritual cowardice" means the pastor secretly disagrees with his denomination but fears the consequences of stating his views. "Culpable ignorance" means the pastor genuinely does not know why women do not preach in his church. He trusts the hierarchy when he ought to have his own answers to the questions of the day.

The strategy of passing responsibility to others also fails pragmatically. The pastor who sheds responsibility for his church's practices chooses the wrong mechanism for peace. He hopes to find peace by saying nothing offensive. But he implies that the visitor should not take the issue too seriously. After all, not even the pastor thinks about it much! But this is unsatisfactory in every way. First, the woman evidently takes it seriously, or she would not have inquired about it. Second, the pastor is confessing his weakness, saying, "We have a practice that is offensive to many people; yet we persist in it without much conviction because we are half loyal to a distant body that tells us what to do." Is it any wonder if women who hear no answers to legitimate questions fail to return?

A pastor's desire to seem reasonable and avoid controversy can be almost overwhelming. But there are dangers in worrying too much about other people's opinions. Leaders ought to try to establish rapport with their audiences, but there is only One we must please. If pastors say things the human audience dislikes, it is unfortunate. But if we say things God dislikes, it is more than unfortunate. We cannot control the way people respond to us, but we can discharge our duties.

When leaders fail to speak, it also harms mankind, since God declares that his commands bless those who obey them. The Lord tells Israel to walk in his ways, love him, and observe the "commands and decrees that I am giving you today *for your own good*" (Deut. 10:12-13, my emphasis). God's commands are good for his people. Old Testament law shaped Israel to be "the kind of society God wants." God redeemed Israel, in part, to make the blessings of obedience visible to the nations. When Israel lived in justice and love, she became a light to the nations.[4] When Israel followed God's laws, she would "show [her] wisdom and understanding to the nations, who will . . . say, 'Surely this . . . is a wise and understanding people'" (Deut. 4:6).

FLAWED CHURCH LIFE

Of course, we can show God's wisdom only if we follow it. Sadly, we do not always do so. Indeed, our errors in ecclesiastical practice complicate discussions of gender roles. Many churches choose their leaders using godless secular standards. They organize their affairs according to local traditions with only faint connection to Scripture. They train their leaders to perpetuate flawed patterns. They elect elders and deacons because they are successful businessmen or professionals. They choose men with nice social skills, nice clothes, and nice families. They neglect spiritual maturity and proven ability to teach and serve. They require the wrong duties of leaders—attending a monthly decision-making meeting but not teaching or overseeing the church. These practices damage the health of the church and undermine the traditional view of gender roles.

If elders [or deacons] are merely successful professionals who have pleasant personalities and give policy advice at monthly church meetings, why can't a woman be an elder? After all, Abigail, Deborah, and Huldah gave good advice on spiritual issues.

If elders [or deacons] need only *know* doctrine but need not teach it, why can't a woman be an elder? After all, Priscilla knew doctrine well enough to correct Apollos privately.

If elders don't oversee the church, why must they distribute the elements at communion? They are supposed to distribute the elements, in part, because they know who is under church discipline and who has never professed faith. But if elders don't know the spiritual condition of the people, why not let anyone serve?

If deacons [or trustees] merely watch over the church property and collect and disburse funds, why can't a woman be a deacon?

CONCLUSION

Our goal is to follow Scripture wherever it leads, both intellectually and practically. It would be naïve to think that we can simply turn to Scripture and start reading with an open mind. We bring preferences to our reading. Still, we can seek openness and receptivity so that the text has its say, and follow where it leads. If we adopt the right methods and have the right desire—to let God's Word affect us—then we can partially transcend our prejudices. If we acknowledge that Scripture is independent of us and precedes us, it can change us.[5]

2

THE MINISTRIES OF WOMEN IN BIBLICAL HISTORY: A SURVEY

A PRELIMINARY IMPRESSION

If we survey the Bible, seeking a general impression of the roles of men and women, we see that God appoints men to most leadership positions. The law said Israel's priests were supposed to be male—the sons, not the daughters, of Aaron (Exod. 29:30). All monarchs were supposed to be male (Deut. 17:14-20). In fact the sons of Aaron were priests, and the sons of David were monarchs (e.g., 2 Sam. 7:12-16). Israel had just one female monarch, Queen Athaliah. But she usurped the throne, murdered her rivals, and dedicated her reign to pagan deities (2 Kings 11).

In the New Testament, the twelve apostles Jesus chose were all male (Matt. 10:2-4). Paul assumed that all elders were male (1 Tim. 3:1-7). The first missionaries and church planters in Acts were all male. All of the traveling companions Paul mentioned in his letters were male: Barnabas, Silas, Luke, Timothy, Titus, John Mark, Epaphras, and Epaphroditus, among others.

But if we perform a second, more careful survey, the picture is not so monolithic. The great majority of prophets and judges were male, but some were women. We remember Deborah the judge (Judg. 4—5) and Huldah the prophetess (1 Kings 22:14-20). Looking deeper, we see an array of women's activities. Women prophesied in public (1 Cor. 11:5) and instructed leaders such as Apollos in private (Acts 18). Paul praised women for their invaluable assistance as he planted churches. Euodia and Syntyche contended at his side in the cause of the gospel (Phil. 4:2-3). He lauded Mary, Junias, Tryphena, Tryphosa, and Persis for their singular aid (Rom. 16:6-13). He also commended women for teaching children (2 Tim. 1:5) and urged older women to instruct younger women (Titus 2:3-4).

Our preliminary impression, our first estimate of the data of Scripture is this: *In Israel and the church, women do all sorts of things, but not everything.* Women take leadership positions, but they do so occasionally, not regularly. Women occasionally serve as judges or prophetesses. They often help establish churches, but they are not monarchs or apostles.

We must discover if this impression should be corrected or refined. We must also define "leadership positions" more precisely. We need not cite everything women do in Scripture, but we will make a list extensive enough to reveal the patterns of women's activities. By analyzing those patterns, we can discern what God ordains and what he does not. Then we can either verify or alter that first impression: Women do many things, but not everything.[1]

WOMEN SERVED AS PROPHETESSES

In Exodus 15, we meet *Miriam*, the first prophetess of the Old Testament. Miriam, the sister of Moses and Aaron, appeared at a high point in Israel's history. After Israel suffered centuries of oppression and a terrible conflict with Pharaoh, God led his people out of Egypt through Moses. When he guaranteed their safety by drowning an Egyptian army in the Red Sea (Exod. 14), Moses led the people in a song of praise to God (15:1-3):

> "'I will sing to the LORD / for he is highly exalted.
> The horse and its rider / he has hurled into the sea.'"

Later in the chapter (15:20-21), we learn that Miriam helped lead the women in their celebration: "Then Miriam the prophetess, Aaron's sister, took a tambourine in her hand, and all the women followed her, with tambourines and dancing. Miriam sang to them:

"'Sing to the LORD / for he is highly exalted.
The horse and its rider / he has hurled into the sea.'"

Miriam's words were virtually identical to Moses' words; her purpose was the same as his. Both led Israel in praise to God. Both helped the people respond aright to a great event in Israel's history. Moses led both the victory and its celebration. Miriam stood beside her brother, leading the women in celebration and praise; so her restatement of Moses' inspired speech became part of Scripture, too.

When Miriam supported Moses this way, she was effective and blessed. Later Numbers 12 says that Miriam and Aaron spoke against their brother Moses, asking, "Has the LORD spoken only through Moses? . . . Hasn't he also spoken through us?" (Num. 12:2). Miriam apparently led this small revolt, and God put her in her place, rebuking her verbally and striking her with leprosy for a week, so that she was sent out of the camp for seven days (12:4-15).

Huldah, a second prophetess, appeared at a low point in covenant history, during the reign of King Josiah (2 Kings 22:8-20). Josiah ordered repairs to the temple after it had suffered decades of abuse and neglect. Josiah's wicked grandfather Manasseh had defiled the temple for fifty-five years, and Josiah's father Amon did evil for two more. Amon was so wicked his own officials killed him and installed his son Josiah, just eight years old, on the throne (2 Kings 21:1-24). Josiah was a godly king, but as a child he did little to reverse the sins of his father and grandfather. Then in the eighteenth year of his reign, Josiah ordered a reform and restoration of the temple (22:1-7).

For more than fifty years, pagan worship had filled the temple. Israel had ignored the prophets and the law, which had conveniently disappeared. But as the temple repairs proceeded, Hilkiah the high priest discovered among the discards "the book of the law," that is, Deuteronomy (Deut. 22:8).[2] Hilkiah delivered it to the king's secretary Shaphan, who read it to the king. As he listened, Josiah became so dismayed at Israel's sins against this law that he tore his robes. He said, "Go and inquire of the LORD for me and for the people. . . . [For] great is the LORD's anger . . . because our fathers have not obeyed the words of this book" (2 Kings 22:9-13). Josiah surmised that the law that condemned Israel's misdeeds also threatened God's judgment. Still, he sought the assessment of a prophet, or rather, a prophetess, named Huldah.

This incident occurred during the fifth year of the ministry of the prophet Jeremiah (compare Jer. 1:2 and 2 Kings 22:3). Further, though we have no precise dates, the prophet Zephaniah was also active around this time (Zeph. 1:1). Nonetheless, Hilkiah and other royal officials sought Huldah to hear the Lord's assessment (2 Kings 22:14).

This choice puzzles some people. If Jeremiah and perhaps Zephaniah were available, why would the officials consult a woman? They speculate: Perhaps Jeremiah was quite young and hardly known. Huldah's husband was a royal official (22:14); so perhaps the officials already knew and trusted her. Perhaps Huldah was one of the prophets who had already declared God's judgment on the sins of Manasseh. If so, then perhaps she would know if repentance could reverse God's judgment (2 Kings 21:10-15). Perhaps, some even guess, Jeremiah was out of town.

These are mere speculations. Clearly, however, the king's officials consulted Huldah, who declared God's word. Israel would suffer punishment for her decades of sin "according to everything written in the book" (22:16-17). Yet, because Josiah humbled himself and wept in penitence, judgment would not befall Israel during his reign (22:18-20).

Notice the outline of this event. When he discovered the law, the high priest took the initiative (22:8ff.). The king led the preliminary response (22:12ff.). The king also made the final decision regarding a course of action (23:1ff.). Yet the king and his officials genuinely consulted Huldah. She had a real influence over the course of events. She neither initiated the action nor determined the action, but she did influence the action.

We see, therefore, that both at a high point and a low point in Old Testament history, a prophetess rose to interpret events and to lead Israel's response to it.

Although she was a queen, not a prophetess, *Esther* resembles Huldah, for she, too, persuaded a king to take proper action. Her king was the pagan Ahasuerus, but she presented the truth wisely, to move him to do justice and preserve Israel in a desperate hour (Est. 4—8).

The ministry of *Anna* the prophetess resembles that of Huldah and Miriam, too. Anna was with Simeon when Mary and Joseph presented Jesus in the temple. Luke links Anna with Simeon, a just and devout man who awaited God's salvation. When Mary and Joseph brought Jesus to the temple, the Spirit guided Simeon to meet them. He took Jesus in his arms and prophesied over him. This child, said Simeon, will be "a light for revelation to the Gentiles and for glory to your people Israel" (Luke 2:32). Jesus "will cause the falling and rising of many in Israel . . . the thoughts of many hearts will be revealed," and a sword would pierce Mary's heart (2:34-35).

Anna came upon Simeon, Joseph, and Mary as Simeon was uttering his oracle (2:38). It seems that Simeon died shortly afterward (2:26, 29), but Anna preserved and repeated his words. She "gave thanks to God and spoke about the child to all who were looking forward to the redemption of Jerusalem" (2:38). She spent so much time in the temple, she almost seemed to live there, and she kept speaking about Jesus. So Anna formed a team with Simeon. Simeon "waited for the consolation of Israel" and declared it. Anna restated it for all who anticipated the redemption of Israel.

Among other prophetesses, we know most about *Deborah*, the prophetess and judge; we will return to her later. The Bible briefly mentions other prophetesses. Isaiah 8:3 notes a prophetess who bore a son named Maher Shalal Hash Baz. God sent the boy as a sign of God's coming judgment on wicked King Ahaz. Acts 8 says that Philip, a deacon of the early church, had four daughters who prophesied, but we know nothing more of them. Sadly, some women joined men in false prophecy. Nehemiah denounces the prophetess Noadiah, who joined male prophets in trying to intimidate him (Neh. 6:14), and Ezekiel condemns false prophetesses in 13:17-24.

We do not know how many prophetesses operated in biblical times. Apparently, Israel accepted the idea that while prophets were typically men, women could prophesy, too. In addition to the casual reference to Philip's daughters in Acts 8, Acts 2 cites the oracle, "Your sons and daughters will prophesy," in the blessed day when the Lord pours his Spirit out on all people (Joel 2:28-32). Paul also assumed that women prophesied in the church at Corinth. He regulated but did not forbid them.[3] He only said that women who prophesy must do so with covered heads (1 Cor. 11:5) and minister within existing authority structures (chapter 5).

In the Bible, the great majority of true prophets are male. All sixteen writing prophets, from Isaiah to Malachi, were male. Further, all miracle-working prophets—such as Moses, Elijah, and Elisha—were male. These men, with others like John the Baptist, led Israel publicly. Yet a number of women were godly prophetesses.

WOMEN DECLARED TRUTHS THAT ARE RECORDED IN SCRIPTURE

Several books of the Bible are anonymous, but no woman wrote a book whose author is stated. Still, the Bible records the words of women, such as Miriam's song and Huldah's word of judgment, and regards them as inspired truth. We should expect this, since several women served God faithfully as prophetesses. The words of women became Scripture on other occasions, too.

Scripture preserves *Hannah's song* of joy at the coming birth of her son Samuel (1 Sam. 2). Hannah's words, standing at the beginning of 1 Samuel 2, introduce many themes from the book. For example, Goliath learned the lesson of 2:9-10a, that it is not by strength that one prevails and that those who oppose the Lord will be shattered. Throughout his career, David saw that God gives strength to his king and exalts his anointed, as Hannah said in 2:10. Each of Hannah's first four statements is prophetic:

In 2:1 she praises God for delivering her from her enemies. Deliverance from enemies is a leading theme in Samuel, as David later declares (2 Sam. 22:2-4, 18-20, 30-46).

In 2:2 she says there is no rock like the Lord. The Philistines learned this about Dagon, their god made of stone (1 Sam. 5).

In 2:3 she says that the Lord weighs the deeds of the proud, as Eli's sons discovered (1 Sam. 3—4).

In 2:4 she says that the bows of the warriors are broken and the strong have stumbled, as Saul saw (1 Sam. 31; 2 Sam. 1:27).

Second, in 1 Samuel we hear from the remarkable *Abigail*. She was the wife of Nabal, a rich Israelite. Nabal was as churlish and foolish as Abigail was wise and beautiful. Nabal had great possessions, but was so harsh and unjust in his relationships that even his wife and servants considered him worthless (25:17, 25). Abigail and Nabal appear in the time when King Saul sought to kill David. While David hid from Saul, he spent some time in Nabal's vicinity. David and his men became a voluntary patrol against marauders living in far southern regions of Israel. Yet, at the time of sheep-shearing when the wealthy traditionally shared their bounty with less fortunate neighbors, Nabal refused even to acknowledge David, let alone invite him to a feast. Instead, Nabal insulted him: "Who is this David . . . ? Why should I take my bread and water, and the meat . . . and give it to men coming from who knows where?" (25:10-11).

David overreacted; he ordered his men to strap on their swords and visit Nabal. As they rode away, David rehearsed Nabal's offense, working himself up until he pledged himself to murder. He concluded that he had watched Nabal's flocks for nothing, that Nabal had returned him evil for good. Enraged, he asked God to curse him if one male from Nabal's household was alive the next morning.

Abigail realized that Nabal's insults had provoked David. She rode up to meet him and defused the crisis with a brilliant speech that combines social skill and perceptive theological argument. First, she disarmed David: "My lord, let the blame for my husband's action fall on me alone." He is a fool, she said, and acts like one. Instead, she asked for the blame—and the forgiveness—for not seeing David's men and treating them with respect (25:24-25). Can David pour his wrath on this innocent, gracious woman who takes the guilt on herself? Abigail knows he cannot and proceeds on that assumption: "Since the Lord has kept you from vengeance and bloodshed," you, David, must trust God to avenge Nabal's offense.

With that settled, Abigail offers a gift (not a payment) to David's men (not David himself). Thus she makes amends without dishonoring David with a bribe (25:27). She soothes David's wounded dignity and admits his complaint but defuses his overreaction. She acknowledges her husband's error and yet preserves him until God judges him (25:25-26, 36-38).

But Abigail sees far past the social situation. She instructs David theologically, reasoning from the character and promise of God to seal David's repentance. Because David fights the Lord's battles (1 Sam. 17, 23), the Lord will build a dynasty for him (25:28). Because David is God's anointed king, God will protect him. The Lord will hurl David's enemies away from him—a brilliant allusion to the defeat of Goliath—as a man hurls stones from a sling (25:28-29). Because God will deliver him, David has no need to avenge himself. Further, when he becomes king, he will not want innocent blood on his hands (25:30-31).

Abigail wins David over, and he repents without reservation. He praises God for sending her and asks God to bless her. "May you be blessed for your good judgment and for keeping me from bloodshed" (25:33). He accepts her gift and sends her home in peace. David judges her speech to be exemplary, and 1 Samuel also helps us to savor Abigail's skill and wisdom.

Abigail knows how to appease anger. She acknowledges David's complaint but corrects his error. The correction is gentle, not confrontational, and yet she is firm. *She reasons from the* law *of God, from the* nature *of God, and from the* promises *of God to persuade a man of God to act like one.* She instructs David and persuades him though he has a position of authority, and she does not. Abigail does not instruct men publicly, but she does instruct a public man. She does not "instruct in theology," but she does use theology in her instruction. She does not declare what must be done, but her declarations changed what was done. Thus God blessed a woman's private counsel of a public man.

Priscilla's ministry of correction is somewhat like Abigail's. Priscilla and Aquila were a husband-wife team who labored with Paul occasionally for years (Acts 18:2-19; Rom. 16:3-5). They hosted a house church in both Rome and Corinth (Rom. 16:5; 1 Cor. 16:19). These faithful Christians heard the power but noted the deficiencies in the preaching of a gifted expositor named Apollos. When they heard him, "they invited him to their home and explained to him the way of God more adequately" (Acts 18:26). Just as people puzzle over the decision to consult Huldah before Jeremiah, they wonder why Acts usually mentions Priscilla before Aquila. Did she speak more or have greater gifts? Did she have a higher social status before their marriage?[4]

We cannot know why Acts mentions Priscilla first, but we do know that Priscilla and Aquila privately instructed a leading Christian teacher. Apollos "spoke with great fervor" and "was a learned man, with a thorough knowledge of the Scriptures." But "he only knew the baptism of John" (Acts 18:24-25). So when they heard him, they took him into their home and taught him (18:26). Because their craft as tent-makers allowed them to travel widely, Priscilla and Aquila assisted Paul in Rome (Rom. 16:3), Corinth (Acts 18:2; 1 Cor. 16:19), and Ephesus (Acts 18:18-26). Thus Paul honored Priscilla and Aquila in Romans 16 as fellow workers for whom the whole church gave thanks (Rom. 16:3-4).

Paul also honored other women in Romans 16, which offers glimpses of the contributions women made in the early church. Paul had never visited the church in Rome when he wrote them a letter to prepare for an impending journey to Rome and beyond. But he knew many Christians there, and he greeted them in chapter 16. Those greetings show women functioning as leaders in the Roman church.

In Romans 16:1-2, Paul commended Phoebe, a "servant" (NIV, ESV) or "deaconess" (RSV) of the church.[5] The Greek term in question, *diakonos*, ordinarily means a servant or helper, but it can also mean deacon. When Paul called Phoebe "a servant [or deacon] of the church in Cenchrea," the close connection of *diakonos* to a particular person may indicate that she holds an office, or it could simply mean she was very helpful. It is hard to tell which view is correct; even complementarian scholars are divided. But the phrase "servant [or deacon] of the church" suggests that Phoebe had a recognized role in her local congregation.[6] Clearly, Paul urges the Romans to receive Phoebe with honor, for she helped many.

In 16:3 Paul calls Priscilla and Aquila his coworkers. In 16:6 he commends a certain Mary who "worked very hard." In 16:12 Paul mentions three women—Tryphena, Tryphosa, and Persis—who also "worked hard" in the Lord. Paul also mentions Andronicus and

Junias. They were probably married since Andronicus is a man's name, and Junias is a woman's. In a sentence that is difficult to translate, Paul calls them prominent either "with" or "among" the apostles (Rom. 16:7).[7] If "with" is correct, Paul means that the apostles held them in high regard. If "among" is correct, he means that they are prominent among the people called "apostles."

Since Junias is a woman's name, some propose that she is a "forgotten" apostle. But Paul does not equate either Andronicus or Junias with the Twelve. Rather he uses "apostle" in the less technical, more ordinary sense of someone selected and "sent out" for a particular purpose. The Bible called Barnabas (Acts 14:4, 14), Silas (Acts 17:1ff.; cf. 1 Thess. 2:7), Titus (2 Cor. 8:13), and Epaphroditus (Phil. 2:25) apostles in the same sense when the church sent them on missions to spread the gospel. So Paul honors Andronicus and Junias for the faithful discharge of vital tasks.

Whatever we say about women and ministry, it should match the biblical record as it recounts the blessed ministries of women through redemptive history. We have seen so far that women have many ministries but not every ministry. They are not monarchs, priests, apostles, or elders, but they do teach privately and shape the course of history. They also work effectively alongside male leaders such as Paul. But let us review our findings for more patterns. Then we can consider whether the biblical pattern is authoritative today, and if so, how to follow it.

PATTERNS IN THE ROLES OF WOMEN

First, women *lead alongside* men. Miriam the prophetess led beside Moses as she directed the women of Israel to sing about God's deliverance. As Miriam led the women, she served under the umbrella of Moses' leadership, restating his words. If she led men, she did so indirectly as they heard the women sing. Similarly, Luke places Anna beside Simeon. She neither preached nor wrote. Rather, she spoke of Jesus to faithful Jews.

Second, women *teach in private*. Abigail privately taught David using reasoning that was socially astute and theologically informed. She knew God had promised that David would reign.

When they met, she applied that prophecy to assuage David's wrath toward her husband, Nabal. Hannah and Mary instructed believers through their songs of praise, recorded in Scripture, at the birth of their boys, Samuel and Jesus. Both praised God for the gift of a child whose miraculous birth presaged a great ministry. Their celebrations of God's goodness foreshadowed major themes in their sons' callings.

Priscilla and Huldah illustrate both patterns, ministering with men in private teaching. Priscilla instructed Apollos, a man of God, in a theological conversation. Like Abigail, she taught Apollos privately, but unlike Abigail, she worked beside her husband, Aquila. Teamed with Paul, she was probably under his authority, too. Priscilla also reminds us of other women whom Paul praised for their faithful work in Romans 16.

The ministry of Huldah confirms our pattern. Huldah spoke privately to the king's emissaries. She did not go to the court; the court came to her. She did not go to preach to them; they came to her. The men came to her house, listened to her, and heeded her counsel. Josiah the king had ultimate authority and chose to follow her counsel. She did not decree a course of action, but she did propose the course that the king and nation followed. So she led without commanding.

Like Huldah, Deborah was a prophetess. She was also a leader or "judge" of Israel. No other woman had such high titles. Therefore, if Deborah's leadership fits our pattern, it is confirmed.

DEBORAH—PROPHETESS AND JUDGE

We meet Deborah in Judges 4 after she succeeded Ehud as a judge in Israel. In her day, Jabin, a Canaanite king, and his general Sisera oppressed Israel (Judg. 4:2-3). Israel cried out to the Lord, and the Lord spoke to Deborah. A prophetess, Deborah was "leading" (NIV) or "judging" (ESV) Israel at that time.[8] "She held court . . . between Ramah and Bethel . . . and the Israelites came to her to have their disputes decided" (4:4-5). The disputes presented for her judgment would be difficult cases, perhaps beyond the ken of local authorities. She apparently dispensed spiritual counsel and issued judgments with legal authority. On the other hand, Judges never says she taught or prophesied publicly, as Jeremiah or Isaiah did. There is no hint that she delivered sermons or publicly proclaimed oracles from God. Like the other women we studied, she taught privately.

Deborah also led or "judged" Israel in another way. When God determined to deliver Israel from Jabin and Sisera, he told Deborah. Through her the Lord told Barak to gather a force of 10,000 men to fight them. Then God would grant victory to Israel. But Barak was reluctant and refused to go alone. He insisted that Deborah go with him (the phrase "with me . . . with you" is repeated three times in Judges 4:8-9). Deborah did not lead Israel into battle; she consented to *go* with Barak into battle (4:9) but did not *lead* the troops. We might say she co-led with Barak since he summoned the troops (4:10) and met Sisera in battle (4:12-14) while Deborah urged him on ("Go! This is the day . . ." 4:14). As he fought, the Lord routed Sisera (4:14b-16). Barak still led, but his reticence was dishonorable. It cost him his glory, and another woman, Jael, had the honor of slaying Sisera (4:9).

Barak needed a strong woman at his side. But Deborah did not respond to Barak's relative weakness by usurping his role. Rather, she encouraged Barak to lead. She strengthened and supported a rather weak male leader. As a prophetess and judge, Deborah was a public figure. But she taught privately, and in time of military conflict she led alongside a man.

PROPHETS WITH LIMITED AUTHORITY

So then Huldah and Deborah were prophetesses but not public preachers or teachers. They did not establish doctrinal or moral standards for the covenant family. They led and spoke privately, like Miriam, Abigail, and Anna. What Huldah and Deborah *said* had authority as they spoke for God, but they did not have the same kind of authority as kings, priests, or apostles. This description sounds strange, but it fits two biblical patterns.

First, quite a few men and women who had no office such as prophet, priest, king, or apostle still spoke God's truth and had their words enscripturated. For example, Joseph had no *position* whatsoever when he stood before Pharaoh to interpret his dreams. He was a slave, just scrubbed clean from years of prison rot. But he declared God's truth and persuaded a king, and so his words became Scripture. Similarly, Jethro had no official position; yet he challenged Moses, Israel's leader, about his workload in a speech that was wise, effective, and enscripturated (Exod. 18:13-26). Many others, including Esther, Mordecai, Job, Zacchaeus, and a Syro-Phonecian woman, spoke God's truth to good effect, though they held no position in Israel, because they influenced those who did.[9] So both men and women can speak words that attain authority although they have no leadership position.

Second, many prophets lacked official, ongoing leadership. The companies of prophets, mentioned in 2 Kings, had no visible authority. Other prophets simply delivered messages and disappeared. For example, an unnamed "man of God" judged the altar that Jeroboam erected in Bethel and vanished (1 Kings 13:1-10). Elijah also tended to appear suddenly in the court of rebellious kings such as Ahab (1 Kings 17—18) and Ahaziah (2 Kings 1).

In Israel *regular* teaching authority lay with the law, not prophecy. Thus the words of prophets always had to be tested (Deut. 13:1-5; 18:20-22; 1 Cor. 14:29). If a prophecy urged disobedience to God's law, it was false. Further, God ordained that priests and Levites, not prophets, teach the law. As Malachi said, "The lips of a priest ought to preserve knowledge, and from his mouth men should receive instruction" (Mal. 2:7).[10] Moses blessed the tribe of Levi—all priests were from Levi—saying, "He teaches your precepts to Jacob and your law to Israel" (Deut. 33:10). Jeremiah 18:18 and Ezekiel 7:26 also link the law to priests, not prophets. If prophets did not necessarily have formal authority as teachers in Israel, we see why prophecy is the one office women sometimes held.

So it initially seems that female prophets contradict the principle of male authority. But when we see Deborah and Huldah exercising their prophetic ministry though private teaching and counsel, it actually reinforces our principle: Women teach and lead in the covenant family, but they do not hold a permanent public teaching office.

CONCLUSIONS

The pattern is clear. Women instructed men privately but did not deliver formal addresses to crowds gathered for instruction. They advised and rebuked men, great and small, but did not issue decrees that bound Israel or the church. Women counseled men, who listened and adopted their ideas. Women taught and prophesied, giving messages with theological content. But Scripture has no example of a woman doing what we today call "preaching." Women led beside men in Israel and the church, but no woman approached the rank of Abraham, Moses, David, Elijah, Isaiah, Peter, or Paul as a principal leader. Women led alongside men but ranked beneath them in authority, not beside them as absolute peers. When Miriam aspired to equality with Moses, God rebuked her.[11] When Barak tried to avoid leadership, Deborah urged him on.

There are three ways to interpret these facts. Option 1: The biblical record is erroneous; women led far more than it records. Option 2: Male leadership was a temporary concession to ancient cultures. It is not a normative pattern for God's people today. Option 3: God ordained men to be the principal leaders of the covenant family, and that pattern remains authoritative.

Option 1: The biblical record of male leadership is erroneous.

Some radical feminist critics say women did much more than the Bible records, especially in the early church. But, they say, by the time the New Testament was written, many decades later, a male hierarchy had taken over, and it suppressed the truth about female leadership.[12]

To accuse church leaders of systematically distorting the history of the early church is to place oneself outside the bounds of orthodox, evangelical Christianity. Christianity is more than an ethical or spiritual system of thought. God's saving acts in history are its foundation, and if those acts did not occur, we are most pitiably deluded. An abundant literature defends the claim that the Bible is historically reliable and written by faithful witnesses.[13]

Option 2: Male leadership is a temporary concession.

Other egalitarians, both radical and evangelical, say male leadership was a temporary concession to woman's lack of education and low social status in antiquity. They say the Bible's history of male leadership ("patriarchy") is an evil God merely tolerated. The Bible's authors "pushed society as far as it could go" without inciting a social upheaval that would cause more harm than good.[14] If Jesus had chosen female apostles and the church had allowed female elders, it would have proved fatal for the church in a patriarchal society. Paul especially had to show his Greco-Roman readers that Christianity upholds the social order.[15] But, egalitarians say, the changes that did occur establish a trajectory showing that God would grant women full equality as soon as society would accept it, which it certainly would today. Scripture gave women legal rights, and the Spirit bestowed gifts for ministry upon them, undercutting the hierarchical system. So the Bible gradually liberates women even as it gradually liberated slaves. It never commanded the end of slavery or of patriarchy, but it sowed the seeds of destruction for both.

There are three problems with this view.

First, many of the allegedly "patriarchal" and oppressive patterns of male leadership are part of Old Testament law—*God's* law. Therefore, Guenther Haas argues, the view that patriarchy is evil leads to "the conclusion that God in Scripture commanded sinful practices." And if an egalitarian says the laws are temporary accommodations to patriarchal culture, designed to end patriarchy, one "is arguing that God prescribes evil that good may come." But Romans 3:8 forbids that very thing. Besides, God repeatedly says the law is the pattern of holiness for Israel. So this view "undermines the authority of the Bible."[16]

Second, Christopher Wright has shown that God shaped Israel into a "paradigmatic society," God's model society. God redeemed Israel, in part, to order their social life "to make visible his moral requirements on the rest of the nations." As Israel lived in "freedom, justice, love and compassion . . . they would function as God's priesthood among the nations."[17] Moses taught Israel God's decrees so that as Israel followed them, she would "show . . . wisdom and understanding to the nations," and would say, "'Surely this . . . is a wise and understanding people'" who are blessed "to have their gods near them . . . [and] to have such righteous decrees" (Deut. 4:4-8). How can

Deuteronomy 4 be true if the Old Testament is systematically patriarchal and patriarchy is evil?

Third, the feminists plead that women's subordination to men is
analogous to slaves' subordination to masters. God vastly improved
the status of both, but, feminists say, instead of ordering the liberation of slaves and the full equality of women, he articulated principles that guaranteed the end of slavery and the end of the
subordination of women. But there are important differences between
slavery and women's subordination:

God never ordained slavery. His law regulates and limits it. But
as the next chapters show, God did ordain the spiritual leadership of
men.

There is, with one exception, a six-year "term limit" on slavery
in Israel (Deut. 15:12-18; Lev. 25:39-43). But there is no stated limit
on the time males should lead churches or families.

Paul tells slaves, "If you can gain your freedom, do so" (1 Cor.
7:21). But he never tells women to gain their freedom from their
elders or husbands if they can.

The narrative pattern we have discovered is explicitly verified by
Paul's statement that he does not permit a woman to exercise authority over a man (1 Tim. 2:12).[18]

*Option 3: God ordained men to be the principal leaders of his covenant
family.*

The pattern of male leadership in the Bible is clear. Evangelical
Christians will not adopt the view that the record is incorrect. If the idea
that male leadership is a temporary concession has the weaknesses I
have proposed, then one option remains: God ordained men to serve
as spiritual leaders in the community of believers. Women bless Israel
and the church when they teach in private and lead alongside men.

Questions remain. Why do ancient patterns guide Christians
today? Didn't Paul end traditional gender roles when he said, "There
is neither . . . male nor female, for you are all one in Christ Jesus"
(Gal. 3:28)? Secular people have even sharper objections. They may
accuse Christians of bigotry, misogyny, or patriarchalism. They ask
how Christianity can claim to be a religion of love and freedom and
say women cannot lead. The next chapters address these questions.

A Note on Method

Egalitarians commonly avoid the implications of biblical narratives showing male leadership by claiming these narratives show God's willingness to accommodate himself to the practices of biblical times. They say narrative patterns do not show that God favored male leadership but that he tolerated patriarchy, a lesser evil, in order to accomplish his redemptive goals, which eventually led to women's liberty anyway. Following Guenther Haas, this chapter pointed out that patriarchy cannot be dismissed as an evil to be tolerated, since patriarchy is part of biblical law. Since God forbids that mankind do evil that good may result (Rom. 3:8), and since his laws flow from his holy character, we cannot dismiss the laws that command male leadership or the narratives that show it.

In addition, I want to affirm that biblical narratives can be programmatic. Chapters 4, 5, and 6 advance this point by showing how Genesis 3, Ephesians 5, 1 Corinthians 14, and 1 Timothy 2 mandate male leadership. I wish, however, to go beyond the traditional—and valid—view that narrative is authoritative when verified by law, and assert that narrative can be authoritative in its own right. I argue this at length in *Putting the Truth to Work: The Theory and Practice of Biblical Application*, 189-212, but mention a few salient points here.

1. The motto, "Direct teaching has priority over narrative," does not appear in Scripture and seems to be contrary to it. When Paul says, "All Scripture is God-breathed and is useful for teaching, rebuking, correcting and training in righteousness" (2 Tim. 3:16), he makes no distinction between narrative and law. Since the Bible is fundamentally the history—the narrative—of God's salvation of his people, it is strange to give law and doctrine priority over narrative. If we want to know God and his ways, narrative leads us there as surely as law or doctrine. Where do we learn more—when we read the command, "Be kind and compassionate," or when we read the narratives of Jesus' kindness and compassion? Which is more revelatory—the statement, "God is love," or the record of God's love for his people? Narrative and discourse are mutually defining; neither one has priority over the other.

2. While we must resist moralistic uses of biblical narrative, Scripture explicitly instructs readers to find moral guidance in narratives. The New Testament repeatedly draws lessons from older narratives. In Matthew 12:1-

8, Jesus tells the Pharisees they should know that God desires mercy and not sacrifice because they read that David ate the shewbread when he fled Saul's court (1 Sam. 21). Paul commanded the Corinthians to learn from the rebellion of Israel in the wilderness: "Now these things occurred as examples to keep us from setting our hearts on evil things as they did" (1 Cor. 10:1-10; cf. Heb. 3:7—4:11). Hebrews 11 recounts the faith and perseverance of Abraham, Moses, and others. They are a "cloud of witnesses," exhorting the church not to shrink back but to continue their race (Heb. 10:35—12:2).

3. Scripture bases many ethical and doctrinal conclusions on narratives. Jesus faced temptation by drawing lessons from Israel's failures in the wilderness (Matt. 4:1-11; Luke 4:1-13). James finds in Abraham and Rahab proof that faith without works is dead (James 2:20-26). For James, Elijah illustrates effective, righteous prayer (5:17-18). Jude cites Cain, Balaam, and Korah to show that those who throw off authority suffer judgment (Jude 8-11). Paul gathers theological lessons from Old Testament figures. In Romans 4, Abraham represents the justified believer. Yet he does not merely *illustrate* justification by faith; he advances the argument. Abraham's great sacrifices mean that no one can claim justification by works more than he. But if even Abraham was justified by faith, then who can be saved by works? From Abraham we learn that works cannot justify (4:9-11), that faith perseveres (4:20), that it empowers obedience (4:17-21), that it trusts God.[19]

4. The imitation of Christ motif has strong biblical support (Matt. 10:24-25; 20:28; Luke 6:40; John 13:15-16; 15:20; Rom. 8:29; 1 Cor. 15:49; Eph. 4:32; 5:1, 25-27; Phil. 2:3-8; 1 Peter 2:18-25; 1 John 2:6; 3:16). It requires believers to draw ethical lessons from the narrative of Jesus' life.

5. Jesus repeatedly chides Jewish leaders for failing to draw moral or theological lessons from biblical narratives. He asks, "have you not read," in Matthew 12:3, 12:5, 19:4, and 22:31, not to inquire after their literacy or reading habits, but to rebuke them for failing to grasp lessons available in biblical narratives.

3

THE ROLES OF WOMEN
IN THE MINISTRY OF JESUS

WOMEN IN ANTIQUITY, WOMEN AND JESUS

Philo, a first-century Jewish philosopher and theologian, spoke for most ancient men when he said marketplaces and public gatherings are suitable for men, but "women are best suited to the indoor life."[1] Whether in Athens or Jerusalem, whether in farmlands or hinterlands, women were rarely in school, rarely in power, rarely in public.

The leaders of first-century Israel had a resource, the Old Testament, that should have led them to challenge this widespread state of affairs, but they missed it. Near Jesus' day, revered rabbi Jose ben Johanan said, "Let thy house be opened wide and let the needy be members of thy household; and talk not much with womankind." Later, an editor commented that this is true "of a man's own wife: how much more of his fellow's wife! Hence the sages have said, 'He that talks much with womankind brings evil upon himself and neglects the study of the law and at the last will inherit Gehenna.'"[2]

Thus the rabbis urged men to keep their distance from their own wives, not to mention other women. Most rabbis thought it was either a waste of time or a positive danger to speak to women outside the ties of marriage and family.[3] Perhaps because their families typically sheltered them, the law did not give women the same legal rights as men either.

The root of such attitudes was the widespread view that women were mentally and spiritually inferior to men. So men said women could not be educated, but they could tempt or entice men to sin. Rabbis believed women had souls at least; so they might go to the synagogue. But hardly any rabbis or philosophers expected women to study or learn. Women could also go outdoors to the market, but they did go not alone or with financial independence.

I am tempted to say that Jesus liberated women from all this. Jesus did liberate women, of course, and so the statement is not false. But it is misleading, as a mother would mislead a child at her first wedding if she directed her daughter's attention to the music, flowers, and dresses and ignored the bride, groom, and vows. The statement misrepresents Jesus' agenda. It sounds too contemporary, too social. Jesus brought women social liberty, but it was a consequence of his prime agenda, not the agenda itself. Jesus came to seek and to save the lost, to give his life as a ransom for many (Luke 19:10; Matt. 20:28).

Jesus did not *refute* Greek or Jewish ideas about women; he *ignored* those ideas. He simply treated women as humans and let the chips fall where they may. He reminded everyone that God created both women and men, so that both bear his image (Matt. 19:3-6). Therefore, he taught women and befriended them. He singled out male lust, not female seductiveness, as a source of sexual sin (Matt. 5:27-32). He broke with custom and applied divorce law identically for men and women (as did Paul).

Women played vital roles in Jesus' life from beginning to end. Mary voiced many themes from Jesus' life in her song of praise (Luke 1:46-56) and gave him birth (2:7). Wealthy women supported his ministry materially (8:3). Faithful women remained with him at his crucifixion (John 20:25-27). Women were the first to witness his resurrection (20:1-18).

The Lord's ministry was "gender blind." He healed men and women, boys and girls alike (Luke 8:26-56). His decision to feature women in many of his illustrations and parables has a similar gender-blindness. In his teaching, women bake bread (Matt. 13:33), grind grain (24:41), and wait for a wedding party (25:1-10). They search for lost money (Luke 15:8-10), pray persistently (18:1-5), and give wholeheartedly (21:1-4).

Jesus' disregard for Jewish traditions also led him to associate freely with women. In Luke, for example, Jesus encountered a grieving widow and mother (Luke 7:11-15), let a sinful woman anoint his feet (7:36-50), and sought out a long-suffering woman who touched his cloak amidst a throng of people (8:43-48; cf. 13:10-16). Going to his crucifixion, Jesus took a moment to address a group of women who mourned his impending death (23:27-31).

Jesus' willingness to ignore custom is part of his resolve to minister to all, regardless of gender, ethnicity, status, or moral history. He was an equal-opportunity party attender, as quick to dine with a self-righteous Pharisee as with an unrighteous tax collector. When someone came seeking healing or counsel, nothing mattered but that person's spirit. He met lepers and soldiers, paupers and rulers. None suffered his prejudice; none enjoyed his deference. He hardly even favored his own family (Matt. 12:46-50). Jesus' freedom from bias extended to women as well. He saw women as persons for whom he came to this world. "He did not perceive [women] primarily in terms of their sex, age or marital status; he seems to have considered them in terms of their relation (or lack of one) to God."[4]

In conversation with women, Jesus was candid and tender. When he met a woman at a well in Samaria, he asked for water, but he moved on to address her five divorces and her cohabitation with a man not her husband (John 4). In a wide-ranging conversation, they discussed her past, her worship, and her salvation. This seems commonplace today, but it was doubly startling then. The woman could not believe a *Jew* spoke to her (4:9). But the disciples were just as surprised that Jesus spoke to a *woman* (4:27). The same candor prompted him to acknowledge and forgive the sin of the woman who anointed his feet with oil, tears, and kisses (Luke 7:47-48).

Jesus spoke tenderly to women. To a woman with chronic bleeding, he said, "Daughter, your faith has healed you. Go in peace" (Luke 8:48; Mark 5:34; Matt. 9:22). He called a woman whose back he straightened a "daughter of Abraham" (Luke 13:16). Jesus even wept with Mary and Martha when their brother Lazarus died (John 11:22-42).[5]

WOMEN IN THE KITCHEN, WOMEN IN THE COMPANY OF MEN (LUKE 10:38-42 ESV)

One of Jesus' most illuminating encounters with women occurs with the sisters Mary and Martha. Both were Jesus' disciples and friends, and they opened their home to him. The story shows how Jesus stretched women's roles without repudiating tradition. Hear Luke's account:

> And a woman named Martha welcomed him into her house. And she had a sister called Mary, who sat at the Lord's feet and listened to his teaching [or, "his word"].[6] But Martha was distracted with much serving. And she went up to him and said, "Lord, do you not care that my sister has left me to serve alone? Tell her then to help me."

> But the Lord answered her, "Martha, Martha, you are anxious and troubled about many things, but one thing is necessary.[7] Mary has chosen the good portion, which will not be taken away from her."

We need to let imagination whisper in the ear of history to appreciate the scene. First, remember that Jesus did not call or write ahead to warn Martha and Mary that he was coming. (In antiquity ordinary people rarely sent letters.) He simply arrived at Martha and Mary's door with at least a dozen men behind him.[8] Custom required the women to provide a generous meal for the travelers. With no advance preparation, with none of the aid a modern kitchen affords, Martha and Mary faced a daunting task. Yet if they worked together, perhaps they could prepare a proper meal in proper time.

But they did not work together. Martha set to the task, but Mary did not. Instead, doubly defying convention, Mary abandoned her domestic duties and sat at Jesus' feet in the posture of a disciple.[9] There she sat, drinking in Jesus' speech while Martha took the traditional woman's role.[10]

Martha, overburdened by her preparations, objected. Distressed that Mary would not help, distressed that her duties pulled her away from Jesus, Martha attempted to enlist Jesus to remand Mary to the kitchen.[11] Frustrated, Martha pleads, "Lord, don't you care that my sister has left me to do the work by myself? Tell her to help me!"[12] In one short outburst, she accuses Mary of sloth and accuses Jesus of indifference.

But Jesus is not indifferent. We can almost hear his compassion as he begins, "Martha, Martha." Yet Jesus unexpectedly takes Mary's side: "Martha, Martha, you are anxious and troubled about many things, but one thing is necessary" (10:41-42 ESV). At first, it seems the contrast is between the *many* dishes Martha is preparing, perhaps elaborately, and the *one* dish that would be enough. But the "one necessary thing" is not food; it is the act of sitting at the Master's feet. That is what Mary chose, and Jesus will not let Martha take it from her.

Jesus' praise of Mary is not a criticism of traditional female work. "Mary has chosen what is better" does not mean, "Martha chose what is evil."[13] Jesus does not condemn Martha's service. Hospitality is good, but at this hour, listening is better. Jesus affirms Mary's right to resist tradition and be a disciple. "For women as well as men, one's primary task is to be a proper disciple; only in that context can one be a proper hostess."[14] Martha chose to *serve* Jesus with physical food. Mary chose to *be served* spiritual food, and Mary chose wisely.

Martha wanted to be a perfect hostess, but Mary wanted to be a good disciple. Jesus said that Mary made the right decision since he was not simply talking—he was delivering "the word"; so his disciples should drop lesser deeds and listen. Martha thought she was a hostess, serving physical food, but Jesus said he was the host, serving spiritual food. In this way, Jesus placed discipleship ahead of traditional women's roles.

Discipleship lessens distinctions between male and female, old and young, rich and poor. This idea is hardly new. Long ago Moses commanded all Israel to assemble once every seven years. Men, women, and children gathered to "listen and learn to fear the LORD" (Deut. 31:12). Similarly, when Jesus delivers "the word," women should put down the kneading bowl and listen. Mary grasped this.

Jesus says it is better to be a good disciple than to be a good hostess. Yet Jesus never *opposes* traditional women's roles. He never disparages food preparation or commands women to abandon traditional service. Indeed, Scripture assumes and affirms roles such as preparing food and caring for family members (Gen. 18:1-8; Judg. 4:17-22;

1 Kings 4:8ff.; Prov 31:10-31; 1 Tim. 5:1-14). Paul says women should be "good houseworkers" (Titus 2:5, see NASB and CEV).[15]

Jesus' visit with Mary and Martha immediately followed the parable of the Good Samaritan, which blesses concrete acts of service for the needy. Living long before the advent of fast-food restaurants, Jesus and the disciples probably arrived hungry. Martha was right to feed them, but a simple meal would have been enough.

This story teaches three lessons. First, we must question the gender roles our culture hands us. Traditions contain both wisdom and folly. No culture gets everything wrong, but none gets everything right either.

Second, Jesus wants women to be disciples. Sometimes women, like men, need to drop everything and listen. Jesus wanted both Mary and Martha to sit at his feet. Later when their brother Lazarus died, Martha was quick to listen and learn (John 11:17-37). Jesus' desire to disciple these women foreshadowed the role of women who witnessed his resurrection (Matt. 28:1-10; Mark 16:1-8; Luke 24:1-12; John 20:2-18).

Third, when Jesus commends discipleship, he does not reject traditional female roles. There is no conflict between femininity and discipleship. Many women attain maturity through marriage and motherhood, much as men become mature through marriage and fatherhood. Marriage and parenting are schools of character and realms of service. In antiquity that work often included making and selling (Prov. 31), not just buying and consuming, but it entailed food preparation and childcare as well. Parenting is kingdom service. Still, on those rare occasions when "womanly duties" and discipleship come into conflict, Luke 10 affirms the primacy of discipleship. Luke 11 makes that point a second time.

A WOMAN'S PRAISE, A WOMAN'S GLORY (LUKE 11:27-28)

One day, while Jesus was engaged in a dispute, a woman in the crowd called out her support, crying, "Blessed is the mother who gave you birth and nursed you" (11:27). This burst of praise for Jesus' mother sounds a bit odd, but the crowd knew what she meant: "Your power is great; your words are true. How your mother is blessed to have a son such as you."[16]

The woman intended to praise Jesus and to declare her loyalty in a distinctly feminine way. Her expression reflected the age-old idea that women find greatness by marrying a great man or bearing a great son. She meant to bless Jesus by blessing his mother. (Even today an older woman occasionally tells a notable man, "Your mother must be so proud.") Her allegiance to Jesus is commendable, but her expression subtly diminishes womankind. It rests on a flawed answer to the question, "How does a woman find greatness?" Her answer is, "A woman finds greatness through connection to a great man."

Jesus could have ignored this small error. Instead he gently corrected her: "Blessed rather are those who hear the word of God and obey it" (11:28).[17] The term "rather" is mild here. It means, "Yes, but there is more." That is, Jesus accepts her praise as far as it goes; Mary is indeed blessed to have Jesus as her son. But Mary's blessedness consists in more than her physical bond with Jesus.[18] She also shares the blessedness of all who hear the Word of God, believe it, and act upon it (Luke 1:45; 8:21). Mary gave birth to Jesus with remarkable faith and obedience to the angel's commission.[19]

To this day, a woman finds her chief blessing through discipleship, and discipleship knows no gender. Women may enjoy blessedness in their own right, not just through marriage or progeny. Every woman can hear the Word of God and obey it. In this sense, Jesus liberated women from the restrictions of traditional female roles.

Yet, as we said before, it can be confusing to say, "Jesus liberated women," for it sounds as if he adopted the feminist agenda of recent decades, and he did not. He never said women should do everything men do, never said men and women are identical except for reproduction and lactation, nor did his actions imply it. Rather, Jesus set a precedent when he appointed males as his first apostles, showing that the church's official leaders should be male. Women may exercise the informal leadership that is open to every believer, but Jesus chose men to lead as apostles.

JESUS AND THE APOSTLES

It is possible to appraise the evidence we have surveyed and conclude that Jesus was a pioneer of feminism. Women were objects of his grace and members of his kingdom. He healed, instructed, and discipled them. He invited them to follow him, give to him, converse with him, and attest his resurrection.[20] Still, Jesus did not level all distinctions between men and women. He chose twelve males and no females to become his apostles. They had male names: Simon (called Peter), Andrew, James, John, Philip, Bartholomew, Thomas, Thaddaeus, Simon, and Judas (Matt. 10:2-4).

Jesus appointed the apostles as his foundational witnesses. He trained them to testify to what their ears heard, their eyes saw, and their hands touched during his ministry (1 John 1:1-4; John 1:14; Acts 1:8; 4:20). After his resurrection, they saw the wounds on his hands and feet. They touched, saw, believed, and testified, for they could not do otherwise (Luke 24:39; John 20:20-25; Acts 4:20).[21] They preached and wrote down the church's foundational message.

Evangelical feminists do not deny this, but they do try to minimize its significance.[22] They claim Jesus' choice of male leaders sets no precedent for Christian leadership today.[23] They reason that temporary conditions related to ancient cultures prevented Jesus from appointing female apostles. Since those conditions belong to the distant past, Jesus' choice of male leadership allegedly belongs to the past as well.[24] Allow me to respond to some crucial feminist ideas:

• Many feminists say that in that culture, it would have offended social sensibilities if Jesus had chosen women as disciples and traveling companions. Reply: Yes, but Jesus violated cultural conventions whenever he saw fit. He touched lepers. He called tax collectors and prostitutes his friends. He healed Gentiles. He violated customs for the Sabbath. He tossed recognized businessmen out of the temple. Jesus violated convention by talking to women, discipling them, and letting them travel with him (Luke 8:1-2). He shattered so many conventions; why should he quail at one more? Besides, "when moral issues were at stake, Jesus did not bend to social pressure."[25]

• Many feminists say women were uneducated, and, supposedly, intellectually inferior; so no one would accept them as public leaders. Reply: Yes, but Jesus and the Twelve were not highly educated either (Matt. 13:54-57; John 7:15; Acts 4:13), and early Christians accepted their leadership. Formal education is not a requirement for ministry.

• Many feminists say travel was dangerous for women. Reply: Yes, but travel was dangerous for men, too. Paul was imprisoned, lashed, beaten, stoned, shipwrecked, sleepless, hungry, thirsty, cold, and naked (2 Cor. 12:23-27). Besides, the apostles' wives sometimes traveled with them, dangers notwithstanding (1 Cor. 9:5).

Thus evangelical feminists deny that Jesus' choice of male disciples sets a precedent. Many reason that if Jesus' choice of male disciples signifies that only males can lead, then the choice of twelve Jewish disciples should signify that only Jews can lead.[26] That is, if the *gender* of the choice is normative, then so is the *ethnicity*. Since we know that Jesus' choice of Jewish leaders does not set a precedent, they argue that his choice of males does not set a precedent either.

This argument rests on an analogy. Jesus' decision to choose men first is the same as his decision to choose Jews first. Since the appointment of Jewish leaders was temporary, they reason, the appointment of males is temporary, too. But the analogy fails. Both historically and biblically, the appointment of Israelites is quite different from the appointment of males.

Historically, the appointment of Israelite disciples is a unique element in God's plan of salvation. In that plan, God made covenants to bind Israel to himself in love. He chose Abraham, the father of Israel, so that all nations might be blessed through him (Gen. 18:17-19; 22:17-18). He chose Moses to lead Israel out of Egypt and to mediate a covenant between God and Israel; so she was his treasured, holy nation (Exod. 3, 19). The prophets, priests, and kings of Israel all prepared Israel to receive salvation through the Son. When God's plan of redemption came to fruition, Jesus was born to "be the shepherd of my people Israel" (Matt. 2:6). Jesus said, "I was sent only to the lost sheep of Israel" (15:24). Therefore, he told his disciples not to go to the Gentiles but "to the lost sheep of Israel" (10:6). Since Israel had the covenant and the promises, Jesus had to go to Israel first and find his foundational leaders there. When Jesus chose twelve Jewish disciples, it was a historical necessity. But when the gospel went to the Gentiles, it became proper to have Gentile Christians lead Gentile churches.

Scripture shows that Israel's privileges were temporary. God prepared Israel to receive a Savior through whom all nations would be blessed (Gen. 12:1-3). After his resurrection, Jesus and the apostles said that the gospel must go to the Gentiles (Matt. 28:19; Luke 24:47; Acts 1:8; Rom. 1:5). When the New Testament lists the qualities of leaders, it never says they must be Jewish, but it does say they must be male (Acts 1:21-23; 1 Tim. 2:12—3:15; Titus 1:5-9). When the gospel went to the Gentiles, Gentiles soon began to lead. The Gentile church had Gentile leaders, including Titus, Epaphroditus, Tychicus, and Luke, who wrote both Luke and Acts (2 Cor. 8:16-23; Phil. 2:25-30; Col. 4:7-14; Eph. 6:21-22; Philem. 23-34).[27] Men such as Titus exercised great authority. Paul left him in Crete to straighten out his unfinished business and to "appoint elders in every town" (Titus 1:5). No woman is ever given such a charge.

The feminist case rests on a supposed analogy between temporary Jewish leadership and temporary male leadership, but the analogy fails at both points.

Historically, God temporarily and foundationally chose to redeem the Jews first and the Gentiles later, and so temporary Jewish leadership is fitting. But he did not redeem men first and women later. So temporary male leadership is not fitting.

Biblically, Scripture never says that Gentiles must not exercise authority, but he does say that women must not exercise authority (1 Tim. 2:12).

The apostles saw no link between temporary Jewish leadership and temporary male leadership. They agreed that Jesus' choice of twelve male apostles was a precedent. When they replaced Judas, they said a male must take his place: "Therefore it is necessary to choose one of the men who have been with us the whole time" (Acts 1:21). In the original, the word for "men" is not *anthrōpos*, the Greek term for a "human," but *anēr*, the Greek term for a "male." Later, the apostles followed the precedent again and had the church choose seven males (*anēr*) to oversee the church's mercy ministry (Acts 6:1-6).

FINAL THOUGHTS

Throughout his ministry, Jesus released women from many burdens. He befriended women, taught them, accorded them legal rights, and offered them the full benefits of discipleship. But Jesus still distinguished between men and women. When he appointed twelve men and no women as his apostles, he followed the precedent, discussed in chapter 2, for formal leadership positions in the church.

Since Jesus loves, serves, respects, and dignifies women as no man ever has, some are perplexed that he did not appoint woman to be apostles. Most contemporaries reason that if two people have the same value, they should have the right to the same functions or roles. The contemporary mind-set is meritocratic. That is, if someone is talented and capable, everything should be possible, with no options closed. Everyone should be able to move to the top of their chosen ladder according to the merit shown in their gifts, training, and experience.

The biblical mind-set has room for merit. Paul recognized the value of social progress (1 Cor. 7:21). But in the biblical worldview, God apportions gifts, ordains places, and oversees the success or failure of human plans (Ps. 39:5-6; Luke 12:16-20; James 4:13-17). Therefore, our prime goal should not be to rise as high as we can, but to be faithful in our God-given roles. Two people may have equal gifts and work equally hard, and yet God may appoint one to lead and the other to follow. Indeed, a follower may have greater gifts than a leader, but unless the leader is corrupt, the follower serves God and mankind best by supporting the leader, not by subverting and overthrowing him.

Everyone experiences this principle. Every coach has worked with a player more talented than he or she is. Every teacher has had a student who is more intelligent than she or he is. But a team becomes weaker if the gifted players rebel, and a classroom falls into chaos if the bright students stage a coup. Some people chafe when this principle is applied to gender roles. It seems unfair that women with talents equal to men should sit under their authority. This reminds us of the last thing Jesus did to liberate women: He has shown how to be equal to someone while yet taking directions.

Within the Godhead, Father, Son, and Spirit are one in power and knowledge, co-eternal and co-equal in every excellence. Yet in the work of redemption the Son subordinated himself to the Father and submitted to him. Jesus declared, "My food is to do the will of him who sent me and to finish his work" (John 4:34). He said, "I have come down from heaven not to do my will but to do the will of him who sent me" (6:38). He said what the Father taught him to say (8:28; 12:49-50). He did what the Father commissioned him to do (5:19, 26, 30, 36; 10:17-18; 14:31; 17:4). In Scripture Jesus' submission to a humbling task is essential to his greatness (Matt. 20:25-28; Phil. 2:5-11). Thus, Jesus showed that there is no shame in a subordinate place. The orders of mankind originate in the Creator himself. If our Lord can submit to the Father without losing dignity or value, then women can submit to male leaders while they have equal knowledge, holiness, and worth.

4

FOUNDATIONS FOR MALE–FEMALE ROLES: GENESIS 1 AND EPHESIANS 5

SO FAR WE HAVE gathered evidence that God appointed men to be principal leaders of Israel and the church. Women like Huldah and Abigail led privately. Miriam and Anna led beside men in authority. Paul confirms this pattern with explicit commands:

> *I do not permit a woman to teach or to have authority over a man. . . . For Adam was formed first, then Eve.* (1 Tim. 2:12-14)

> *Women should remain silent in the churches. They are not allowed to speak, but must be in submission, as the Law says.* (1 Cor. 14:34)

Notice that Paul grounds his teaching in Old Testament precedents—in the creation of Eve and the law of Moses. But there is also a puzzle here, since no law explicitly requires that women be silent. Paul might be thinking of laws that ordain men to hold Israel's leadership offices:

The law says a king, not a queen, must lead the government and the army (Deut. 17:14-20).

The law says that the priests were the sons, not the daughters, of Aaron (Exod. 29). Male priests led temple worship and instructed Israel. "For the lips of a priest ought to preserve knowledge, and from his mouth men should seek instruction—because he is the messenger of the LORD Almighty" (Mal. 2:7).

Fathers bore responsibility to lead their families, as the stories of Abraham (Gen. 18), Eli (1 Sam. 3), and David (2 Sam. 13—14) show.

But these principles hearken back to something more foundational, the creation accounts of Genesis. The creation order is the first reference point for male-female relations (1 Cor. 11:8-9; 1 Tim. 2:13).[1] If man led woman from the beginning, then men should also lead the church.

GENESIS 1—2 AND MALE LEADERSHIP

Genesis shows that at creation male and female had equal value and status but different roles. Genesis has two complementary narratives of creation, one running from 1:1 to 2:4, the other from 2:5-25. The first accents the equality of man and woman; the second reveals the difference between them.

Genesis 1 says that God created man and woman side by side, in his image and likeness. He charges them to rule the world for him. Shoulder to shoulder, men and women govern the earth for God. They rule its animals, cultivate its plants, and develop its riches.

> *"Let us make man in our image, in our likeness, and let them rule over the fish of the sea and the birds of the air, over the livestock, over all the earth."* . . . *So God created man in his own image, in the image of God he created him; male and female he created them.* (Gen. 1:26-27)

Genesis 2 retells the story of creation with a special focus on the sixth day. It shows that while God created man and woman at nearly the same time, he formed Adam slightly earlier. Genesis 2:7 says, "The Lord God formed the man from the dust of the ground and breathed into his nostrils the breath of life, and the man became a living being." Next God set him the tasks of tending the garden of Eden and naming the animals (2:15-20). Then he created Eve (2:21-22).

In ancient Near Eastern culture, listeners would assume that because God created Adam first, Adam led the relationship. Primogeniture—leadership by the firstborn—was the way of the world. The first son gained a double portion of the family wealth. He "became the head of the family . . . . exercising authority over the household as a whole."² He led the family's social and spiritual life (Deut. 21:15-17; 2 Kings 2:9). There were exceptions, but they had to be noted. The challenge to primogeniture creates the tension between Jacob and Esau and between Joseph and his brothers (Gen. 25—33, 37—45).

The principle of primogeniture is sprinkled throughout Scripture. God delivers Israel because Israel is God's firstborn (Exod. 4:22; Jer. 31:9). Paul links Jesus' authority over creation to his supremacy as the firstborn (Col. 1:15-18). Jesus is the believer's pattern because he is "the firstborn among many brothers" (Rom. 8:29). Paul assumes primogeniture when he says women must not have authority because Adam was formed first (1 Cor. 11:8-9; 1 Tim. 2:13).³

When Adam named Eve, it fit the paradigm of primogeniture (Gen. 2:23). To name something, in ancient Near Eastern cultures, was to state its nature and to exercise authority over it. When Adam named the animals, he manifested his rule over them (Gen. 2:19-20). Naming signifies authority throughout Scripture. For example, God renamed "Abram" as "Abraham," which means "father of a multitude." The name reinforced the promise that old, childless Abraham would one day have many heirs (Gen. 17:5; Rom. 4:17-18). Similarly, Nebuchadnezzar, king of Babylon, renamed his Jewish captives. Daniel and his friends became Belteshazzar, Shadrach, Meshach, and Abednego (Dan. 1:1-7). To this day the ability to assign a nickname and make it stick can indicate authority. When Adam named Eve, he displayed his leadership (Gen. 2:23).⁴

God's ban on the fruit of the tree of knowledge contains another hint that Adam is the representative leader. When God tells Adam, "You must not eat from the tree of the knowledge of good and evil, for when you eat of it you will surely die," the Hebrew verbs are singular and masculine (2:17). But when the serpent tempts Eve and she quotes God's command ("You must not eat . . ."), the "you" is *plural* (3:3). That is, Eve knows that when God told Adam, "If you eat, you will die," he told her too, even if she wasn't there. What God said to Adam, he said to Eve.

After the Fall, God treats Adam as the party chiefly responsible for the disaster. The man bears the brunt of God's inquiry. In 3:9 God asks, "Where are you?" using a masculine singular Hebrew pronoun. In 3:11 God asks, "Who told you that you were naked?" using a singular again. In 3:13 God turns to the woman, and in 3:16-19 he punishes both of them. But God speaks of Adam alone in 3:22-24, expressing concern that the man "become like one of us" so that he must be driven out of the garden. Thus, Genesis shows that *in his relationship with Eve, Adam led both at creation and after the Fall*. That is how Paul interprets Genesis in 1 Corinthians 11:8-9 and 1 Timothy 2:13 (see chapters 5 and 6).

Male leadership is God's original plan. It is not due to the Fall and curse. Therefore, when we work to reverse the consequences of sin, we do not attempt to banish male leadership; we labor to see that it functions according to God's original design.

GENESIS 1—2 AND MALE-FEMALE EQUALITY

The value of Eve and the leadership of Adam are both evident from the beginning. Adam is the first one formed; Eve is his peer and complement. Genesis 1 says that both man and woman are created in the image of God and rule the world for him. Genesis 2 conveys the same point when it describes Adam's brief bachelor life and the creation of Eve.[5] While he was alone, God charged Adam to work the garden and care for it (2:15). Moses also mentions resources of gold, onyx, aromatic resin, and rivers outside the garden (2:10-14), hinting that mankind would eventually pass beyond Eden's borders. Meanwhile, Adam must tend Eden (2:15-17). Splendid as the earth and the task were, Moses implies that something was amiss:

The LORD God said, "It is not good for the man to be alone. I will make a helper suitable for him." Now the LORD God had formed out of the ground all the beasts of the field and all the birds of the air. He brought them to the man to see what he would name them; and whatever the man called each living creature, that was its name. So the man gave names to all the livestock, the birds of the air and all the beasts of the field. But for Adam no suitable helper was found. So the LORD God caused the man to fall into a deep sleep; and while

he was sleeping, he took one of the man's ribs and closed up the place
with flesh. (2:18-21)

There is a riddle here. In Genesis 1 all six days of creation ended
with the refrain: "And God saw that it was good" (1:4, 10, 12, 18, 21,
31). Now we read, "It is *not good* for the man to be alone" (2:18,
emphasis added). This is unexpected. Sin has not arrived; what can
be wrong? We are relieved perhaps to see that God proposes a rem-
edy for Adam's problem: "I will make a helper suitable for him." Yet,
surprisingly, God does not immediately make that helper. Instead,
apparently ignoring the problem, he orders Adam to name the animals. We are baffled, but there is no sense that Adam is troubled—
yet. The process of naming the animals then begins the resolution.

To name the animals well, Adam must give them descriptive
names. That requires Adam to observe and ponder: "What is the
essence of this beast? What is a fitting name for it?" The verses
describing the process are repetitive. God brought the animals to
Adam "to see what he would *name* them; and whatever the man *called*
[one], that was its *name*. So the man gave *names* . . ." (emphasis
added). The task, the repetition implies, took time. Then suddenly
Adam's singleness, his lack of a helper, reappears: "But for Adam no
suitable helper was found." Why does Genesis return to the problem
of loneliness now?

As Adam named the animals, he had to notice that they came in
pairs so that they could multiply. All had companions—except him!
Where was his partner? He delighted in God's creatures, but he surely
noticed that none was his suitable companion. Consider the domestic canine. It is pleasant to romp and play with a pup, and it is relax-
ing to pat a dog that snoozes contentedly by our side. But dogs are
limited. If we want to frolic, dogs are fine; but if we want a conversation, they fail us. We can relate to dogs at *their* level, but they cannot
rise to ours.

Adam had to sense this problem as he named the animals. God
had Adam name all the animals *so he would see his aloneness as loneli-*
ness. Work and animals would never fulfill Adam. He needed more,
and now he knew it, as the parade of animals impressed Adam with

both his superiority and his solitude. He saw no companion among the animals. Adam was seeking, but not finding, "a suitable helper" (2:20). Now that Adam sees the situation God's way, God can fashion the woman, the companion suited to the man's needs. When He finishes, God leads Eve to Adam, presenting one last creature for him to name.

When Adam meets Eve, he breaks into poetry. Now at last he cries, "This is now bone of my bones and flesh of my flesh" (2:22). Eve is Adam's companion and partner. She is not a threat due to her equality, nor a menace due to her differentness. Her capacity to commune with him brings joy (2:23). The woman, bride and wife, is the helper Adam needed because she is *of* his flesh and yet *other than* his flesh. Thus Adam rejoices at Eve and marries her. She completes him.

The phrase "I will make a helper suitable for him" (Gen. 2:20) has been interpreted different ways. Chauvinists say, "You see, this proves that women exist to help men." Feminists retort, "No, it proves that men need help!" But the truth is happier than gender warriors suggest.

In biblical parlance, a "helper" is simply one who serves and need not be an inferior. After all, God often calls himself "Israel's helper" (Exod. 18:4; Deut. 32:29; Ps. 10:14). God did give Eve to Adam to support his work of caring for creation, but he made her strong enough to help. By helping us, God dignifies all helpers.

There are two lessons for our gender debates. To correct chauvinists, we say God designed women to help men, but *women are able to help because they are strong*. To correct feminists, we say God designed men to need women, but *women must be willing to help*.

Chronic problems in the gender debates would be resolved if we better understood God's character and ways. In God's world, the Almighty is a helper, and the Lord of all is servant of all (Matt. 20:25-28). In God's world, subordination does not signify inferiority. God sovereignly appoints a place for everyone, and a subordinate post may have nothing to do with weakness.

This point is essential to healthy male-female relations at home and at church. First, let men grant women dignity for their strength. Second, let women live with humility in their service. Third, let women walk with nobility in their Christlike labor.

We do not think this way today, of course. In cases such as the parent-child relationship, the superior is stronger and wiser. But two people can have the same ability and virtue while one subordinates himself to the other. In academia, for example, department chairmen commonly petition to be "demoted" so they can get back to their scholarship. In a marriage, when husband and wife have similar abilities, they will divide their labor to create order and get jobs done, without worrying about who gets the prestigious tasks. In our home, I am better at comforting the children, and my wife is more mechanical. We think that is fine.

JESUS, SUBORDINATION, AND EQUALITY

Marriage, work, and church life afford ample opportunities to live out the principle of subordination between equals. But Jesus illustrates it best. Jesus is the Son, the second person of the Godhead. He is fully and truly God, co-equal and co-eternal with the Father. He is perfect in knowledge, power, and virtue. As Lord and Redeemer, he merits worship and praise. He is in no way inferior to the Father or the Spirit; yet he subordinated himself to the Father's direction and the Spirit's leading while on earth. He went where the Spirit led and spoke when the Spirit came upon him (Matt. 4:1; Luke 4:14). He performed miracles when the Spirit's power was present to heal (Luke 5:17; 6:19; 8:46). Jesus often declares his subordination to the Father in John's Gospel:

My food is to do the will of him who sent me and to finish his work. (4:34)

By myself I can do nothing. . . . I seek not to please myself but him who sent me. (5:30)

I have come down from heaven not to do my will but to do the will of him who sent me. (6:38)

My teaching is not my own. It comes from him who sent me. (7:16)

The one who sent me is with me . . . for I always do what pleases him. (8:29)

Make no mistake, the same chapters in John clearly indicate Jesus' deity. He is the judge of the world and the author of eternal life, which he gives to all who believe in him (5:21-24, 39-40). He is the bread of life (6:40), the water of life (7:37), the light of the world (8:12; 9:5), the preexistent God (8:58). He sets people free from their sins (8:34-36) and deserves the same glory as the Father (5:23; 12:23).

The lesson is clear. If Jesus, who is equal to the Father in every way, chose to subordinate himself to the will of the Father, then women can choose to subordinate themselves to others when God so directs. If Jesus submits himself to the Father while equal to him in every way, a woman can submit to male leaders while equal to them in every way. The subordination of the Son to the Father is a model of the subordination of wives to their husbands. Review the quotations in John: If Jesus could say these things to the Father, women can respect men whom the Lord appoints as their leaders.

Genesis 1 and 2 demonstrate both the equal value of men and women and the leadership role of men. When God creates both man and woman in his image, we see their equality. When God creates the man first, we see man's leadership. When Adam is lonely and needy without Eve, we see male-female partnership. We see that men and women are equal but not identical. Men and women have equal worth but differing roles. Men have leadership without superiority. Like Jesus, women experience subordination without inferiority.

GENESIS 3—SIN AND GENDER RELATIONS

Egalitarians argue that Adam and Eve were originally equal in their nature and tasks. But Adam led from the beginning. God formed Adam first, and Adam named Eve, his companion and helper. Adam and Eve briefly experienced the ideal of equal value but varied roles. Eve held a subordinate role without suffering oppression, but this condition dissolved when sin arrived. The Fall began when Eve entertained the voice of the serpent, it ripened when Adam failed to protect his wife, and it culminated when Adam followed Eve into rebellion.

Since Adam and Eve married, the Fall poisoned both marriage and gender relations. This effect became apparent when God called on

Adam, who tried to blame both his wife, for tempting him, and God, for giving him this woman in the first place. "The woman you put here with me—she gave me some fruit from the tree, and I ate it" (Gen. 3:12).

The Bible never romanticizes marriage. It is a society of sinners. Jesus came not to praise the family but to redeem it. The first couple exchanged harmony for struggle and affection for tension.

We traditionally call Genesis 3:14-19 "the curse." But if we look carefully, we see that God only curses the serpent and the ground. For woman and man, he announces pain and disruption, but he also promises grace that limits suffering.[6]

> So the LORD God said to the serpent, "Because you have done this, cursed are you . . . ! You will crawl on your belly and you will eat dust all the days of your life. And I will put enmity between you and the woman . . . he will crush your head, and you will strike his heel."

> To the woman he said, "I will greatly increase your pains in child-bearing; with pain you will give birth to children. Your desire will be for your husband, and he will rule over you."

> To Adam he said, "Because you listened to your wife and ate from the tree . . . cursed is the ground because of you; through painful toil you will eat of it all the days of your life. It will produce thorns and this-tles for you, and you will eat the plants of the field. By the sweat of your brow you will eat your food until you return to the ground . . . for dust you are and to dust you will return" [emphasis mine].

See how much grace God places in this declaration:
- God places enmity between the serpent (the mouthpiece for Satan) and the woman. Surely it is good for there to be hostil-ity between mankind and Satan. It is good that we fear and hate Satan.
- The curse brings warfare between the seed of the woman, Jesus, and the serpent. That war is blessed, for Jesus bruises the serpent's head even though the serpent bruises Jesus' heel (ESV).
- The woman will suffer pain in childbearing, but at least she will have children. Adam and Eve will die for taking the fruit, but they will not die at once; nor shall the human race perish.

- The man will suffer painful toil and sweat in his labor, but at least he will not starve. We will fight weeds (and technological malfunctions), but we will not perish.

When God announced his judgment, he applied it to the man in his work and to the woman in her relationships. The statement, "Your desire shall be for your husband, and he will rule over you," reflects this application to the woman. But is this judgment pure doom, or is there grace there, too? The answer turns on the nature of the woman's "desire" and the man's rule.

The term for "desire" appears just three times in the Bible—in Genesis 3:16 and 4:7 and in Song of Solomon 7:10. In the Song, "desire" is sexual. So some believe the curse is that woman's sexual desire becomes irrational so that she has relations with her husband though she knows it leads to pain in childbirth. Others say "desire" signifies an emotional and economic dependence that drives her to submit to her husband even if his leadership is insensitive or abusive. Egalitarians say that women trade their equality with men for subjection to them. Complementarians say that the woman's light subordination to man's rule becomes a heavy servitude. The common thread is that women are willing to submit to their husbands in a destructive way. Sadly, experience confirms that women can wrongly remain in relationships with violent, oppressive men.

But a second explanation of Genesis 3:16 proposes that the woman's "desire" for her husband is an urge to control him, not love him. The next passage, Genesis 4, uses the same term "desire" in a negative, nonsexual way. There Cain, overwrought by God's rejection of his sacrifice, turns his rage against his brother Abel. God reasons with him, "Why are you angry, and why has your face fallen? If you do well, will you not be accepted? And if you do not do well, sin is crouching at the door. Its desire is for you, but you must rule over it" (Gen. 4:6-7 ESV). This translation of 3:16 and 4:7 shows that the main Hebrew terms are identical; the sentence structures are also similar.

3:16: "Your *desire* shall be *for your husband*, and he shall *rule over* you."

4:7: "Its *desire* is *for you*, but you must *rule over* it."

Sin desires to dominate Cain, but he must fight to master it.

Similarly, wives desire to dominate their husbands. Susan Foh says, "The woman has the same sort of desire for her husband that sin has for Cain, a desire to possess or control him."[7] Typically, husbands resist and stymie the wife's desire for mastery.

Events in Genesis support this view, as women are more prone to rebel against their husbands than to submit too meekly. For example, we see Rebekah ignoring Isaac's will in Genesis 27. We also find Rachel and Leah striving for control over their shared husband, Jacob, in Genesis 29 and 30. Today there are some overly submissive women, but we also have ample experience of defiant women, of homes and workplaces where warlike women battle bellicose men.

Genesis predicts strife between husband and wife. Conflict is an element of sin's disruption. If a husband is cruel and vindictive, his "victories" in marriage combat can deepen the curse. But his mastery may also contain the grace we noticed in other judgments. If the man thwarts the woman's desire to overthrow God's order, they retain a semblance of God's plan. Yes, men often abuse their strength. But many rule well and bring the gift of a well-ordered life.[8]

To say it another way, some think a woman's "desire" for her husband is innocent, if somewhat disordered. Wives desperately seek companionship, which husbands generally do not return. This view says that wives have unsatisfied longings for their husbands' affection. They plead, "Darling, don't go to work today; linger with me on sheets of satin." But men retort, "Nay, woman, I go forth to tame the world, to slay its dragons." With her desire for fellowship thwarted, woman is prone to accept man's domination.[9] So women want a lover and get a lord. The man's cold strength is the woman's enslavement.

But it is more accurate to think that the woman's "desire" signals an urge to dominate her husband, leading to a struggle she will probably lose. Wives tell husbands, "You better get to work," and husbands retort, "I'll work when I please." The struggle is a bitter fruit of sin, but the man's victory contains one small grace: It preserves some order.

CONCLUSIONS

The Fall does not *cause* male leadership; it perverts it. The complementary roles of leader and helper are not inherently evil, though sin does pervert them. Since male leadership is not a result of sin, we should not try to reverse it at home or church. Men, instead of leading sacrificially, vacillate between lazy abdication and harsh domination. Women, spurning the role of strong helper, vacillate between combativeness and servility.

Christians must labor to reverse the effects of the Fall. But we need to know what we are doing—or *undoing*. We do not bring peace to the gender wars by annulling male leadership. To eradicate male leadership to solve male-female tension makes no more sense than eradicating work to solve the problem of sweat, or eradicating reproduction to remove the pain of childbirth. Obstetricians reduce pain, but childbirth continues. Air conditioners reduce sweat, but work continues. And loving service reduces strife between men and women, but male leadership continues. Sin has perverted God's structure for male-female relations, but grace can restore it.

Genesis shows that male leadership is a result of God's original plan, not a consequence of the Fall. Male leadership in the church is part of God's design for creation. Therefore, we should expect men to lead the church and the family today. If men take responsibility and lead sacrificially, and if women use their strengths to help, we will return, at least partially, to God's original plan.

A book on women in ministry could bypass Ephesians 5 since marriage is its theme. But, like Genesis, Ephesians shows that male leadership is part of God's design for men and women in close relationships. It also explains how men lead well and how women follow well; so we will study it briefly.

EPHESIANS 5—GENDER AND MARRIAGE

Few texts are more feared, even reviled, than the dreaded imperative: "Wives, submit to your husbands" (Eph. 5:22). There are reasons for this. Many men abuse Paul's command, citing it as a pretext for selfish domination of women. But some women resent the idea that they should ever submit to *anyone*, including their husbands.

I often speak at marriage conferences but almost never focus on the submission of wives. Still the question often arises in question-and-answer sessions. In my experience, more women complain about husbands who *refuse* to lead than complain about husbands who lead oppressively. More men abdicate than dominate. They arrive home exhausted by work, flop on the sofa, open the paper, turn on the television, and tune out the family. Their bodies have arrived, but their minds are still en route. If the children become unruly, they may rouse themselves to shout a bit before sinking, sloth-like, back into their diversions. Abusive domination is a less common but more severe problem. Abdication brings frustration, but domination brings devastation.

Submission of wives does not imply domination by husbands, as a careful look at Ephesians shows. In context, the command "wives submit" develops two broader imperatives. Ephesians 5:1-2 reads, "Be imitators of God . . . and live a life of love, just as Christ loved us and gave himself up for us." Ephesians 5:18 says, "Do not get drunk on wine. . . . Instead, be filled with the Spirit." Grammatically, the next five verbs are participles that describe the character of a Spirit-filled life. Spirit-filled people will demonstrate the Spirit's influence by "addressing one another in psalms and hymns and spiritual songs, singing and making melody to the Lord with all [their] heart, giving thanks always . . . submitting to one another out of reverence for Christ" (5:18-20 ESV).

The phrase "submitting to one another" stands as a banner over Ephesians 5:22—6:9, the longest description of family life in the Bible. "Submitting to one another" is a striking phrase, an apparent oxymoron. Submission is one-directional. We submit to *authorities*— to God, king, governor, or officer. We submit to parents and laws. Submitting occurs when one person who is lower in rank yields to another who is higher in position or power. Submission means that one person bows to the will of another. But how can two people submit to each other? They cannot both outrank the other. Can parents submit to children? Can husband and wife *each* submit to the other? There are two possible answers:

First: Believers should *submit to whatever authority* is over them. On this view, the command to submit to each other does not mean that everyone should submit to everyone, as if all authority structures cease. Rather, Paul means that each Christian should yield whenever someone has authority over him or her. "Submitting to one another" does not mean parents should submit to their children just as children submit to parents. Parents should *serve* their children so self-lessly that it may *appear* that the parents are submitting. But irreversible authority structures remain. Parents can still tell children when to go to bed, and children may *not* reply, "Fine, but *you* should go to bed, too."

Second: All fixed authority relations are relativized so that no one has the right to exercise authority over anyone else except by temporary necessity or mutual agreement. So husbands have no general duty to lead their wives, pastors have no intrinsic authority over their churches, and employers have no objective authority over employees.

There are reasons to favor the first view, that "submitting to one another" means all Christians should submit to the relevant authorities, not that everyone submits to everyone. If these arguments are valid, then authority structures remain at home and church.[10] The reasons are semi-technical, and so readers may wish to skip the proof, in smaller print:

Reason 1: The term "submit" (*hypotassō*) means to subject, subordinate, bring under control, or obey. Excluding Ephesians 5, submission is one-directional in all New Testament uses. One person, who is lower in position or power, yields to a person of higher position or power. Therefore, "submitting to one another" does not mean all Christians submit to everyone; it means they submit to whatever authorities are appropriate. That is, "submitting to one another" means to submit whenever there is a rightful authority to submit to.

Reason 2: The chief reason to speak of mutual submission is the pronoun "to each other." The Greek term typically requires full reciprocity—but not always. It is reciprocal in Philippians 2:3: "Consider *one another* better than yourselves," and Mark 9:50: "Be at peace with *one another*." But other times "each other" is not fully reciprocal. In Galatians 6:2, "Carry *one another's* burdens" does not mean everyone should trade burdens with everyone else. Galatians 6:5, "Each one should carry his own load," shows that total reciprocity is not in view. Rather, those who have lighter burdens carry others' burdens *when appropriate*. Similarly, Christians should submit when appropriate. Likewise, in Revelation 6:4, "Men slay *one another*" does not mean all murders end in double death, but that warring men slay whomever they can. Similarly, Ephesians 5 commands that we submit to whomever we can.

Reason 3: The text itself limits the extent of the submission so that it falls short of total mutuality. Thus wives are not told to submit to all men but to *their own* husbands. Further, Paul tells children to obey and slaves to submit, but he never tells husbands, parents, and masters to submit to wives, children, or slaves.

Reason 4: Paul's other writings show that authority structures remain. Paul commands Christians in Rome to submit to governing authorities. Paul orders the church to submit to their overseers. But he neither commands the government to submit to the people nor tells overseers to submit to the people (1 Thess. 5:12).

So Ephesians 5 neither teaches full reciprocity nor ends authority structures. Wives submit to husbands, children obey parents, and slaves obey masters, but not visa versa. Still, Paul's directions do alter the concept of authority. If husbands sacrifice for their wives, if parents do nothing to exasperate their children, if masters never threaten but treat slaves respectfully (5:25; 6:4, 9), if authorities wield power for others, the spirit has changed even if the structure has not.

Authorities remain; yet if they lead benevolently, their authority will appear to fade. When a husband loves his wife, when parents nurture their children, when masters forgo threats, when authorities bend to the needs of their subordinates, casual observers might think they have abdicated. In the world, the powerful lord it over others for their own benefit. Not so in the family of faith. To a widow newly married to a Christian husband, to an orphan newly adopted by a Christian father, all would seem new if they left the sway of a typically self-indulgent lord. Their needs matter. Arbitrary demands are fewer. Christians should exercise authority with enough love that all things seem new. Still, we are not free to create whatever arrangement seems workable. Men still bear responsibility to direct the family for its good.

Finally, marriage is different from other authority relations. Paul tells children and slaves to obey; he tells wives to submit, not obey, suggesting that the husband-wife relationship is more nearly reciprocal. Remember that parents can tell children to go to bed as they discern their best sleep schedule, but children cannot order their parents to sleep. Yet marriage is so nearly reciprocal that a wife can summon her husband to bed (1 Cor. 7:3-5!).

THE WIFE'S THEME

Still, we cannot escape it. Paul does say, "Wives submit to your husbands as to the Lord. For the husband is the head of the wife as Christ is the head of the church. . . . Now as the church submits to Christ, so also wives should submit to their husbands in everything" (Eph. 5:22-24). Literally, Paul says wives must submit to *their own* husbands, not to men in general. Scripture never says women must submit to men in general. Further, when Paul says the husband is the head, he means that the husband is the leader or authority, not the tyrant.[11]

The wife *accepts* a husband's leadership in two ways. First, she listens to him, expecting him to lead, not chafing under the indignity of it all. She understands that her submission does not undermine her dignity, for it offers a unique opportunity to be like Christ, who is equal with the Father and yet submissive to his will.

Second, she *respects* her husband. If there is one thing a man needs from his wife, it is respect. So many women show the opposite, making little jokes about their husbands' incompetence, ignorance, and oafishness. If he protests, she says, "I was just kidding." There is a woman who submits but who makes it perfectly clear that it is beneath her dignity to do so. That brings dishonor both to her husband and to herself.

Men do abuse submission, of course. Some seize it to make demands about food, money, or sex. Others use it to silence and control their wives. Paul forbids such things. Almost every principle here applies to gender relations at church. This chapter is already long, and so I will not spell them out; I trust you to see and claim them.

THE HUSBAND'S THEME

The love of Christ is the standard for husbands: "Husbands, love your wives, just as Christ loved the church and gave himself up for her, to make her holy . . . and to present her to himself as a radiant church, without stain or wrinkle or any other blemish, but holy and blameless."

This love is spiritual, not managerial. Jesus does not aim to "manage" the church so that its events start on time, its budget stays balanced, and no one gets upset. He aims to make it pure and radiant. Just so, a husband's first concern is not horizontal, to manage his wife, but vertical, to purify her. It is possible to study marriage and church and fix on methods for a better life in an utterly selfish way. Management folk have such helpful techniques. They say:

- Give compliments freely. People will feel good about you and compliment you later.
- Smile. It relaxes the face muscles, makes people positive, and creates a good atmosphere.
- Tell the truth. Share useful information with others, and they may share with you. Never lie. The truth will come out anyway, and so disclose it yourself with your spin.

This sort of advice has a veneer of concern for others, but it is self-serving. And it is doubly disappointing when a husband wants only to manage his wife. Happiness may follow good leadership, but holiness and maturity should be a husband's first goal. Godly headship means leading "*the* way"—God's way—not "*my* way."

Christ's love is the husband's model. Paul does not specify what this means but leaves us to imagine how a husband can imitate Christ's love for the church. We could survey the four Gospels for a complete answer, but I will mention two things.

Loving leaders exercise their prerogatives for the benefit of others. Jesus did not use his divine prerogatives to grasp this world's pleasures. He claimed nothing. He had nowhere to lay his head, no guaranteed food supply or income stream. He humbled himself to the point of death on the cross. Likewise, husbands should use their prerogatives sacrificially. For example, when husbands and wives differ, loving leaders will choose purchases and activities for their wives' joy more than for their own. They watch romantic comedies because their wives like them and cannot sleep after wrenching dramas. They clean the kitchen because their wives hear "I love you" in the clatter of dishes. Loving leaders honor their wives' talents and goals. They decline promotions that advance their careers slightly at the price of a move that disrupts their wives' lives greatly.

Loving leaders perform concrete acts of service. Jesus' principal service is his death and resurrection to atone for sin. But he performed lesser services, too. When the Twelve gathered for their last supper, Jesus took a servant's role and washed their feet (John 13:1-17). Jesus did not descend to the church's level; he went lower. The implications for male-female relations in the home and the church should be obvious.

One Saturday morning, I hired a student to help with a project at my house. It took longer than we planned, and so he unexpectedly stayed for lunch, which was a potpourri of leftovers. Among the dessert options rested one small piece of strawberry-rhubarb pie. My wife urged me to take it. "You've worked hard all morning; you deserve it."

"Yes, but you like strawberry-rhubarb pie more than I do; so you take it," I replied, citing our semiofficial principle: "Whoever likes the last piece most gets it."

"Yes, but you haven't had much to eat, and I know you like it, too," she responded.

"I do like it, but you like it *more,* and I will enjoy this brownie."

I thought I was making progress until I was interrupted by a howling laugh from our student guest. Startled, we turned to him.

"I've never heard anything like this," he said. "At my house whoever has the fastest hands grabs what he can and stuffs it in his mouth before anyone can stop him."

My wife and I had not thought our little debate was remarkable, but we realized we had stumbled onto something good. She wanted to put me first, to respect my work, and I tried to put her first, to respect her taste for this pie.

I tell this story to illustrate the atmosphere love can create. Women have learned to be wary of male leadership because men often wield power selfishly. But the gospel and grace of Christ can make all things new. Men can lead for others, and women can flourish as a result. That is the hope the Lord sets before us.

5

WOMEN, MEN, AND MINISTRY IN CORINTH

WHEN PAUL WROTE 1 Corinthians, he addressed a group that was both gifted and confused. A port city in Greece, Corinth was also an official Roman colony famed for its trade, wealth, and immorality.[1] The Corinthian Christians overvalued their freedom, which threatened to become license. Some viewed their sexuality as a mere bodily function and thought they were free to join prostitutes (6:12-20).[2] Others reacted against sexual license. Some hesitated to marry or contemplated divorce; others abstained from sex within marriage (7:1-40).

In responding to these issues, Paul broke with the sexual counsel of his day by laying down one *standard* for both men and women. Yet he gave men and women different *roles*. He affirmed women's gifts and expected them to pray and prophesy (11:5). But he also said, "Women should remain silent in the churches" (14:34). This leaves us wondering how Paul expected women to prophesy and at the same time to be silent. We suspect that we are missing something.

This chapter focuses on the gifts and silences of women, but Paul's remarks about sex and marriage clarify his approach to gender. They show that "Paul was never a modern egalitarian," but neither did he advocate "strong forms of patriarchy." Paul reformed the family, commanding husbands to love their wives and forbidding parental harshness. He treated wives as responsible members of the household, and yet he expected husbands to lead.[3] His counsel regarding women and ministry stressed both woman's responsibility and man's leadership.

SEXUAL LIBERTY, SEXUAL LICENSE, AND SEXUAL DUTY IN CORINTH (1 CORINTHIANS 5—7)

The Corinthians seized Paul's gospel teaching that believers are set free from sin and from the demand to obey the law to be saved (Rom. 6:18, 22; 8:2, 21; Gal. 5:1, 13). But their concept of liberty threatened to promote license rather than holiness, and in Corinth opportunities for indulgence abounded. As in many Greco-Roman cities, brothels operated openly near city centers. Upper-class parties offered the trio of gluttony, drunkenness, and sexual license. For pagan thinkers, a man's adultery was hardly considered wrong unless it involved a woman with high status, and then the prime issue was the violation of a prominent man's honor.[4] A master or a mistress might take any slave, male or female, for sexual purposes. We do not know how frequently that happened, but legally everything was permitted.[5]

Pagan philosophers defended such behavior. Demosthenes, speaking of marriage, said, "Mistresses we keep for the sake of pleasure, concubines for the daily care of our persons, but wives to bear us legitimate children and to be faithful guardians of our households."[6] At a wedding speech, Plutarch offered the bride justification for her husband's future adulteries. He said Persian kings keep their wives at state dinners but dismiss them when they "get drunk . . . and send for their music-girls and concubines." This is proper, Plutarch says, since it keeps "licentiousness and debauchery" from their wives. Therefore, if a husband dallies with another woman, the wife "should not be indignant," for "it is respect for her which leads him to share his debauchery, licentiousness, and wantonness with another woman."[7]

Add a mistaken concept of Christian freedom to this chaotic environment, and abuses easily follow. So in 1 Corinthians 5:1-10 we learn that a believer took his father's wife (his stepmother), and part of the church was proud of it. Next, Paul had to correct those who believed that the body's desire for sex is like a desire for food—a drive to be satisfied (6:12-13). Indeed, some Corinthian Christians used the slogan, "All things are lawful," to justify self-indulgence (1 Cor. 6:12; 10:23).

Paul advanced a series of arguments to halt the perversion of Christian liberty. Sexual sin is not beneficial. It is a sin we commit against our own body (6:12a, 19) and a "freedom" that enslaves

(6:12b). Besides, the body is not made for immorality but for the Lord (6:13). Nor is sexual sin a private affair. It perverts our union with Christ (6:15-17). Paul says, "You are not your own; you were bought at a price." We should glorify God with our bodies (6:19-20).

Throughout, Paul assumes that the moral standards for men and women are identical. The implicit evenhandedness of 1 Corinthians 6 becomes explicit in chapter 7. There Paul addresses Christians who sought to avoid immorality by shunning sex altogether, even in marriage. He advises, "The husband should fulfill his marital duty to his wife, and likewise the wife to her husband. The wife's body does not belong to her alone but also to her husband. In the same way, the husband's body does not belong to him alone but also to his wife" (1 Cor. 7:3-4). This statement is striking. First, compared to other marriage advice, it is remarkable that Paul even addresses the wife as a morally responsible agent. Second, Paul tells husbands and wives that they have identical rights and duties. Contemporary Jewish and Greco-Roman laws gave women far fewer rights. Sexually, wives were expected to be chaste while husbands had adventures. Further, Paul says, husbands do not own their wives. Neither man nor woman may say, "I have the right to do what I will with what is my own."[8]

Paul perfectly balances the rights of men and women. He commends celibacy to widowers and widows if they can practice self-control, but he urges both to marry if they cannot (7:8-9).[9] Wives should not divorce their husbands, and husbands should not divorce their wives (7:10-11). Neither should instigate divorce with an unbelieving spouse (7:12-13). Yet neither should prevent an unbelieving spouse from leaving if the spouse resolves upon it (7:15-16). We notice the symmetry at every point, but it was most striking in Paul's day when free men had all the rights and women had few.

Paul's equitable treatment of men and women here prepares us for 1 Corinthians 11 and 14. There Paul granted women crucial rights, but he still distinguished male and female roles. Notably, Paul permitted women to pray and prophesy but required that they show submission to their husbands as they spoke (11:4-15). Paul permitted women to prophesy (11:5) but not to weigh or judge prophecy (14:29). We need to discover why and what sort of prophecy this might be.[10]

PROPHECY WITH HEAD COVERINGS IN CORINTH
(1 CORINTHIANS 11:3-16 ESV)

> *3But I want you to understand that the head of every man is Christ, the head of a wife is her husband, and the head of Christ is God. 4Every man who prays or prophesies with his head covered dishonors his head, 5but every wife who prays or prophesies with her head uncovered dishonors her head—it is the same as if her head were shaven. 6For if a wife will not cover her head, then she should cut her hair short. But since it is disgraceful for a wife to cut off her hair or shave her head, let her cover her head. 7For a man ought not to cover his head, since he is the image and glory of God, but woman is the glory of man. 8For man was not made from woman, but woman from man. 9Neither was man created for woman, but woman for man. 10That is why a wife ought to have a symbol of authority on her head, because of the angels. 11Nevertheless, in the Lord woman is not independent of man nor man of woman; 12for as woman was made from man, so man is now born of woman. And all things are from God. 13Judge for yourselves: is it proper for a wife to pray to God with her head uncovered? 14Does not nature itself teach you that if a man wears long hair it is a disgrace for him, 15but if a woman has long hair, it is her glory? For her hair is given to her for a covering. 16If anyone is inclined to be contentious, we have no such practice, nor do the churches of God.*

This passage poses several questions. In what sense is man the "head" of woman (11:3)? Why must women cover their heads while men uncover theirs (11:4-5)? How is woman "the glory of man"? Does Paul believe men embody God's image more than women (11:7)? How do angels affect hair styles (11:10)? Given how much hair styles change across centuries and civilizations, what can "nature" teach us about hair (11:14-15)? What head covering did Paul want Corinthian women to wear? What might he ask of Christian women today? Questions like these have stimulated a vast, complex literature. Yet one point is clear: Especially in worship, Paul wanted married women to show respect for their husbands by the way they adorned their heads.[11] To prove this, we must first set the contexts for Paul's teaching.

At a literary level, Paul finished a section on freedom, from 6:12

to 10:31. Paul affirmed Christian freedom but had to control potential abuses. Here Paul says that women are free to prophesy, but he
checks a possible abuse—that women might prophesy in ways that
dishonor their husbands.

At a cultural level, we recall that Corinth was a Roman colony.
Destroyed by a Roman army in 146 B.C. and re-founded by Julius
Caesar in 44 B.C., nearly a century before Paul's visits, Corinth owed
much to Roman ways. Therefore, even though most residents of
Corinth were still Greek, we should focus on Roman customs as we
consider women's head coverings. Scholars debate whether the covering Paul required was a cloth or a certain hair style.[12] But surviving
statues, relief carvings, and references to hair in literature are consistent.[13] In portraits adult women (typically wives) wore their hair
curled or braided and up on their heads.[14] So if the head covering
Paul commends for wives is a hair style, it should be fairly long and
pulled up on the head.

When husbands and wives are shown together, the women's
heads are usually covered. They wear cloth shawls on top of the head,
not face veils.[15] But "girls, maidens, harlots, and immoral wives" went
bareheaded.[16] For an adult, short hair might signify prostitution or
lesbianism. So when Paul says, "If a wife will not cover her head, then
she should cut her hair short" (11:6), his readers know that a woman
with shorn or shaved hair has been humbled, as a punishment for
adultery or harlotry, for example.[17] Unusual hair, whether shorn or
unbound, could signify mourning. But long, loose hair could also
indicate rejection of a husband's authority—sexual promiscuity, "an
invitation to lust."[18] When Paul tells women to cover their heads, he
encourages them to retain the commendable values of their society.
They must not dress in ways that bring dishonor to their husbands.
If a woman does not have her literal head covered, she shames her fig-
urative head—her husband (11:3-6).

Greek, Roman, and Jewish men wore their hair short. For men,
"long hair [was] characteristic of homosexuals" and barbarians.[19]
Men rarely covered their heads in public, but Roman portraits show
that elite men did cover their heads during religious activities by
pulling a corner of their toga over the back of their heads. Even

Augustus and Nero appear in statues offering sacrifices in that posture.[20] When Paul forbids men to cover their heads, David Gill suggests, he urges them not to flaunt their status. That would cause divisions and status-seeking in the church (cf. 1:10-12; 6:1-8). Instead, by wearing nothing on their heads, they proclaim that Christ is their head (11:3).[21]

Among other things, Paul wants the Christians of Corinth to wear their hair according to local customs for respectable people. He demands nothing that is culturally difficult, nothing to alienate a neighbor needlessly.[22]

Whether we decide the covering is a veil, a hair style, or (most likely) a shawl, everyone agrees that Paul instructs married women to wear head coverings. Some of Paul's arguments are hard to follow due to our limited knowledge of ancient customs. But Paul intended everything to persuade the Corinthians to comply. The main point is clear at least.

11:3-5a

After thanking the Corinthians for holding fast to true doctrine, Paul exhorts them to order their male-female relations by his principles (11:2). He first cites a line of primacy: " . . . the head of every man is Christ, the head of a wife is her husband, and the head of Christ is God." This order explains why women cover their heads and men do not.

When Paul says, "the head of every man is Christ," *head* is a metaphor. Some think *head* means "source," but the most thorough studies indicate that *head* typically means either "authoritative headship"[23] or whatever is first, prominent, or outstanding, whatever is "determinative or representative by virtue of its prominence."[24] Paul uses *head* literally later, but the metaphors of headship or prominence fit well here. As chapter 4 showed, the Father exercises a kind of authority over the Son, even though the Son is eternally God.[25] As the Father has a kind of primacy over the Son, as the Son exercises authority over men, so men (especially husbands) have a kind of primacy over women (especially their wives).[26]

The Father and the Son share one divine nature, just as men and women share one human nature.[27] But even as there is an order in the Godhead, so there is an order for men and women. Paul says they must reflect that order in their appearance, especially when they pray or prophesy. Men manifest leadership by uncovering their heads. Women manifest submission to leadership by covering theirs.

If women refuse to cover their heads, they dishonor their "heads" in two senses. They dishonor themselves, that is, their physical head. They also dishonor their husbands, their metaphorical heads. When we disgrace authorities, we shame both ourselves and that authority. Rebellious students dishonor themselves and their teachers. Unruly children dishonor themselves and their parents. Rebellious wives dishonor themselves and their husbands.

11:5b-6

The themes of prayer, prophecy, and decorum indicate that the topic is worship. The setting might be formal worship, but Paul probably envisions women praying and prophesying in a looser, private gathering.[28] (The first reference to public worship is probably in 11:18: "When you come together as a church. . . .")

At any rate, Paul says that a woman who prays or prophesies with an uncovered head brings such shame on her head that she might as well shave it entirely. As much as male and female are one in Christ, God created distinctions between them that must remain visible. If a woman throws off the shawl, given by the culture to differentiate male and female, she might as well throw off the long hair given her by nature.

11:7-12

However our new life in Christ changes us, we remain created beings. Paul says that God created man first and created the woman from man and for man (11:8-9). Yet no one should think men are independent of women. We are mutually dependent. Whereas woman came from man at creation, man now comes through woman at childbirth (11:11-12). This reminder should keep men from abusing their authority. Two enigmas remain, in 11:7 and 11:10.

In 11:7 we understand the statement that man is "the image and glory of God," but how is woman "the glory of man"? Paul cannot believe man is the image of God, and woman is not, for he knows God made mankind, male and female, in his image (Gen. 1:26-28; Gal. 3:28). Of the many explanations offered for this statement, two seem plausible. The first says that while men and women both bear God's image, man gives God more glory because he imitates God's rule as he leads the family and the church.[29]

The second explanation of 11:7 notes that God receives glory when man manifests God's attributes. But just as man glorifies or honors God by reflecting God's attributes, so woman glorifies man by exhibiting man's attributes. To explain, a human exalts God when he or she mirrors God's character. Similarly a woman glorifies a man by revealing his character—although not by mirroring in this case. Rather, as husband and wife encounter each other in relationship, as their similarities and differences emerge, we see who man and woman truly are. Let me draw on some stereotypes that have been objectively verified. Men, more than women, can focus so intently on tasks that they do not hear a phone ringing or a baby crying just ten feet away. The average woman is much more likely to hear such things. Men are prone to philosophize about the world's woes while women actually search for lost keys. These differences do not prove either men or women are superior, but that they are different. Men and women reveal their character in their differences and in relationship to each other. Full humanness, Karl Bath said, is not "male or female" but "male and female." Man and woman are fully themselves as a complementary pair.[30]

The second enigma is in 11:10. It says women ought to have a symbol of authority on their heads "because of the angels."[31] The Greek term (angelos) most often means "angel" in the Bible, but it can also mean "messenger," and Bruce Winter argues it means messenger here. He reasons that Roman authorities were suspicious of Christians as a secretive sect. Yet meetings were open to the public, to visitors (1 Cor. 14:23-25). A Roman visitor might be shocked to hear a woman prophesying in church since women were not expected to speak in public meetings. Paul let them do so, but, he says, they should at least show their submission to men by wearing a head covering—"because of the messengers." Every visitor was a potential message bearer, describing the conduct of Christian gatherings. For their sake and for the sake of the Christians' reputation, women who spoke should do so with deco-rum—with their heads covered.[32]

11:13-16

Paul invites the Corinthians to agree that his judgment is correct. Nature itself, he declares, teaches men to keep short hair and women to grow long hair. An educated man, Paul knew that men from many cultures had long hair and that Jewish men grew theirs long for Nazirite vows. So he is not requiring everyone to conform to Greco-Roman customs. Rather, he says, nature teaches men to dress and behave like men and women to dress and behave like women. In that culture, men should not wear head coverings because it makes them look like women. Women should not shave their heads because it makes them look like men. The issue is not hair per se, but the nat-ural desire to identify with one's own gender.

Ancients and moderns both feel this desire. Epictetus asked, "Are you a man? . . . Very well then, adorn as a man, not as a woman." But if a man wants to look like a woman, says Epictetus disapprovingly, we exhibit him and say, "'I will show you a man who wishes to be a woman rather than a man.'"[33]

I once read a review of a documentary movie about Isaac Mizrahi, a designer of women's clothes. It reported that as a child, Mizrahi reg-ularly "pinched cash" from his parents while they slept, and with it he bought fabric. Since ordinary boys would spend stolen loot on sporting goods or food, it seemed that the writer was hinting that this designer was not an ordinary boy. The article added that Mizrahi "whipped up a special purple suit to wear on his first trip to Paris" when seventeen. The reader was hardly surprised to learn that Mizrahi was gay four paragraphs later. In our culture, *women* wear purple suits; men who dress in purple suits are not advertising their masculinity.[34]

Paul wanted men and women to give visible tokens that men lead and that women exercise their gifts within that leadership. In that cul-ture, a head covering implied a submissive woman. Head coverings no longer signify much in contemporary Western culture. If a woman wore a shawl on her head today, people might read it as an outdated style or as odd raingear. We must find culturally appropriate ways for women to show respect to their husbands.

In our culture, no single symbol signifies submission to authority. But if a married woman took off her wedding ring, wore revealing clothing, and reverted to her maiden name, people would deduce that she was rejecting her husband's authority. Conversely, a woman respects her husband by wearing a ring, dressing modestly, and speaking gently. In all we do, our external conduct should match our internal convictions.

So Paul wanted women to pray and prophesy. Yet in first-century Corinth, Paul wanted women to wear head coverings to affirm their submission to God's order for church and marriage.

A QUESTION OF METHOD

The last section said men must still lead the church, but women need not wear head coverings. Someone may ask, "Who has the right to pick and choose among biblical commands? How can you say head coverings are optional but male leadership is mandatory?"

Because our culture is so different from the Bible's, Christians must always labor to determine when to obey a command literally and when to seek the principle behind it and apply it nonliterally. I have written about this elsewhere; let me state the fundamentals here.[35]

First, we can distinguish principles from rules. Principles guide a wide range of behavior without specifying particular deeds. For example, "You shall love your neighbor as yourself" and "Seek first the kingdom of God " are principles. Rules require definite actions in specific cases. They embody or illustrate principles. "Greet one another with a holy kiss" (Rom. 16:16; 1 Cor. 16:20) is a rule. The principle is "Greet one another warmly." We apply it by hugging or shaking hands. Here is another rule: "When you build a new house, make a parapet around your roof" so that no one falls off it and dies (Deut. 22:8). The principle is "Do not kill; preserve life by taking precautions to prevent accidents." We apply this principle by putting banisters beside staircases.

In 1 Corinthians 11, the rule—a definite action in a particular case—is that women should cover their heads as they prophesy. The principles are: 1) women should use their gifts, including prophecy; and 2) women must respect men, especially their husbands, as God-ordained leaders of the home and church. In ancient Corinth, women showed respect for husbands by wearing head coverings. Today women show respect for their husbands in other ways.

This conclusion does not pick and choose among God's commands; it follows guidelines of sound interpretation. The use of head coverings is a rule that embodies the principle of male leadership. We can dispense with head coverings because they *manifest* the principle. We cannot dispense with male leadership because it *is* the principle. This point also holds for 1 Timothy 2 (chapter 6 in this book).

SILENCE OF WOMEN IN CORINTH (1 COR. 14:26-35)

26What then shall we say, brothers? When you come together, everyone has a hymn, or a word of instruction, a revelation, a tongue or an interpretation. All of these must be done for the strengthening of the church. 27If anyone speaks in a tongue, two— or at the most three—should speak, one at a time, and someone must interpret. 28If there is no interpreter, the speaker should keep quiet in the church and speak to himself and God. 29Two or three prophets should speak, and the others should weigh carefully what is said. 30And if a revelation comes to someone who is sitting down, the first speaker should stop. 31For you can all prophesy in turn so that everyone may be instructed and encouraged. 32The spirits of prophets are subject to the control of prophets. 33For God is not a God of disorder but of peace. As in all the congregations of the saints, 34women should remain silent in the churches. They are not allowed to speak, but must be in submission, as the Law says. 35If they want to inquire about something, they should ask their own husbands at home; for it is disgraceful for a woman to speak in the church.

The setting is the church at worship. It is an active congregation with abundant gifts. But the use of gifts must be orderly to ensure that the church is edified. Part of proper order is that women must remain silent, at least for a while (14:34). That prompts a question. How can Paul expect women to pray and prophesy (11:5), expect everyone to offer a hymn, a teaching, a revelation, or an interpretation (14:26), and yet tell women to remain silent (14:34)?[36] We do not expect Paul to contradict himself. How can women exercise their gifts in worship and yet remain silent in some sense? There are two plausible options.[37]

Option one holds that there are two kinds of worship in chapters 11 and 14. In chapter 11, women pray and prophesy during private or informal worship in which all share. Their prophecy is roughly what we call testimony or sharing today. In chapter 14, the worship is more structured. It may be like the synagogue worship (Luke 4; Acts 13) where one person is invited to bring the main exhortation. A few others may speak, and none of them may be women.

This view makes four valid points. First, Paul would never sanction a free-for-all in public worship where men and women express whatever they wish. Second, even if he let women share, they must neither upstage and dishonor their husbands nor act like peers with the church's male leaders. Third, church gatherings can be formal or informal; acts that are proper for a woman in one setting may be improper in another. Fourth, unless the church totally broke with the patterns of worship from believers in synagogues, recognized leaders would expound the word with authority at some point in worship. During that time, women should not speak.[38]

But this view does not adequately harmonize 14:26 and 14:35. How can Paul say everyone has a hymn or word of instruction in 14:26 and also say women must be silent in 14:35 if there is no qualification or limit on that silence?[39]

Option two harmonizes 14:26 and 14:35 by proposing a limit on the command of silence in 14:35. Specifically, *when Paul says women must remain silent, he means silent during the testing of prophecy.* The testing of prophecy is the theme of 14:29-35.[40] Paul wanted women to use their gifts, but he also wanted all teaching to be tested. That task belonged to elders (also called overseers), especially teaching elders. We know they are male, for they must be "the husband of one wife" (Titus 1:6; 1 Tim. 3:2).[41] Close analysis of 1 Corinthians 14 supports the view that women may prophesy (11:5) but must remain silent when prophecy is tested (14:34).[42]

Theme (14:26)	When you come together, everything must be done to edify the church.
Issue 1: Tongues (14:27-28)	*The number:* Two or at most three should speak. *To edify the church:* Let one interpret. If there is no interpreter, let him keep silent.
Issue 2a: Prophecy (14:29)	*The number:* Two or three prophets should speak. *To edify the church:* Let the others weigh what is said.
Issue 2b:	Additional *note on the number* that prophesies (14:30-33a)
On the Speaking	If a revelation is made to one, let the first be silent. You can prophesy one by one.
The Goal	Everyone will be instructed and encouraged. The spirits of prophets are subject to the control of prophets.
The Reason	God is not a God of disorder but of peace.
Issue 2c:	Additional *note on the weighing* of prophecy (14:33b-35)
On the Weighing	As in all congregations, women should remain silent.
On Women's Silence	They are not allowed to speak, but must be in submission. If they want to inquire, they should ask their husbands at home.
The Reason	It is disgraceful for a woman to speak in the church.

This outline shows how the silence of women applies to the weighing of prophecies. When leaders sift prophecy, then women must "be in submission, as the Law says" (14:34). "The Law" Paul cites in 14:34 is God's will, expressed at creation, that Adam must lead Eve (chapter 4). When Paul says women should ask their husbands at home if they want to know anything (14:35), he refers to the time when elders assess prophecies (14:36). If women wish to inquire about the testing, they may ask at home; they must be silent during the testing itself. This is the order "in all the congregations of the saints" (14:33b). If anyone disagrees, Paul notes ironically, they must think God has spoken to them alone because every church does it his way (14:36-38).

The term Paul chooses for silence also suggests that the women's silence is not absolute. Greek words for silence overlap, and we must not exaggerate differences between them.[43] But our word here, *sigaō*, rarely means total speechlessness. It can mean to keep something to oneself (Luke 9:36), to listen (Acts 15:12), or to be silent after speaking (Luke 20:26; Acts 15:13). The word appears in 14:28, 14:30, and 14:34. First Corinthians 14:28 says that if someone who is speaking in tongues has no interpreter, that person should be silent (*sigaō*)—temporarily stop speaking. First Corinthians 14:30 says that if one prophet is speaking and something is revealed to another, the first should be silent (*sigaō*)—temporarily stop speaking. And in 14:34, while prophecy is tested, Paul says women should temporarily stop speaking.

Outside the testing, women may pray, prophesy, sing, and teach. Churches gather for formal or informal worship. During formal times, the church's prime teachers would hold forth. Then the women might say little. Yet even when women did share, they would not preempt their husbands or church leaders.

Someone may ask why Paul lets women prophesy but not test prophecy. If we focus on prophets such as Moses, Samuel, and Isaiah, we think of prophets as authority figures and conclude that Paul gave women high authority when he let them prophesy. But most prophets were outsiders, prone to appear and disappear (1 Kings 17:1; 18:12). They were voices in the wilderness, lacking official, ongoing leadership. Elijah, Elisha, Jeremiah, Ezekiel, Hosea, and John the Baptist were ignored or abused, not honored (Matt. 23:29-37).[44] Priests were the regular authoritative teachers (Lev. 10:11; Deut. 21:5; 33:10; Mal. 2:6-7).

Women can also prophesy because apostles and elders, not prophets, are the prime authorities in the New Testament. Prophets were God's principal spokesmen in the old covenant, but apostles are the principal spokesmen in the new.[45] For example, in Acts 15 the *apostles and elders* determined the proper response to a theological crisis and then deputized *prophets* to carry the message (Acts 15:2-6, 22-32). Paul also subordinated prophets to himself, showing that apostles outrank prophets (14:37-38). Moreover, Paul assumes that elders, not prophets, will succeed the apostles when they die (1 Tim. 3; Titus 1).[46] Thus prophets do not bear primary authority in the church.

To return to the scene at Corinth, there are two dangers. First, there may be chaos if several prophets speak at once or if someone speaks in a tongue but has no interpreter (14:27-28). Second, false teaching may go unchecked if someone erroneously claims to speak at God's direction. To prevent chaos, Paul commends self-control. The Corinthians must stifle an impulse to speak if another is already speaking or if there is a tongue but no interpreter. Each must speak in turn. Even so, there must be no more than two or three tongues (14:27-28) and no more than three prophecies for a session (14:30-33).

To prevent false teaching, "the others should weigh carefully" what the prophets say, for not everyone who thinks he speaks God's word does so (14:29). It is necessary to weigh or sift speeches that claim to come from God lest the church accept false teachings.

But who are "the others" who test prophecy? They could be other prophets, but that is unlikely. First, Greek writers would use the term "the rest" [of the prophets], not "the others" if they wanted to say the remaining prophets do the testing. Second, the gift of discernment is separate from prophecy (12:10). Third, God appointed teachers to evaluate prophetic words delivered to the church.[47]

Someone may ask how these "others" have the right to test a prophet's speech. The answer is vital to a proper grasp of women's roles. It is necessary to test prophecy because people can falsely claim to speak for God. Moses warned about false prophets (Deut. 13:1-10) and insisted that Israel investigate when they heard of prophets who led the people astray (13:14). Prophets might also believe they speak for God and yet merely voice their impressions (1 Kings 22:1-37). Believers must test all things (1 Thess. 5:21; 1 John 4:1), for there are many false prophets (Matt. 7:15; 24:11, 24; 1 John 4:1; 1 Tim. 4:1). Many teachers seek only to please people (2 Tim. 4:3). Further, spoken prophecy in the New Testament is not identical to written prophecy in the Old (above). Spoken prophecy might report revelations from the Spirit to edify the church, but preaching and teaching had more authority and perhaps less potential to confuse one's subjective impressions with the Spirit's revelations.[48]

Everyone should be discerning (Job 34:2-6; Ps. 19:12; Matt. 16:3; Phil. 1:10; Heb. 5:14). But elders are especially responsible to guide the church to true doctrine (Acts 15:1-35; 20:17-31). Among elders, some especially "labor in preaching and teaching" (1 Tim. 5:17 ESV). Whether they label them pastors, teachers, ministers, or even priests, churches know God calls some men to proclaim and guard the truth. Paul wanted every church to have men who labor in the Word, teach, and discern (1 Cor. 12:10, 28-29). He appointed such men—elders—in every church (Acts 14:23) and told other church planters to do the same (Titus 1:5).[49] Thus it is fitting for women to prophesy but neither to preach nor test prophecy. In today's terms, women may testify or teach informally. But the task of preaching and guarding the Word belongs to male elders.

SUMMARY

So then women exercise vital gifts, but do not hold final authority. The prophetic labors of Moses, Samuel, Elijah, Isaiah, and Jeremiah differ from those of Miriam, Deborah, Huldah, or the women who prophesied in Corinth. Just as female prophets led under the umbrella of male leaders, so Corinthian women spoke under the umbrella of leaders who tested prophecy. For church order, the gifts of teaching and discernment carry more authority than prophecy. Paul distinguishes prophecy from teaching (Eph. 4:11; 1 Cor. 12:28), and so must we. A woman who prophesies and has her words weighed is like a woman who teaches occasionally at the invitation of church leaders. Both speak without supplanting men who promote and guard doctrine. Paul expects women to bless others if they operate under the sponsorship of the church's pastors and elders (chapter 8).

First Corinthians 5—7 shows that there is one ethical standard for all believers, whether male or female. Our roles and responsibilities differ, but we enjoy equality before God's law. First Corinthians 11:5 and 14:26 show that God also distributes his gifts to men and women. Everyone should use these gifts in an orderly way. Order means that prophets speak in turn. Order also means that women prophesy in ways that show respect for their husbands. And order means that elders test what prophets say, to ensure its veracity. At that time women must remain silent. But Paul does not silence women globally. He wants them to speak and pray to bless the church.

6

1 TIMOTHY 2

I HAPPENED TO GET a haircut the day I started this chapter. I brought a book about the apostle Paul, and my cutter (he was too inexpensive to be a stylist and too young to be a barber) noticed the title. "So what do you think of Paul?" he asked, quickly adding, "I think he's an opinionated bigot." This he learned in Religion 101. So it goes for Paul. He said, "I do not permit a woman to teach . . . ," and that is enough to label him a misogynist in some circles. Men have certainly used Paul to promote male domination and to excuse misogyny. But is Paul guilty of bigotry? We must read him in context to see.

1 TIMOTHY 2:9-15 IN CONTEXT

Paul said he wrote 1 Timothy so that "you will know how people ought to conduct themselves in God's household . . ." (3:14-15). The conduct he has in mind has three parts: pure doctrine, proper gender relations in the church, and proper leadership in the church. A peaceful church shuns pointless controversies (1 Tim. 1:6), holds to the gospel, and fights for the faith (1:12-19; 6:12-14). A healthy church also prays (2:1-8), behaves modestly (2:8-10), adopts proper gender roles (2:9-15), and has sound leadership (3:1-13).

There is a close link between chapter 1, with its interest in doctrine, and chapter 2, with its focus on gender relations.[1] The instructions about prayer are doctrinal; we should pray for *all* since Christ gave himself for *all*. Prayer for all "pleases God our Savior, who wants all men to be saved and to come to a knowledge of the truth" (2:1-6a). This prayer corrects heretics who believed the gospel was only for the elite.[2] But Paul's gospel is for everyone: Christ Jesus came into the world to save sinners; he is the one mediator (1:17; 2:3-6). Neither heretical teaching nor Christian misconduct may thwart this message.

Paul lays down standards for good conduct in 2:8-10 and for good teaching in 2:11-15. Men must contend for the gospel but not be contentious (1:18; 2:8). Women must beautify themselves with good works, not rich robes. Paul's desire to preserve the gospel and to assign proper gender roles are related. He wants the right people to fight heresy and present the truth. There are good reasons to believe that 1 Timothy 2:9-15 especially guides believers who gather for worship.[3] So the church faces heresy by standing firm in the gospel, maintaining good conduct, retaining proper gender roles, and following qualified leaders, especially in worship (2:1—3:13).

1 TIMOTHY 2:9-15 IN EXEGESIS[4]

1 Timothy 2:9-10. Woman's Apparel

I also want women[5] to dress modestly, with decency and propriety, not with braided hair or gold or pearls or expensive clothes, but with good deeds, appropriate for women who profess to worship God.

"I want women to dress modestly" means that women should adorn themselves with good deeds, not immodest clothes.[6] "Expensive clothes" might display a high social rank or a desire to rise in status. Greeks and Jews also viewed extravagant dress as a sign of promiscuity and disregard of a husband's authority.[7] In the early church, "the rejection of external adornment was part and parcel of a woman's submission to her husband and a recognition of her place among men in general." But ostentatious adornment indicated "sexual infidelity and materialistic extravagance."[8]

Modesty is the principle. When Paul cites braided hair, gold, and pearls, the point is not that pigtails are sinful, but that elaborate displays of wealth take attention *from* God who is worshiped *to* a well-dressed "worshiper." If men were prone to disrupt the church through angry disputes, women were prone to disrupt it through physical displays.[9]

1 Timothy 2:11. Woman's Learning—the Permission
  A woman should learn in quietness and full submission.

Modern readers can hardly see 1 Timothy 2:11 without 2:12: "I do not permit a woman to teach . . ." But 1 Timothy 2:11 both liberates and restrains. First it permits, even commands, "Let a woman learn" (ESV).[10] First-century Greek and Jewish cultures generally considered women mentally inferior. They judged women's education a waste of time at best and a cause of temptation at worst. As we saw before, the Mishnah advised men not to talk much to women lest men bring evil on themselves, neglect the law, and finally inherit damnation. Near Jesus' day, Philo, a Jewish philosopher influenced by Greek thought, said that Satan wisely attacked Eve through her senses, "For in us mind corresponds to man, the senses to woman." He also said that the masculine soul devotes itself to God the Creator while the feminine soul attends to things created.[11] But Paul believed women must listen and learn.

Paul stresses how women should learn—in quietness and submission. "Quietness" means in a quiet manner, not in absolute silence.[12] "Submission" means that they accept the doctrine taught by the church leaders. Quiet and submissive listening shows that women respect their teachers and accept the teaching. This kind of submission is only sensible. Neither men nor women can learn if any are noisy and insubordinate.

Feminists say that after women learn enough, they will begin to teach. Therefore, they reason, when Paul prohibits women from teaching in 2:12, it is a temporary ban that applies only until women are well instructed.[13]

It is true that women can impart what they know to others, as Abigail and Priscilla did. To anticipate chapter 7, women rightly *function* as teachers, sharing their knowledge, perhaps rather frequently, to edify others (Rom. 15:14). But feminists believe that well-instructed women should hold the teaching *office* as elders or preachers. This view rests in part on a distinctive interpretation of the phrase "I do not permit" in the next verse, 2:12.

1 Timothy 2:12. Woman's Teaching—the Prohibition

I do not permit a woman to teach or to have authority over a man; she must be silent.

Paul's counsel seems clear: Women may learn but may not teach or exercise authority over men. Yet almost every word of 2:12 is contested. For one thing, Paul sometimes lets women teach men. He permits female prophets to speak in Corinth and lists female coworkers who must have said *something* as they toiled. He declares that all Christians have gifts they must exercise for the common good, knowing one must speak to exercise most gifts. How shall we reconcile Paul's prohibition here with his permission elsewhere? There are two possibilities: The prohibition may be temporary, or it may be partial.

Egalitarians say the prohibition is *temporary*. They note that the verb *permit* is in the present tense. Therefore, they say, Paul only prohibited teaching in the present, when women were uneducated. When that was remedied, they could teach. Unfortunately for this argument, the next sentences declare why women may not teach, and Paul cites the order of creation, not a lack of education. Further, some wealthier women *were* educated.[14] Besides, if the problem were lack of education, Paul could have said, "Women may not teach *until* they are educated."

It is misleading to say the present tense of "I do not permit" means the injunction is temporary. The use of the present tense does not imply matters will change later. Suppose I see my daughter licking ice cream from her bowl and say, "I do not permit you to lick your bowl." She ceases at once; yet the next time she eats ice cream, she licks her bowl again. If I say, "I told you 'I do not permit you to lick your bowl,'" I will hardly be pleased if she replies, "Yes, Father, but you used the present tense, so I thought you forbade licking in the present only, without reference to the future." No, prohibitions ordinarily stand 1) until further notice, and 2) unless something in the context shows that the prohibition is temporary. If I tell a child, "I do not permit you to open your presents until Christmas morning," it is clear when the prohibition ends. But Paul uses no "until." If I tell a child, "Don't touch that plate," as I take it out of the oven, I mean,

"Don't touch it while it is hot." After dinner, the child may touch the cool plate to wash it. But Paul gives no hint that his prohibition will end as circumstances change. When Paul says, "I do not permit a woman to teach," he delivers a permanent principle, not a temporary preference.[15]

Complementarians say Paul's prohibition is permanent but partial. Thus women may teach privately, informally, and occasionally. But, Paul says, they should not present the essentials of the faith as authoritative church leaders. The task of guarding the gospel occupied Paul's letters to Timothy (1 Tim. 6:20; 2 Tim. 1:12-14). That task belongs to the elders or "overseers" who are male; they are "the husband of one wife" (1 Tim. 3:2. The terms "elder" and "overseer" are interchangeable in Titus 1:5-7 and Acts 20:17, 28).

Paul's language indicates that the complementarians are correct. Paul forbids a certain kind of teaching, not all teaching, when he says women must not teach or exercise authority over men. Specifically, he means women should not teach the gospel fundamentals in the church assembly. There is a wide-ranging and technical debate about the terms "teach" and "exercise authority;" an appendix takes readers a bit deeper into the discussion that I will summarize shortly.

Three factors indicate that Paul forbids only public, authoritative instruction in doctrine. First, other Scriptures show women teaching, but none show them preaching or teaching the assembly of believers. Second, the context is worship in the church. Therefore the teaching is what leaders do when the whole church gathers. Third, Paul's language suggests that he forbids women to teach doctrine and to exercise ruling authority in the church. Let us consider that language now.

The verb translated "teach" (*didaskō*) means just that, to teach or instruct someone. But in Paul's letters—especially in 1 Timothy, 2 Timothy, and Titus—what is taught is usually the foundational doctrines of the faith.[16] (Timothy and Titus were Paul's most trusted pastoral representatives; the three letters to them form a cluster called "the Pastoral Epistles.") A clear example of teaching that has doctrine as its content is found in 2 Timothy 2:2: "The things you have heard me say in the presence of many witnesses entrust to reliable men who will also be qualified to *teach* others." Similarly, in Titus 1:9 (ESV) Paul says that an elder must "hold firm to the trustworthy word as *taught*, so that he may be able to give instruction in *sound doctrine* and also to rebuke those who contradict it."

The noun *teaching* is very similar. For example, Paul says God called us through the gospel to share in the glory of Jesus. Then he adds, "So then, brothers, stand firm and hold to the *teachings* we passed on to you, whether by word of mouth or by letter" (2 Thess. 2:14-15). The teachings or "traditions" (ESV) are the message of the apostles carefully handed down by spoken words and letters (Gal. 1:6-12).

So when Paul says, "I do not permit a woman to teach," he means men must preach the gospel truths that are the heart of the faith. The preachers are the church's elders. They are apt to teach and lead exemplary lives, proving their ability to lead by caring for their wives and children (1 Tim. 3:1-5). Some elders work hard in the Word—preaching, teaching, and defending the gospel (5:17). The point is not that men must do all the teaching or that women must never teach men anything. Rather, Paul says that men who are tested, approved, and consecrated by the church must preach, teach, and defend the gospel of Christ (2 Tim. 2:24-26).

Paul also says that women must not "exercise authority." The Greek word (*authenteō*) is difficult because it is rare, appearing just once in the New Testament and only a hundred times or so in all ancient literature. It sometimes has negative connotations. Some say Paul means that women must not "usurp authority over men" or "abuse their authority over men." But most evidence indicates "rule" or "exercise authority" is the best definition.[17] In a telling example, the great Greek preacher John Chrysostom says that women must not teach men because Eve "once taught Adam wrongly" and must not exercise authority over man because "she once *exercised authority* wrongly." "Exercise authority" is our word, and when Chrysostom added "wrongly" to it, it shows he felt our word did not, by itself, have a negative force. If *authenteō* does not intrinsically mean to abuse or usurp authority, then Paul is forbidding women to rule or govern the church.[18]

Third, the grammatical structure points also to the translation "exercise authority." The terms "teach" and "exercise authority" are joined by the Greek conjunction *oude. Oude* is a negative word that means "and not," "neither," or "nor." *Oude* also has an interesting grammatical feature. When it links two verbs, both are bad in themselves, or both are good in themselves. It never links a negative and a positive verb.[19] Consider these sentences:

You may neither eat your food nor drink your juice until we pray.	"Eat" and "drink" are both positive. They will be linked in Greek by *oude*.
Neither steal nor destroy your brother's toys.	"Steal" and "destroy" are both negative. They will be linked in Greek by *oude*.
Neither call nor bother me.	"Call" is positive, "bother" is negative. They will not be linked in Greek by *oude*.

In our passage, Paul links "teach" and "exercise authority" with *oude*. This means both are positive or both are negative. Since "teach" is clearly positive, "exercise authority" must be positive, too.[20] It is correct, therefore, to translate 2:12, "I do not permit a woman to teach or to have authority over a man." Paul is not merely forbidding women to rule wickedly—by domineering or usurping authority; he is forbidding them to rule in a church context. Women may lead in various ways. But just as men bear final responsibility for the doctrine of the church, so men bear final responsibility for the direction of the church.

THE REASONS FOR MALE LEADERSHIP: THE APPEAL TO GENESIS

Creation

For Adam was formed first, then Eve. (1 Tim. 2:13)

Paul explains that male leadership is part of God's original plan. It rests on God's created order, not the Fall or the curse. By citing creation, Paul appeals to first principles. Jesus reasoned from creation when he faced a challenge about marriage and divorce (Matt. 19:3-9; Gen. 1:27; 2:24). Paul previously cited Genesis to explain male-female roles in 1 Corinthians 11. The appeal to creation indicates that male leadership rests on something essential to men and women.

Evangelical feminists claim that this verse is difficult to fathom.[21] Yet somehow critical feminists understand what Paul is saying; they simply believe he is wrong.[22] Paul appeals to the principle of primogeniture (chapter 4), which was well known to his original readers. Leadership by the firstborn is assumed throughout the Bible. It was the way of the world.[23]

Evangelical feminists say that Paul wanted the men to lead because the women were uneducated. But Paul does not mention ignorance. He does not say, "Uneducated women may not teach." Besides, not all the women of Ephesus (where Timothy labored when he received Paul's letter) were uneducated or deceived; Priscilla was there (2 Tim. 4:19). Paul makes no exception for women who were educated.

Some egalitarians are unimpressed by arguments from creation. They prefer to reason from redemption, saying the equality of men and women in redemption transcends their differences at creation. They cite Galatians 3:28: "There is neither Jew nor Greek, slave nor free, male nor female, for you are all one in Christ Jesus." They say an emphasis on creation leads to a stress on order and submission, whereas redemption accents "freedom, mutuality, and equality."[24] A vision of a new creation, when people of "every nation and social standing . . . [and] of both genders" are reconciled, must "transform the present," they claim. For Christ did not establish the church merely to "mirror original creation, but to anticipate . . . God's new creation."[25]

This has a certain appeal, but Scripture explicitly says *the order of creation will not change until Jesus returns* to judge and restore creation. *Then* our bodies will change (1 Cor. 15:22-23). *Then* marriage will end (Matt. 22:30). And Scripture has clearly prescribed the gender roles that govern this age (Eph. 5:22-33; Col. 3:18-19; 1 Tim. 5:14).

All Christians agree that men and women are one in Christ. But our oneness in Christ does not eradicate differences in abilities, interests, personal history, or gender. We are equal in redemption, in value, and in purpose, but we have different gifts and roles.[26]

Deception

> And Adam was not deceived, but the woman was deceived and
> became a transgressor. (1 Tim. 2:14 ESV)

No one has an easy time explaining this verse. In the past commentators often said it means men should lead because women are prone to deception.[27] But, we must ask, if women are prone to deception after the model of Eve, would that make man prone to rebellion after the model of Adam? If so, how would that qualify Adam to lead? It would give us a church in which rebels instruct fools.[28] Further, if women are easily deceived, either they lack intelligence so that they are easily duped, or they are intelligent but lack proper interest in the truth so that they are willing to be duped. These ideas cannot be right. Women neither lack intelligence nor interest in the truth.

But egalitarians have trouble with verse 14, too. They take the deception of Eve to parallel the deception of Christian women in Ephesus. They say women who are deceived by false doctrine cannot teach, but when they are not deceived, they can teach. But this explanation does no justice to Paul's statement. He does not say, "Deceived women cannot teach." Further, it seems, Paul should not forbid *all* women to teach because *some* were deceived—and it is hard to imagine that *every* Christian woman in Ephesus was deceived. Moreover, the argument that Ephesian women could not teach because they were deceived works only if no Ephesian men were deceived. If men were deceived, Paul should prohibit their teaching, too. But he does not. It is hard to imagine that all the women and none of the men were deceived. Indeed two men, Hymenaeus and Alexander, did blaspheme and wreck their faith (1 Tim. 1:19-20). So even if most women were uneducated and deceived, certain men were deceived, too. If the problem were simply deception, Paul would forbid that deluded *men or women* teach, but he forbade women in general. Paul also refers to creation. Therefore he must have God's created order in mind.

The traditional interpretation of 2:14 can follow two paths. The first view says that women may not teach men because God established an order in which men lead (2:12-13). When men fail to retain their leadership role and fail to teach women, men subvert God's order, causing chaos, deception, and sin. By the first view, verse 14 supports verse 13 by declaring what may happen if we ignore it.

The second view says verse 14 adds a new thought to verse 13: Eve's deception refers beyond the Fall itself to something that represents womankind. If Eve's deception disqualified all women from leading, perhaps Paul has some aspect of woman's nature in view when he insists on male leadership. That aspect cannot be generic inability, since Scripture never implies that women are less intelligent or virtuous than men. If they were incapable, Scripture would not let them teach other women or children. But when Paul begins, "And Adam was not deceived," the "and" rests on the "for" of verse 13 and implies Paul has a reason for entrusting doctrine to male elders.[29] Perhaps women are generally less likely to challenge dubious ideas than men. Perhaps they are less willing to challenge another person's beliefs in public. It is not a flaw to avoid controversy, but *if* there is a difference, it could make women less suited to defend doctrine since defense sometimes requires confrontation. And Eve's sin did include a failure to confront Satan with the difference between his counsel and God's command.

The problem with the second view is that if we say, "Women may not lead because . . . ," some will think we believe women are inferior. The strength of the second view is that it explores the differences between men and women. The problem with the first view is that it refuses to explore male-female differences. The first view offers just one explanation as to *why* God appointed men to lead: For his own reasons, God chose to organize human societies through representative systems rather than pure democracies. He ordained leaders and authorities in the home (parents), in the church (elders), and in Israel (kings and priests), and male leadership is part of God's order.

These statements are true, but they are hardly persuasive in a marketplace of ideas, such as a university campus. If there is a persuasive argument to be made for male leadership, and we refuse to make it from fear of misunderstanding, then we are not serving others as we should. I explore this issue at length at the end of chapter 10. Let me say here that men principally lead because God chose to structure his world through leaders. But I ask that we at least explore whether God has fashioned differences between men and women so that even while they are equal in ability and character, their differences let them flourish within God's order.

Roles of Women

> But women will be saved through childbearing—if they continue in faith, love and holiness with propriety. (1 Tim. 2:15)

At first glance, this verse seems even harder than 2:14. Why does Paul suddenly shift from gender roles to salvation and childbirth? Worse, it sounds as if Paul has forgotten the gospel. Does he believe men are saved by faith and women saved by the work of childbearing? What then happens to women who never give birth? If childbearing saves, why does Paul commend celibacy (1 Cor. 7:7-8)? But let us proceed, assuming that Paul is consistent and that 2:15 concludes his discussion of gender roles.

Above all, Paul does not mean that motherhood brings eternal salvation. Like the English word *save*, the Greek word *save* (*sōzō*) has several possible meanings. In English we save souls, but we also *save* leftovers, time, money, and floundering swimmers. The Greek term often has the same sense of preserving or delivering. So the "saving" of women is not their eternal redemption but their *preservation* through the process of childbirth.[30] Childbearing, further, is not an isolated action. It is the unique work of women, the feminine role par excellence. It represents other female roles—nurturing children and caring for a household. Paul does not promise that Christian women will never perish in childbirth. Rather, God blesses and preserves women as they accept the roles he gives them.

Jesus and Paul encouraged women to transcend traditional roles of service in the home and family, but they never disparaged those roles. When false teachers forbade marriage and all that goes with it (1 Tim. 4:3), Paul affirmed marriage, motherhood, and even housework: "I counsel younger widows to marry, to have children, to manage their homes . . ." (1 Tim. 5:14). He told older women to "train the younger women to love their husbands and children, to be self-controlled and pure, to be busy at home, to be kind, and to be subject to their husbands, so that no one will malign the word of God" (Titus 2:4-5). The phrase "busy at home" (NIV) or "working at home" (ESV) is literally "good houseworkers."[31] So when Paul says women are saved through childbearing, he blesses the uniquely female role that also represents other traditional female roles.

This idea suggests how 2:15 is both consistent with the gospel and concludes Paul's theme. Childbearing is not a work that *merits* salvation, but it is part of the work God plans for women as they work out their salvation (Eph. 2:8-10; Phil. 2:12). When women willingly bear children and care for them, they walk in their God-ordained life pattern. "Women will be saved through childbearing" means that God preserves women who thrive when they embrace traditional roles.

The Bible never says women should stay at home, barefoot and pregnant. It never advocates the cloistering of women, common as it was in antiquity. Women had vital tasks with Jesus and Paul and probably left home for some of them. Proverbs praises the woman who invests in real estate, starts a vineyard, and makes fine garments for her family, for the poor, and for sale (31:16-24). When Paul says, "If *anyone* does not provide for his relatives, and especially for his immediate family, he . . . is worse than an unbeliever" (1 Tim. 5:8), he does not mean that men must bring home the bacon. He says, "if *anyone*," including widows and single or divorced women who head households. All must plan to ensure that their families have what they need. No Scripture says men must earn money while women stay home and spend it. Our culture, not Scripture, declares a man successful when he earns so much that his wife need work at nothing but carpool and decor.[32]

Still, at least during the childbearing and child-rearing years, Paul urges married women to work in the home. The Bible grants women freedom to work, but it also affirms their traditional roles. If I may illustrate personally, my wife, trained as a musician, worked full time as an administrator for several years until shortly before the birth of our first child. For the next thirteen years, she stayed at home, caring for our small children and teaching piano lessons. When our youngest entered elementary school, she accepted an offer to teach music three days a week at the Christian school our children attended. Similarly, I know a youngish mother with a career in interior design. She is glad the field lends itself to part-time work during the years of early motherhood. Sometimes a woman simply must work full time outside the home. But Paul affirms that God blesses the roles of wife, mother, and homemaker.

CONCLUSIONS FOR MALE-FEMALE PARTNERSHIP

Because 1 Timothy 2 occupies a central place in all discussions of women and ministry, we have examined it in detail. We have concluded that the text means what it says. Women should learn the faith and share their knowledge in some settings (Titus 2:4). But they should not become the principal instructors and defenders of the faith. This has been God's plan and order from the beginning, one in which women thrive as they live out their faith.

7

THE GIFTS OF THE SPIRIT AND
THE ROLES OF WOMEN

IT WAS PAINFUL TO BEHOLD. The Bible study leader was a sweet fellow, but first he got lost in his notes. Then he misspoke—badly enough that a tape could have led to a heresy trial. Now he paused, too long, and it began to look like the start of a meltdown. Just then his wife, full of calm and reason, came to the rescue with a comment so exquisite and discreet that the heresy and embarrassment melted away. The lesson continued, but more than one person wondered if the right person was leading. This is the kind of scene we must remember as we move from Bible studies to practical proposals for women's ministries. This chapter studies spiritual gifts—to begin the shift from theory to practice for women's ministry. We start with the basics concerning gifts.

BIBLICAL SURVEY OF SPIRITUAL GIFTS

Principles, Lists, and Terms

God bestows grace and power to equip believers to live as heirs and heralds of his kingdom. He has distributed gifts to every believer, male and female alike. No Scripture suggests that the gifts are gender-specific.

Paul and Peter list the gifts of the Spirit in Romans 12:3-8, 1 Corinthians 12—14, Ephesians 4:7-13, and 1 Peter 4:10-11. The lists, which vary in size and content, mention about twenty gifts, including teaching, prophesying, serving, encouraging, leading, giving, healing, and tongues. The lists are not exhaustive inventories. No two lists are identical, and gifts such as music, hospitality, and artistry never appear in the lists, even though they are treated as gifts elsewhere (1 Cor. 14:26; 1 Peter 4:9; Exod. 31:2).[1]

Paul calls our abilities "gifts" (Eph. 4:7-8), "ministries" (1 Cor. 12:5), "workings" (1 Cor. 12:6), "manifestations of the Spirit" (1 Cor. 12:7), "spiritual things" (1 Cor. 12:1; 14:1), and "measure of faith" (Rom. 12:4).[2] But his favorite term is related to "grace" (*charis*) and means "grace-gifts" (*charismata*; Rom. 12:6; 1 Cor. 12:9, 29-31).[3] God's grace empowers our work for him and leads us to focus on the Spirit, who endows people to minister his grace for the common benefit of his people (1 Cor. 12:7-11; 14:12).

All gifts are significant. A gift is greater only if it allows more strategic service (1 Cor. 12:31; 14:1-5). Gifts in some senses do, and in some senses do not, belong to us. We receive something from God, but it is not our possession or trophy. We are stewards of God's grace (Rom. 12:6; 1 Peter 4:10). The Spirit bestows upon women the stewardship of all his gifts, including prominent gifts such as prophecy (1 Cor. 11:5; Acts 21:8-9). Prophecy is more than prediction. It strengthens, encourages, comforts, and edifies believers (1 Cor. 14:3-5). It also reveals the secrets of human hearts (1 Cor. 14:24-25). The New Testament has six gift lists.

New Testament Gift Lists

ROMANS 12:6-8	1 CORINTHIANS 12:8-10	EPHESIANS 4
Prophesying	Wisdom	Apostle
Serving	Knowledge	Prophet
Teaching	Faith	Evangelist
Encouraging (or exhorting)	Healing	Pastor
Contributing	Miraculous powers	Teacher
Leadership	Prophecy	
Showing mercy	Distinguishing spirits	
	Tongues	
	Interpretation of tongues	

1 CORINTHIANS 12:28-30	1 CORINTHIANS 14:1-28	1 PETER 4:10-11
Apostles	Prophesy	Speaking
Prophets	Tongues	Doing
Teachers	Interpreting tongues	
Workers of miracles		
Gifts of healing		
Helping		
Administrating		
Tongues		
Interpreting tongues		

The Nature and Use of Gifts

A gift is a *capacity* and *desire* for ministry, given by God for regular, *fruitful* use for the church. "Capacity" means that gifted people effectively advance God's kingdom. Gifted leaders actually mobilize people for causes. Gifted teachers are clear and compelling, so that people learn. Encouragers listen, speak, and act to lift spirits (1 Cor. 14:3-5; Rom. 12:8).

"Desire" means that we usually take pleasure in our gifts. Yes, prophets may need to deliver bitter words of woe. But there is usually joy in prophecy. Leaders govern diligently, says Paul. Those who show mercy "do it cheerfully," and givers "give generously" (Rom. 12:8). The phrase "let them give generously" literally reads "let them give *with simplicity*." That is, if someone has the gift of giving, they need no return; they simply give. Giving itself is the reward. Givers say, "Please take this money," or "Please borrow our car. You will minister to us if you do." Leaders take pleasure in helping others accomplish goals. The merciful are *glad* to help others. The gifted feel alive when they exercise their talents, even if it brings hardships, as apostleship did for Paul. But if the "owner" of a skill dislikes the work, it probably is not a gift, in our sense.

"Fruitful" means the exercise of a skill strengthens the church (1 Cor. 14:3). The gifts bring God's people to maturity. They edify the body of Christ (Eph. 4:12-13). Conversely, someone may be a talented musician but fail to bless the church if he seeks to entertain rather than inspire worship. True gifts are God-centered.

CATEGORIES OF GIFTS

The gifts are diverse; yet we can classify them to facilitate our understanding of women's ministries.[4] Let me propose three categories: There are: 1) gifts of speaking and doing, 2) gifts that are more supernatural or more natural, and 3) gifts that are more public and more private. When we chart the gifts this way, we find women exercising gifts in most, but not all, spheres.

Gifts of Speaking and Serving

Peter divides gifts into two categories, speaking and serving. "*If anyone speaks*, he should do it as one speaking the very words of God. *If anyone serves*, he should do it with the strength God provides." Through the gifts of words and deeds, we administer God's grace (1 Peter 4:10-11). All use their gifts to serve others. It is not just elite believers or office-holders who exercise gifts. Indeed, for most gifts, there is no office. Yet the two categories—gifts of speaking and serving—do correspond to two church offices. Elders lead the ministry of words, and deacons lead the ministry of deeds.

Speaking and Doing Gifts

SPEAKING GIFTS	SPEAKING AND DOING GIFTS	DOING GIFTS
Apostleship	Faith	Administration
Discernment	Leadership	Creativity
Encouragement		Giving
Evangelism		Healing
Knowledge		Miracles
Prophecy		Hospitality
Shepherding		Mercy
Teaching		Service
Tongues		
Interpretation of tongues		
Wisdom		

Women appear to exercise every gift in these lists except apostleship. Yet, as we have seen, they must teach privately, not publicly, and lead in ways that do not claim authority over the church.

Gifts More Natural or More Supernatural

All gifts are supernatural, but gifts such as miracles, prophecy, and tongues are more obviously so. With them the manifestation of the Spirit is sudden, without preparation or training. With gifts such as leadership, teaching, and encouragement, God appears to heighten or consecrate "natural" (that is, regular and ongoing) human abilities such as intelligence and speaking skill. As gifted teachers prepare lessons, they use normal human skills that they hone through training.[5] But we do not prepare, methodically working through procedures, to perform a miracle or utter a prophecy. Power comes immediately from the Spirit.[6]

More Supernatural and More Natural Gifts

MORE SUPERNATURAL	NATURAL AND SUPERNATURAL	MORE NATURAL
Discernment	Evangelism	Administration
Healing	Faith	Creativity
Miracles	Mercy	Discernment
Prophecy		Encouragement
Tongues		Giving
Interpretation of tongues		Hospitality
		Knowledge
		Leadership
		Service
		Shepherding
		Teaching
		Wisdom

Note: Every gift has natural and supernatural elements. Prophets receive words from heaven but still use natural means (writing implements) to write them down. Christian teachers prepare lessons by studying; yet the Spirit enables them to grasp spiritual truths, perhaps in times of great need. We must not be rigid with our categories; still, some gifts are more directly from the Spirit than others.

Prophecy, the most supernatural speaking gift, is given to women. Prophets, we recall, are not regular, ongoing authorities. They spoke as the Spirit moved. Elijah, Elisha, Jeremiah, and others show that many prophets never became established authorities. Prophets who were established authorities typically performed another role, too. So, besides being prophets, Moses was a deliverer, Samuel was a judge, and Isaiah was a royal counselor.

Miracle-working is another clearly supernatural gift. No woman ever performs a miracle in Scripture. In 2 Corinthians 12:12, Paul says miracles attest that someone is an apostle. Apostles like Peter and Paul, and other agents of God's redemption such as Jesus, Moses, and Elijah performed signs that authenticated their leadership roles. It seems that women never perform miracles in Scripture because they do not have such leadership roles.

Gifts More Public or More Private

We differentiate between public gifts, used in leadership, and private gifts, used with individuals or small groups. Apostles, evangelists, teachers, and leaders exercise gifts publicly, in ways that exercise authority over the people of God. Serving, encouraging, and giving are more private gifts. With gifts such as hospitality, mercy, and shepherding, we do not rule; we come alongside to serve individuals or small groups. In Corinth tongues were for private use, and prophecy was for public speech (1 Cor. 14).

More Public and Authoritative Versus
Less Public and Authoritative Gifts

MORE PUBLIC/AUTHORITATIVE	POTENTIALLY PUBLIC OR PRIVATE	LESS PUBLIC/AUTHORITATIVE
Administration	Discernment	Creativity
Apostleship	Encouragement	Giving
Miracles	Evangelism	Healing
Leadership	Faith	Hospitality
Prophecy	Knowledge	Mercy
Teaching	Service	Shepherding
	Tongues	
	Interpret tongues	
	Wisdom	

Note: Gifts such as evangelism, discernment, and encouragement, in the middle column, can have either public or private use. And since private gifts such as creativity and service can become public, we must not overdo our categories. But a difference between public and private gifts remains.

Clearly, women can exercise most gifts in most ways. But Scripture reserves some of the most public, authoritative speaking gifts for men. This fact becomes clear if we classify gifts using the categories from all three tables above. Because the Spirit grants gifts to living men and women, our charts will oversimplify things, and the precise spot for most gifts will be debatable.[7] The use of a gift will vary with the person who possesses the gift and the circumstances in which he or she uses it. Thus many gifts could have more than one place on our graphs (see footnote).[8] When in doubt, I let the use of a gift in the ongoing life of the church be my guide.

Speaking Gifts in Church Leadership

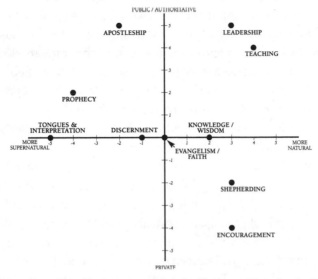

Comment: Many speaking gifts are open to women, but the most public and authoritative ones are for men: apostleship, teaching (of the whole church), and leadership.

Doing Gifts in Church Leadership

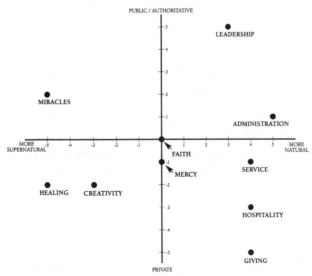

Comment: As with speaking gifts, almost all doing gifts are open to women. On both charts gifts in the upper right quadrant are for men. These public/authoritative and more natural gifts set the direction for the ongoing life of the church. The church uses such gifts the most in its ordinary life.

Gifts as Heightened Forms of Regular Duties

A second look at the gift lists shows that God expects all believers to participate, at least occasionally, in most gifts. A chart at the end of this chapter presents the evidence that most gifts of the Spirit are also qualities or activities that are required of all believers. Wisdom, knowledge, discernment, faith, evangelism, teaching, generosity, and mercy are all called gifts; yet every believer should pursue such things.

That means gifts usually entail a *heightened* capacity for something others can do to a lesser degree.[9] Let us call this "The Principle of Participation": The Principle of Participation implies that no one should use a theology of gifts to dodge glamourless tasks such as kitchen or nursery duty claiming, "Not my gift." Anyone can serve. But the Principle of Participation can also lead to uncertainty. We may not recognize at once who has a gift and who is simply helping. There may be a fuzzy boundary between the "The Gifted" and "The Helpers." That means women and men may effectively participate in a ministry, and like it, without having a gift. They may wrongly conclude something is their special calling when they are simply serving well.

But the Principle of Participation also frees women for ministry. It teaches us to expect women to share in every ministry. Yes, God calls certain men to the offices of leading and teaching, but there are many ways to lead and teach. If everyone participates in most gifts, then women can do at least a little of almost anything. They can lead and teach to an extent even if they hold no official position.

THE EXERCISE OF GIFTS

The Principle of Participation has crucial ramifications for women's ministries. It implies that women should be involved in every field of service. Women should be represented on all kinds of ministry teams even if they do not lead those teams.

Furthermore, because some gifts overlap, we should expect women to be at hand for every type of service. The Bible is not overly precise about gifts. No two gift lists are identical, and many gifts are left undefined. We are uncertain, for example, about the boundary between gifts such as wisdom and knowledge (1 Cor. 12:8), between "healing" and "miraculous powers" (1 Cor. 12:9-10), or between serving and helping (Rom. 12:7; 1 Cor. 12:28). Since the boundaries are fuzzy, we expect women to offer aid when working in the vicinity of their main gift.

For example, leadership teams should include women (and men) with the related gifts of wisdom and administration. Anyone with great wisdom or high administrative skill has a trace of leadership gifts. People gifted in those areas need each other. So even if a church does not ordain women to formal leadership offices, they can help lead by wise counsel and administrative ability. One way to harness this idea to women's ministries is to distinguish between *function, role,* and *office* in ministry.

Function

Christians may briefly exercise almost any spiritual function. Everyone is capable of serving; everyone occasionally functions there. A crusty old grump may see a sad person and say an encouraging word. A middle-aged traveler can share her faith on an airplane even if she is no evangelist. A teenager can tell a friend why she is staying pure until marriage, whether she is gifted to teach or not. So women can perform many functions as needs arise, at least temporarily.

Role

When someone has skill and desire for a task, when their labors meet needs, so that wise people ask them to serve again, their work is more than a function. Regular, fruitful service is a role. When work becomes customary, joyful, and effective, it may express a gift that leads to a role in the kingdom.

People can also fill a role temporarily even if they are not especially gifted. For example, my gift is teaching, not administration, but administrative roles fall to me occasionally. Years ago, as solo pastor of a small church, I had to administer the calendar, budget, and nursery. Today I am a professor, but also dean of faculty, so I have administrative work again. As needs arise, people with modest ability may find such roles thrust upon them.

If someone's role perfectly suits his or her gift, the person may stay in that position. With most gifts, there is nothing loftier than a long-standing role. There is no office, no ordination, or ceremony to set them apart. There is no office of Giver or Encourager (Rom. 12:8; 1 Cor. 12:28). Anyone can lead in those areas. Women may surpass men in gifts such as service, encouragement, and administration. Almost every well-oiled organization has women in key administrative posts. At every well-run conference I have seen, a woman's hand was near the helm.

Office

A role becomes an office when the church recognizes, calls, and con-secrates someone for a formal leadership position. Officers meet known criteria for a position described in Scripture. Today offices include elder, deacon, and perhaps evangelist. In the past, there were prophets, priests, kings, and apostles. As we have seen, the Bible requires that priests, monarchs, and apostles be male. Women may be prophets, but they exercise the prophetic role privately. Huldah did not go to the court; the court came to her. Deborah did not rise up to preach; she sat under a tree to judge.

An office is a formal position, formally bestowed. Officers meet criteria published in Scripture. God calls them, and then they are tested and consecrated to lead God's people. Today God equips elders to teach, lead, and shepherd. He equips deacons to serve and to lead the church's service. To lead well, they must function in many areas. Tough guys must encourage, and shy men must learn to lead a bit.

The work of officers shifts around, too. Speaking personally again, the name of my *office* is "teaching elder." As a pastor I had to *function* as an administrator, evangelist, and shepherd. That trio faded in my early years as a professor, but as dean, I accepted the *roles* of administrator and leader again. My work as a leader has a "teacherly" texture, depending on knowledge and persuasion.

Whatever their gifts are, most men and women move around this way, staying near their prime gift, but adopting new roles and func-tions as needs arise. A teacher may become a shepherd, but he exer-cises care largely by sharing the truth. A shepherd may become a leader, but her authority flows from her care for people.

CONCLUSIONS

Christians may fulfill almost any kingdom task, as needed. Students can instruct their teachers, shy believers give an account of their faith, and those who lack empathy can encourage others. Women may carry out almost any spiritual function. They may exercise vital roles as they use their skills to meet needs and advance the kingdom. If skills grow and bear fruit, women should stay with a role. If they excel for a long period, they may become informal leaders even if they never hold office.

Scripture says God has given men the ordained offices of teaching and leading the church, but he has given encouragement, service, administration, and many other gifts to women. With their gifts, they should do all sorts of things, if not everything. As long as they do not usurp final leadership authority, they will greatly aid the work of elders and deacons. Therefore, we should rejoice when women lead by using their gifts, for the Spirit distributes these gifts to build up the body of Christ for the common good.

Gifts and the Principle of Participation

GIFT NAME	GIFT IN ACTION	EXAMPLE, TEXT	FOR ALL BELIEVERS?
Administration 1 Cor. 12:28	Organizing kingdom activities	Nehemiah Neh. 1—6	All must live orderly lives. Col. 2:5, Prov. 28:2
Apostleship Eph. 4:11	Giving eyewitness testimony to Jesus' work and its meaning	The Twelve Matt. 10, *passim.*	No. We build on their work; we do not share in it.
Creativity Exod. 35:31-35	Using art and music especially to lead God's people in worship	Bezalel, Oholiab & friends, Exod. 36:2	Not clear in Scripture, but many have some creativity
Discernment 1 Cor. 12:10 1 John 4:1-3	Distinguishing between truth and error, knowing whether something is of God or of the evil one	Paul, Galatians 2 Peter, Acts 8:18-24	All must test all things and hold fast to what is good. 1 Thess. 5:21
Encouragement Rom. 12:8	Motivating fellow Christians to walk with God, by word and deed	Barnabas, Acts 4:36, 9:26-30, 11:22-26	All encourage each other daily, 1 Thess. 5:11, Heb. 3:13, 10:24-25

Evangelism Eph. 4:11	Presenting the gospel to unbelievers with clarity and power, to elicit a response	Peter, Acts 2—4, 10 Paul, Acts 13—18	All witness to Christ at opportune time. Acts 8:4, Matt. 28:18-20
Faith 1 Cor. 12:1	Trusting in God's provision or victory, sur-passing what ordinary eyes can see	Elijah, 1 Kings 17—19 Paul, Acts 21:21-26	All believe in God. John 14:1 All walk by faith. Rom. 4:12
Giving Rom. 12:8	Supporting God's work materially with gen-erous, timely, cheerful contributions	Macedonian believers, 2 Cor. 8	All give according to the ability and resources given; tithing
Healing 1 Cor. 12:29	Calling effectively on God for physical heal-ing, especially in the family of faith	Elders pray for the sick, James 5:13-18	All Christians pray for each other. Col. 1:3, 4:3 James 5:16
Miracles 1 Cor. 12:10	Representing God's power, as it works to show his grace and authenticate his servants	Jesus, the apostles, many prophets	No. But all can pray for God to display his power today.
Hospitality 1 Pet. 4:9	Ministering to guests, especially strangers, to mediate grace	Gauis, 3 John 5-8	All show love by welcoming strangers. Heb. 13:2, Rom. 12:13
Knowledge 1 Cor. 12:8	Sharing the truth, publicly or privately, to give others the knowledge they need	Apostles, elders, deacons, 1 Tim. 3:9	All must know the faith. Prov. 8:10, 10:14, 2 Pet. 3:18
Leadership Rom. 12:8	Guiding and directing God's people with understanding of his purposes for them	Elders, 1 Tim. 3:1-7, 1 Thess. 5:12	Not clear. But the godly often have goals to pursue. Phil. 3:14, Exod. 3
Mercy Rom. 12:7 1 Cor. 12:28	Exercising compassion, by forgiveness or acts of kindness	Dorcas, Acts 9:36 Jesus, Mark 1:41	All forgive each other. Matt. 6:12. All show mercy. Col. 3:12, James 3:17
Prophecy 1 Cor. 12, 14	1) Speaking God's very words, as with prophets of old, "Thus says the Lord." 2) Speaking to comfort and guide the church, as directed by the Spirit	1) Isaiah to Malachi, Moses, Elijah 2) Timothy 2 Tim. 4:1-5	1) No, but Spirit poured out widely in early church. Acts 2:16-18 2) Not publicly, but any friend can be fervent in private. Prov. 27:9

Service	Putting oneself at the service of others to meet needs in a direct way	Jesus (came to serve) Matt. 20:28	All disciples serve, just as Jesus did. Matt. 20:28, Rom. 15:2
Shepherding Eph. 4:11	Overseeing the flock of God, caring for individual Christians	Apostles, John 21:16 Elders, Acts 20:28, 1 Pet. 5:2	All who have authority should tend and nourish those under their care. Matt. 18:5-20, James 5:19-20
Teaching 1 Cor. 12:28	Communicating spiritual truth to facilitate growth in knowledge, faith	Elders, 1 Tim. 3:2 Apollos, Acts 18:24-28	All may teach or instruct each other. Rom. 15:14, Col. 3:16
Tongues 1 Cor. 12, 14	Miraculous ability to present truth in a hitherto unknown human language. Possibly a private prayer language (debated)	Many in Corinth 1 Cor. 12, 14	Debated. Paul wishes all spoke in tongues, but it may be rhetoric. Are tongues below teaching? 1 Cor. 14:5
Interpret tongues 1 Cor. 12:10, 14:5	Understanding and presenting a message spoken in an unknown tongue, to edify all who hear it	Certain Corinthians 1 Cor. 12, 14	No, since tongues may go uninterpreted. 1 Cor. 14:1-5
Wisdom 1 Cor. 12:25	Using insight and understanding to guide people to the best course of action	Solomon, Proverbs	All believers should seek wisdom. Prov. 1—10, James 1:2-5

Conclusion: Even by the most restrictive count, all believers may share in at least fourteen of the twenty-one gifts listed here. Clearly then, women may share in most gifts.

Comments

1. As noted in the chapter, there is only indirect warrant for listing hospitality and creativity as gifts. They do not appear on the lists given by Paul and Peter.
2. A number of gifts may be defined in different ways. Prophecy has especially been defined in distinct ways. As preaching is sometimes called a shadow of the prophets' speech, some see healing, as a result of prayer and laying on hands, as a shadow of the greater miracles and healings during biblical times. Slight shifts in definitions move several more gifts into the "for all" category. For example, the Greek word *apostle* roughly means "one who is sent." It is used at least once in Romans 16:7 of someone who is sent on a spiritual

task. Thus any Christian man may be an apostle in a secondary sense if he is willing to be sent on a task by God.

3. Charismatics believe most or all gifts continue to this day—miracles, healing, tongues, and interpretation. Some believe God still appoints apostles to lead the church and have a level of authority like a bishop's. Charismatics also define several gifts more supernaturally. They may view knowledge and wisdom as prophet-like certainty of future events or important truths that would otherwise be inaccessible to us.

4. In my view, it is impossible to argue either that all gifts continue or that all have ceased. The gifts of apostleship ceased when the work of redemption was completed and the apostles finished their ministries of teaching and writing the Gospels and Epistles. The miracles that attest that someone is an apostle ceased at that time. But, to name just four, gifts of teaching, leadership, service, and giving clearly continue. We must examine gifts one by one to evaluate their status. Further, gifts such as healing and discernment may continue but in a different form in our age.

8

MINISTRIES OF WOMEN IN THE CHURCH: TRADITIONAL IDEAS AND FRESH PROPOSALS

WITH OUR SURVEY OF Scripture complete, we now consider how women should use their gifts in the church today. Before we plunge ahead, we should review the principles that lead to our practices.

ROLES OF WOMEN IN SCRIPTURE

In Scripture most leadership positions fall to men. Priests and monarchs were supposed to be male. Jesus chose twelve men as apostles. In Acts the first missionaries and church planters were male. Paul assumed that all elders were male (1 Tim. 3:1-7). Yet women exercise quite an array of ministries. Deborah served God as a judge of Israel. Miriam, Huldah, and Anna were prophetesses. Paul permitted Corinthian women to prophesy in public (1 Cor. 11:5). The praise that Miriam, Hannah, and Mary offered to God became part of Scripture. In private settings, Abigail instructed David, Esther guided Ahasuerus, and Priscilla taught Apollos. Women also became Paul's invaluable coworkers as he established churches. They contended at his side, working hard for the gospel (Phil. 4:2-3; Rom. 16:6-13). Paul also urged women to teach children and other women (2 Tim. 1:5; Titus 2:3-4).

Women never took ongoing leadership positions in Israel or the church. For example, in the crisis caused by Josiah's discovery of the law in the temple, Huldah did not go to the court to preach to the king and people; the court came to her, and she spoke privately to the king's emissaries. The men listened and heeded her counsel so that she led without commanding. This is typical of women's leadership roles. Women counseled, taught, and judged, but almost always privately. Their messages had theological content, but they did not preach or teach from positions with formal authority. Women taught in private and led alongside men.

ROLES OF WOMEN IN CHURCH HISTORY

Historical studies cannot resolve theological debates since Scripture should be the church's supreme authority. Still, as chapter 10 will show, calls for women's ordination were almost nonexistent until the latter half of the twentieth century when feminism arose. But church leaders always agreed that women had gifts that should be used privately. Tertullian let two prophetesses, named Priscilla and Maximilla, minister beside him for years. After Jerome agreed to instruct two noble women, he marveled at their aptitude and boasted that they privately refuted two heretics who troubled the church. In the Middle Ages, gifted women led women's movements. Some became counselors to kings and popes. Many Protestants granted women the right to teach privately.

THEOLOGY OF GIFTS

The Principle of Participation says every believer should share in activities that are the special province of a gifted few. Gifts of the Spirit are heightened abilities to perform tasks that any disciple may perform occasionally. So there is a gift of teaching, but all Christians can instruct each other. Discernment, faith, liberality, and service are gifts, but all should exercise them to a degree.

We also distinguish levels of activity. Every believer can function in any sphere. But when someone has talent and passion for a certain service, where they labor fruitfully, that service becomes their role. Finally, a man takes an office when the church calls him to lead the church as a deacon or elder. Most gifts express themselves in roles, not offices.

We also divided gifts into modes of activity: There are gifts of speaking and doing, gifts that are more supernatural and less so, gifts that are more public and more private. Looking at gifts this way, we found that women exercise gifts in every category except in the quadrant of the most public and least supernatural gifts.

WOMEN'S MINISTRIES IN THE CHURCH

Churches that expect men to lead should still engage women in a wide variety of ministries. Some traditionalists use the slogan, "A woman should be free to do anything an unordained man can do." This is almost tolerable as a generalization, but we must refine it three ways. First, mature, gifted men must be free to test a potential call to leadership by teaching and overseeing in tasks that ordinarily belong to elders or deacons. Second, women must not be encouraged to take roles, roles that would otherwise be acceptable, if those roles cause them to upstage their husbands and undercut their authority at home. Third, the generalization only works if the local church knows what elders and deacons are supposed to do and acts accordingly.

With these caveats, we say women may join any ministry except those that are distinctive to elders or deacons. So, for example, women can organize, recruit, and advise. They can always lead "from alongside" as coworkers, meeting needs, gaining knowledge, and disseminating it to influence decisions. They can gain skills and pass them on to others as mentors. In worship they may pray, suggest hymns, and offer testimonies.

In small churches, volunteers perform most tasks. Larger churches often hire staff for specialized ministries. Churches should be free to employ women in various positions. We can begin with jobs that are clearly fitting for women and proceed to others.

- *Women's Ministry Proper.* Most churches appoint someone to oversee the discipleship of women. This ministry could include evangelism, discipleship, and services for women with special needs. Women's leaders may be volunteers, but larger churches might hire a woman to lead this ministry. Paul specifies that older women should train the younger women in household duties, "to love their husbands and children, to be self-controlled and pure, to be busy at home, to be kind, and to be subject to their husbands" (Titus 2:4-5).[1]

- *Children's Ministry/Christian Education.* Women raise children in the nurture of the Lord at home, and so we expect them to teach children at church. Women will be at least as adept as men at training children. If women teach children at church, we expect some to organize children's programs as well. In a large church, a paid children's minister should be male if he also pastors parents and exercises authority over the church's teachers. But if a children's minister primarily coordinates and administers Christian education, women may oversee it.
- *Youth Ministry.* Churches frequently minister to teenagers with extensive small-group and one-on-one discipleship. Teenagers need wise people of both genders in their lives. Thus married couples are often effective with teens. Yet for one-on-one meetings it is (ordinarily) best for women to mentor younger women and for men to mentor younger men. (People often ask when it is that a male child becomes a man so that men should instruct him. I sometimes want to say, "At fifteen years, seven months, three days," to show the absurdity of such a question. Maturity varies from child to child and place to place.)
- *Counseling.* We expect mature women to disciple adolescents and young women through the ordinary process of growing in wisdom. By the same logic, whether professionally or informally, women should also counsel women who have a troubled path to maturity. Further, it is difficult to see why a woman could not also counsel married couples and families. A woman could even counsel a man in a clinical setting if her skills met his needs.
- *Christian Schools.* The vast majority of Christian elementary schoolteachers are women. Even in upper grades, most teachers are women. (Rambunctious boys would profit from having more male teachers to understand them, settle them, and model manhood for them.) But since women do the bulk of the teaching, we expect some to rise within the ranks to lead Christian schools as principals and administrators (I cannot see why principals need to be elders).
- *Mercy Ministry.* Mercy ministry covers everything from disaster relief to literacy training, from pro-life counseling to meals

for the ill, from hospital visitation to substance abuse prevention. Mercy ministry is overseen by deacons and elders but *performed* by the whole church, including deacons' wives (1 Tim. 3:11) and other women (Rom. 16:1). Mercy ministry is theologically grounded; thus deacons must "keep hold of the deep truths of the faith with a clear conscience" (1 Tim. 3:9). But mercy workers are not essentially theologians; so anyone can coordinate or administer this ministry.

- *Music Ministry*. Music is a spiritual ministry since music leaders help lead worship and often disciple their musicians. But the church has not insisted that these leaders be trained in theology and ordained. Churches rightly seek spiritually mature music leaders, but both women and men may lead the music ministry under the direction of a church's pastors.

- *Church Administrators*. In small churches, the pastor and secretary know every member and activity, and church administration is time-consuming but straightforward. In large churches, the management of buildings, budgets, calendars, and communication grows complex. Some churches want ordained ministers to oversee administration since it entails theological oversight. But others view administration more as a business function. Pastors should help ministries set a course, but must one be ordained to write checks, organize conferences, and improve ministry structures? If administrators need not be elders, they need not be males. Of course, those who work in music, administration, mercy, or education should be theologically astute. Their faith should inform all they do. But the *essence* of their work is not theological.

- *Writing and Performing*. Women write articles, magazines, and books. They write music that conveys Christian ideas, whether their audiences are predominantly Christian or not. Visual artists can also express their faith in their work. None of this is ministry as traditionally defined, but churches should support it. I know a musician who has written, produced, and played in hundreds of recordings for mainstream and Christian musicians. He has written implicitly Christian love songs that reflect biblical views of love, to offer an alternative to the suggestive lyrics that dominate popular music. Whether artists are male or female, the church should support such work.

These proposals represent the kinds of ministry that suit godly women. There are many others: personal evangelism, work on mission teams, and visitation. Churches should support women in any ministry that matches church goals. They should entertain initiatives from women with a passion for kingdom service. Suppose several women want to minister to single mothers. Wise elders will assist them by listening to their ministry plan, suggesting refinements, telling them what joys and sorrows to anticipate, and helping with funding, if necessary. The church can oversee without controlling everything.

Finally, I must mention remuneration. Anecdotal evidence indicates that women rarely receive generous salaries from churches. If a woman is an administrator, she is probably called a secretary or an assistant. Women sometimes receive lower pay when they do the same work as men when, for example, a youth program employs both a man and a woman. Further, work that was done by female volunteers sometimes becomes a paying job when a man takes over. Such things should not be done in a righteous society. Commonsense feminism rightly says, "Equal pay for equal work." If a church would pay a man for a job, they should pay a woman. If the hours, training, duties, and skills are the same, the pay should be the same, too.

VOLUNTEER SERVICE AND WORSHIP

Since volunteers do most work in most churches, a review of unpaid labor is essential. In the New Testament, Paul cites women who labored for the gospel such as Euodia and Syntyche in Philippi (Phil. 4:2), Priscilla in Corinth (1 Cor. 16:19; Acts 18:18-26), and Mary, Junias, Tryphena, Tryphosa, and Persis in Rome (Rom. 16:6-16). They were not apostles, elders, or teachers, but they did help advance the gospel. In principle, *the scope of women's ministry today should be as broad as it was in the apostolic era.* Unfortunately, we know little about their work. Women should not be apostles or preachers. But they should have ministries broad enough to gain the praise Paul's letters bestow on women.

Let us first affirm traditional women's church work. It is good for women to teach children in Sunday school and to disciple teenagers. Older women rightly train younger women to love their husbands and work faithfully at home (Titus 2:3-5). It is good for women to work in nurseries and kitchens. But nurseries need male workers, too.

When 1 Corinthians 14:26 says, "Everyone has a hymn, or a word of instruction . . ." Paul seems to expect everyone, including women, to be active in worship. It goes without saying that women can participate in all corporate activities, such as singing, praying, and confessing the faith. But should women have a solo voice, leading the congregation? Consider a few possibilities:

- Women could be *song leaders* guiding worship by singing at a good pace with a true voice. They could also help select music and highlight lyrics in music before the church sings it.
- Women should have the same rights as men to share a *testimony* or word of encouragement, especially in less formal settings.
- The preacher should read his text before expounding it since the reading prepares for the sermon. But we read Scripture for other reasons during worship. Why not let women *read Scripture*? Oddly, some churches let teenagers read Scripture on "Youth Sunday" and let children recite texts during Christmas but forbid adult women to read. Why may a girl recite Scripture at seven and seventeen but not at twenty-seven? Perhaps tradition, not Scripture, leads some evangelical churches to forbid women to read Scripture in worship.

Ushering stands at the fringe of worship. Women often serve as greeters, but why are female ushers so rare? Is the passing of bulletins a sacred task? Are the deacons afraid that women will purloin loose change from the offering plate? Is ushering a painless way to get men involved? Or is this task a self-perpetuating male enclave? It can be daunting for a single female visitor to meet a line of large men at the sanctuary door. The passage into church might look more welcoming to single women and children if a few women leavened the dark-suit brigade.

Ecclesiastes 4:9 (ESV) blesses team ministries, saying, "Two are better than one, because they have a good reward for their toil." So a team of friends or a husband-wife team can bear good fruit. Some women still want to be a pastor's or missionary's wife. But couples may also lead Bible studies together or plan ministry events together. Both know their own strengths and know when to count on their spouses so that the work is effective.

THE CONTROVERSIAL QUESTIONS

May Women Teach the Bible to Men?

No one doubts that women may teach women since Paul plainly urges it in Titus 2:3-5. But we must ask if women may teach men too, in semiformal settings such as Sunday school or Bible studies. My answer is, "Occasionally, but not regularly." Let me explain.

Abigail, Huldah, and Priscilla show that women can teach men privately. But none of these women taught groups of men in a formal, regular way. Joel said the daughters and servant girls of Israel would prophesy in the last days (Joel 2:27-28), and women prophesied in public in Corinth. But their prophecies did not have the same authority as public teaching. Men tested their words (1 Cor. 14:29-35). When they prophesied, women had to wear something on their head to signify (in that culture) that they submitted to male authority (11:3-11).

In first-century Corinth, a woman who spoke wore a head covering to show her submission to authority. But what is the equivalent of a head covering today? What sign can a woman use, while teaching, to show submission to her husband or elders? Not head coverings, for hats are seen as fashion statements today. Indeed, I doubt that there is *one* visible "sign" contemporary women can use, although wedding rings and modest clothing and demeanor can advertise submission to authority.

Private meetings—like those Abigail, Huldah, and Priscilla had with David, the priests, and Apollos—are no problem. Body language and vocal patterns easily convey whether a speaker is advising or commanding. But can a woman teach men in public? If so, how might she show she is not usurping authority?

In our culture, the answer lies with the format. Before someone gives a guest lecture, we hear an introduction. The host says, "We invited Miss Clement to speak to us about adolescence." The presenter then lists the training, experience, and achievements of Miss

Clement. These convey several things: 1) the host has confidence in the speaker; 2) the audience should listen to her; and 3) the speaker is under the authority of the host, who chose the topic and weighed her qualifications to speak. The host ordinarily has the first and last word. He explains the purpose of the gathering. At the end, he may recapitulate salient points and note what the participants should glean from them. The host is in charge throughout:

He chooses or approves a topic and invites an apt speaker.

He oversees the planning. He invites Miss Clement to address adolescence and may help craft the theme and direction of her talk.

The host sets the schedule, including the length of the speaker's presentations.

The speaker is the expert but not the sole authority. She comes as invited. She speaks *at a set time, for a set time, on a set topic*, at the pleasure and under the authority of the host.[2]

If this analysis is correct, women who accept tokens of submission to authority should be free to instruct groups of adult men and women as a guest speaker does. Her words are weighed by others, by responsible men.

Thus a woman may teach men, as a guest, under church oversight. The social dynamics will reflect the nature of the situation. For example, an elder opens and closes the session. Listeners pose questions to the speaker, leading to open-ended discussions. The elder has the right and duty to correct errors even if that causes social discomfort. The woman will speak in an area of expertise, to help the church overcome a weakness. As she speaks, whether in monologue or dialogue, a wise woman will adopt a manner that shows she does not claim theological authority.

If this is correct, then a woman should not teach indefinitely, week after week, month after month, year after year, in a class that becomes "hers." If a talented woman teaches a mixed group indefinitely, she inevitably shifts from guest speaker to regular teacher. If regular teachers have talent, they inevitably accrue authority. (This holds for men, too. Unqualified men should not act as if they have authority and teach month after month. If they are gifted to teach, let them be trained, tested, and approved as elders.)

I have been a guest speaker hundreds of times and a long-term supply preacher eight times. I know authority inexorably accumulates when one speaks week after week. Eventually, the "guest" is setting the agenda for the messages. He starts speaking without an introduction. Leaders stop describing the invitation and qualifications. Between the first and fourth months, the speaker gains control and authority. For this reason, I believe women should serve the church as guest teachers for a limited time on a topic of expertise, but not by teaching groups of men and women for long periods of time. Obviously, this reasoning has implications for women's Bible studies; so we must consider them.

May Women Preach?

All our studies indicate that God appointed men to preach the Word. In Scripture every preacher is male. In the Old Testament, most public proclamations come from prophets such as Moses, Isaiah, and Jeremiah. Their task was to declare, "This is what the Lord says." The ministries of Miriam, Deborah, and Huldah are telling here, for each is a prophetess, but none preached. Perhaps some male prophets did not preach either, but the salient point is that no women did. In the New Testament, the apostles most closely resemble the prophets. They were all male, as were the next generation of teachers, such as Stephen and Timothy.

In the old covenant, God appointed male priests and Levites to perform the regular teaching of God's law (Lev. 10:11; Deut. 33:10). King Jehoshaphat sent priests and Levites to teach the law throughout Judah (2 Chron. 17:7-9), and King Josiah sent Levites to "all Israel" (2 Chron. 35:3). Priests also judged proper behavior (Deut. 16:18; 17:8-11; 1 Sam. 14:19, 36; 22:11-15). Hosea denounced priests who failed to do this (Hos. 4:4). Malachi said, "The lips of a priest ought to preserve knowledge, and from his mouth men should receive instruction" (Mal. 2:7).

When the apostles died, ending the apostolic age, the church needed ongoing teaching authorities again. For a transitional period, Paul delegated to Timothy, Titus, and others the responsibility to preach and organize churches in his place. As Paul's agents, Timothy and Titus had more authority than pastors do today, but Paul did direct them to establish a succession of preachers and teachers. Timothy must entrust the gospel to faithful men who will be able to teach others (2 Tim. 2:2). Titus must appoint elders to hold fast to sound doctrine and "refute those who oppose it" (Titus 1:5, 9). This ministry belongs to elders, particularly elders who labor in the Word (1 Tim. 5:17). Each elder was male—"the husband of one wife" (1 Tim. 3:2 ESV). Thus the church's preachers should be ordained men, gifted and tested for sustained preaching and teaching.

If all this is correct, implementation issues remain. Elders must help female speakers speak without lapsing into preaching. They must help ordinary Christians realize that a woman is not usurping authority simply because she speaks forcefully and quotes the Bible. We must develop a format that tells our culture, "This is not preaching." For example, whatever we label the event, if a woman stands behind a pulpit and delivers a monologue featuring Bible exposition on a Sunday, hearers will perceive it as a sermon. If the event is structured like a worship service, whatever the other circumstances may be, the "talk" will probably seem sermonic and authoritative.

Conservatives need courage and honesty here. Traditionalists with weak convictions can find ways to let women do what they want and so avoid society's censure. At worst, they give a string of clues that indicate an event is a sermon, and then label it a talk or an exhortation. If criticized, they insist that the woman was not preaching and claim victory by definition: Women cannot preach; the speaker is a woman; therefore, she was not preaching. Such equivocation is cowardly and ineffective.

It is also cowardly and ineffective to stifle women to avoid criticism from ultra-conservatives. Timid men keep women down. Strong men delight in partnerships with strong women.

What If There Is No Man?

In rare cases, there will be a choice between having a woman speak and having no one at all. A man ministering to an isolated group may die, leaving his wife in the field. An isolated people may ask a solo female translator to describe her faith. Should she serve as their teacher? Philippians implies that she should. In 1:12-18 Paul says that as long as Christ is proclaimed, it is better that men preach the gospel from defective motives than that no one preach at all. Yet an apparent crisis situation may not actually be one; patience may bring a male leader. Furthermore, if a woman does lead in a crisis, she must work to end the crisis by seeking a male leader, rather than functioning indefinitely on her own.[3]

Women's Bible Studies

It is precarious for a man to comment on women's Bible studies, but trusted female friends tell me that some women can teach women's classes for years and remain under the authority of church leaders, and some cannot. In my former home church, the pastor's wife has taught a well-attended Bible study for sixteen years. They meet for eight months per year. She is seminary-trained, intelligent and forceful, and yet she never portrays herself as a rival authority or conducts a semi-autonomous ministry. When I asked her how she remained under authority, she had several thoughts:

- She guards against autonomy by explicitly teaching against it. Therefore, she taught through 1 Timothy and explained God's design that male elders lead the church.
- She relates church authority structures to family structures. She says it is a blessing for women to be under authority, especially their husbands'. She explains that women are not speechless doormats but are blessed when they live within their roles.
- She refers to the pastor's sermons most weeks, connecting her teaching to the pulpit ministry. This is easier since she is the pastor's wife, but all wise women speak respectfully of their pastors. She also finds it easy to follow the elders because they have a positive attitude toward women and their service.
- She does not pretend to be an authority on everything. She gladly says, "I don't know." She invites her husband to teach her class occasionally.

When women tilt toward autonomy, we cannot simply accuse them of power lust. Some women do seek authority aggressively and create ministries that become their private enclaves. There are women's ministries that have virtually become churches themselves, with the size, meetings, budgets, and structures that practically describe an all-female church. Yet other women resist authority because domineering elders squelch women's gifts and initiatives. I don't believe that a certain amount of blockish behavior grants women the right to overthrow God's structures. Still, if elders honor women, it is easier for women to honor elders. If men respect the insights of women, it is easier for women to respect the guidance of men.

Women as Deacons

It is difficult to tell if the New Testament teaches that women should be deacons or not. The first seven deacons were all male (Acts 6). Yet Phoebe was called a "deacon" (*diakonos*) in Romans 16:1, where the term may either mean a servant or a formal deacon. In 1 Timothy 3:11, Paul interrupts his comments about male deacons to address their female counterparts. They should be "worthy of respect, not malicious talkers but temperate and trustworthy in everything." But it is almost impossible to determine if these women are deacon's wives or deaconesses (see Appendix 1).

Whatever the uncertainties, we know two things. First, deacons lead the church by planning, but even more by action. The work of an elder is to love people by words. The work of a deacon is to love people by deeds. Paul says deacons must hold to the "deep truths" of the faith, but they need not *teach* them. The work of deacons is grounded in truth, but deacons are action figures, not professors.

Second, vexed as some debates about texts and offices are, all parties agree that women should help guide diaconal work. We may debate whether to label women deacons or deaconesses, deacons' assistants or deacons' advisors. The main thing is that women whom God calls to practical service and to planning should be free to do so.

A PAUSE TO REVIEW

We need to discuss newer ways for women to serve, but let us review key conclusions. First, the church's regular teachers are ordained men, elders who are gifted, trained, and tested. God appointed elders to carry out the sustained, foundational doctrinal instruction. This includes preaching, regular adult teaching, discipleship, and instruction of new Christians.

Second, women teach other women and children. Leaders may also invite them to speak on chosen topics to edify the church. This conclusion may please no one. It sounds liberal to conservatives, since it lets women teach men, and sounds conservative to liberals, since it restricts that teaching. Yet this position follows biblical principles: 1) God called elders to be the church's principal teachers. 2) The Principle of Participation implies that any Christian may briefly function as a teacher. Unordained men and women may speak as needed, especially when they are experts, even if they lack an elder's authority.

It bears repeating that the church would suffer less tension over women's issues if it operated properly. If elders never teach, if they do nothing but vote at monthly decision-making meetings, no wonder women chafe under their authority. Further, if elders merely make decisions, and good decisions flow from wisdom, and churches have wise women, why not have women elders? But if a man is qualified to teach, and his life verifies his words, he should become an elder and lead by word and deed. If he is working hard, he will seek the aid of talented women.

WOMEN AS ADVISORS

Let me propose one more thing—an advisory ministry for godly women. Conservative churches often ask women to serve with deacons, whatever they call these women. This practice is logical since men need women to share the work of caring for the needy even if the women are not ordained. Suppose the deacons hear that certain children have no food. Given the abundance of food in the West, there is probably serious disorder in the home. There may be no husband or father; there may be substance abuse or gambling. Clearly, a visit to bring food and to investigate is appropriate. On such a visit, a husband-wife team has an advantage over an all-male team, at least in speaking to the mother.

Although the case is less obvious, I believe women should do something similar with elders. Female advisors could help elders watch over the church. Remember the duties of an elder from 1 Timothy 3:1-7, Titus 1:5-9, 1 Peter 5:1-4, and James 5:14-16:

- Elders watch over doctrine and morals. They set a course for the church.
- Elders care for the needy. They comfort mourners, visit the sick, feed the hungry, and instruct the ignorant.
- All elders are apt teachers. Some have special gifts and work hard in the Word.
- Elders set a worthy example to the people of God.

When a group exceeds the size of 150, it becomes impossible for everyone to know everyone. Then elders need trusted eyes and ears, especially to care for women and children. Married men do not easily oversee single and divorced women. Because mature women naturally and properly retain closer contact with them, they can help oversee them.

Someone may say, "Elders can gain this information by talking to their wives." True, but not all elders are married. (Since Jesus was single, we must either permit single men to be elders or set standards that Jesus did not meet.) Further, wise women may not be married to elders or may not be married at all. Besides, elders do not always consult their wives as well as they could. Above all, by consulting wise women, leaders can act on the point that women like Deborah, Abigail, and Priscilla dispensed excellent and timely counsel.

Some conservative churches have taken steps in this direction. They have dinners for elders and their wives to discuss church life. They use ministry teams and place women on teams for education, worship, evangelism, and outreach. The wives of deacons advise and share in the work of deacons. Christian schools place women on regular boards or advisory boards.

These practices are commendable, but we can do more. We could try to list fields where men need the input of women. But where would men *not* want insight from discerning women? We even profit from talking to women about men's issues, let alone world mission, youth work, children's ministry, and pastoral care.

Men will have questions. Should pastors then consult women about their preaching? Why not—at least to learn more about the church's needs? Will women gain too much authority if men consult them so? This alleged problem was not on Josiah's mind when he consulted Huldah or on David's mind when Abigail talked sense into him! Will the presence of women disrupt the atmosphere of meetings formerly run by men alone? Maybe, but some all-male men's meetings could use a little disruption. Of course, there are times when elders need to meet alone. But the addition of a gifted woman need not unravel a men's meeting. Women's relational sensibility can balance the goals-and-management perspectives of men.

The New Testament specifies that the elders who oversee and direct the affairs of the church must be male (1 Tim. 3:1-5; 5:17). Other passages assume church authorities will be male (Acts 15:22-23; 1 Cor. 14:29-34). But the New Testament never specifies that every leader must be male. In Romans 12:6-8, leadership stands in a list of gifts that are open to the entire church.[4] Those who work hard and teach well, wise people who live well, inevitably become leaders, at least informally (Heb. 13:7; James 3:13). I cannot tell churches how to draw on the wisdom of women, but we should try to find ways to do so. Men will know the church and guide it more effectively if they consult all leaders, whether male or female, whether officially recognized or not. Elders should gain the counsel of godly women if they want to direct the affairs of the church well.

AN ALTERNATE VISION OF LEADERSHIP

A notion of church leadership, loosely based on Paul's churches where men and women worked beside each other, lies behind these proposals. It is a grass-roots, decentralized approach. Centralized churches choose men with a blend of social skills, career success, and spiritual interest for leadership posts. The main duty of these men is to attend monthly leadership meetings where they discuss issues and make decisions. The church watches closely. "Who is an officer?" and "What happened at the meeting?" are vital questions. Good men who dutifully attend meetings may get pulled away from their hands-on ministry. Less noble men attend meetings, lobby for their views, vote, and go home, thinking their work is done.

Decentralized churches encourage new ministries to sprout so that unofficial leaders can emerge. These leaders know each other's gifts, skills, and passions.[5] They cooperate in the present. Then for the future they mentor the next generation of leaders. Women do not need to agitate for recognition because all leaders are recognized for their gifts and ministry experience whether they have a title or not. Titles and "the monthly meeting" decline in importance. The ordination of elders and deacons verifies the rise of new leaders more than it creates them. Elders are proven teachers and shepherds, learned and holy men.

As the importance of the monthly meeting diminishes, some elders may be excused from it to focus on ministry. Meanwhile, others, not necessarily ordained and not necessarily male, may occasionally attend the meeting, lending wisdom and administrative skill. They may not vote, but voting might decline in importance if decisions emerge by consensus more than by ballots or decrees. Leaders make decisions through influence and gentle authority (see chart below), rather than through power and coercion, as everyone with expertise has a voice.

Forms of Leadership and Decision-making

INFLUENCE	AUTHORITY	POWER
Basis: knowledge, expertise, and experience	Knowledge, experience, position, and office	Ability to coerce, punish; fear of punishment
Mode: inform, advise	Inform, advise, command	Command, threaten
Result: Advise, then wait	Build consensus to decision	Issue decree

THRIVING IN OUR PLACES

I close with the story of a runner named Kenny Moore, a 1972 Olympian, and his coach, William Bowerman. Bowerman revolutionized long distance training while coaching track at the University of Oregon from 1949 to 1974.[6] Though he hardly recruited, Bowerman's teams won four national championships. He did everything he could for his runners. He created lighter running gear and designed shoes for them on his wife's waffle iron. The shoes were so good they helped launch Nike, which Bowerman co-founded with Phil Knight.

But Bowerman's runners remember him most for tailoring their training to each one's needs and skills. Bowerman saw potential in Moore, a two-miler who had enjoyed little success. His personal best time of 9:15 meant he never won a race—until Bowerman analyzed his training and took charge one day. Bowerman chided Moore for training too hard, for running until he was always injured or sick. Bowerman demanded that Moore change. Either he alternated easy three-mile jogs one day and mildly taxing workouts the next, or he was off the team. Moore submitted; three weeks later Bowerman entered him in a two-mile run against Dale Story, the NCAA cross-country champion. Story's time was thirty seconds better than Moore's best, but Bowerman ordered Moore not to chase him and to begin no faster than 4:30 per mile. In Moore's words:

> I gave myself to his plan. I ran 4:30 for the first mile; Story ran 4:19 and led by 70 yards. Bowerman called, "He won't be able to hold it; see what you can do."
>
> I began to gain, and the crowd . . . 10,000 strong, saw me coming and got up and [shouted]. With half a mile to go I had no real will left, only that thunder that would not let me slow. Into the last turn, Story still had 10 yards. Then he looked back, his shoulders tightened, and I learned for the first time how much competitive savagery lay deep in my heart.
>
> I outkicked him by a second, in 8:48, ripping 27 seconds from my [previous] best, finishing in bedlam, crowd and teammates pressing the air out of me, people shouting that everything was possible now, the Olympics were possible now. Bowerman was there with wild blue eyes and a fiendish grin, and I knew what he would say: "See! I told you so! You just needed rest!"
>
> But he didn't. He bent to my ear. "Kenny," he whispered, "even I never thought you could run that fast. Even I."

Everyone needs coaches like this, mentors who help us discover our design. I propose that women will do better than they imagine if they live according to their divine design. In that design women exercise all sorts of gifts. They lead, but they do not vaunt themselves to solo leadership. Rather they lead through relationships. They lead under the protection of loving and sacrificial male leadership. In that context they thrive.

PART TWO

9

EGALITARIANS AND COMPLEMENTARIANS: A COMPARATIVE STUDY

THE CHIEF GOAL OF this book is to survey Scripture to discover how women should use their gifts in ministry today. Chapters 1 to 8 completed that task. Yet readers who have fought a round or two in the gender wars may want more theory, more of the theoretical and historical underpinnings of complementarian and egalitarian views. Chapters 9 and 10 offer to meet that interest. This chapter compares the mind-sets of traditionalists and feminists.[1] The next chapter presents a short history of the church's theory and practice concerning women and ministry.

WHY WE DISAGREE

Ideally, Christians will conduct the debate over gender roles with humility and respect. We will pursue the truth with zeal but conduct discussions with gentleness, to achieve better understanding. Unfortunately, many Christians approach the topic with pride rather than humility. They say things such as, "Everybody knows . . ." and "No one could possibly believe . . . ."

When we think our views are manifestly correct, we are prone to regard the other side as fools or scoundrels. Fools cannot recognize what should be obvious, and scoundrels willfully misunderstand what should be clear. Such overconfidence hardly promotes dialogue.

This book makes a case for a fairly traditional view of gender roles. It seeks to inform fellow traditionalists and to persuade inquirers that God created mankind to thrive when men and women take complementary rather than identical roles. But whether I persuade anyone or not, it helps to identify the way each side thinks.

All evangelical Christians, whether feminist or traditionalist, claim that the Bible is on their side. Not all self-identified Christians make this claim. Critics who deny the authority of Scripture usually judge the Bible to be a "patriarchal" book. Traditionalists believe the Bible is *"patricentric"*—that is, it emphasizes that husbands and fathers are responsible for the welfare of their households—but not *patriarchal* since it teaches servant leadership. Some critics would call this a distinction without a difference. They believe male leadership always suppresses women.[2] For example, the *Women's Bible Commentary* says that Luke appears "progressive" since it "contains a great deal of material about women." But in fact, Luke is "extremely dangerous" because it "portrays them as models of subordinated service, excluded from the power center of the movement" and because it claims "the authority of Jesus . . . to legitimate male dominance in Christianity."[3]

Yet many critical feminists believe the Bible has resources that can promote the liberation of women.[4] Feminist biblical scholar Elizabeth Schussler Fiorenza says she searches the Bible for a "canon within the canon" that will support the heart of spiritual feminism, "the quest for women's power." For her, "woman's own experience and vision of liberation" is her final authority. But Scripture can still function "as a resource for women's struggle for liberation."

We can portray the three main positions toward Scripture and women this way:

CRITICAL FEMINIST[5]	EVANGELICAL FEMINIST	EVANGELICAL TRADITIONALIST
The Bible is traditionalist. Its patriarchalism oppresses women.	The Bible is feminist. Its egalitarianism liberates women.	The Bible is traditionalist. Its advocacy of loving leadership lets women thrive.
The Bible is wrong.	The Bible is right.	The Bible is right.

We might wonder which column in this chart is more troubling: the first, where critics say the Bible is traditional and wrong, or the second and third, where evangelicals believe the Bible is right but draw opposite conclusions about its message. How do such things happen? Allow me to make a few more comments on the critics; then we will focus on evangelicals.

Critics say no thinking citizen can submit his intellectual faculties to an alien, ancient authority that has angels in heaven, miracles on earth, and divine intervention everywhere.[6] Furthermore, they say, true submission to Scripture is impossible. If someone adheres to the Bible, it is their choice to do so. Whether we admit it or not, we retain the throne.

Paradoxically, this posture can make critics more objective interpreters of Scripture. Someone who is dedicated both to Scripture and to a particular view of gender roles will be tempted to interpret the Bible to agree with his view. But since critics claim the right to reject biblical teachings, they may be more free to see that a passage teaches a view they reject.

For example, the critic Elizabeth Schussler Fiorenza says, "The general injunction for all members of the Christian community, 'Be subject to one another in the fear of Christ,' is clearly spelled out for the Christian wife as requiring submission and inequality."[7] Similarly, when Luke Timothy Johnson reads 1 Timothy 2:12—"I do not permit a woman to teach or exercise authority over a man"—he takes Paul's statement at face value. "Paul defends male prerogatives and perspectives out of patriarchal reflex, especially when his sense of orderliness and proper decency is threatened." He simply believes Paul is wrong and that leaders must say so "within the public discourse of the church."[8]

We note, therefore, that critical feminists often interpret the Bible as evangelical traditionalists do. They call it patriarchal and erroneous; we call it biblical and correct.

I am not claiming that evangelical feminists lack objectivity and that traditionalists have it. No one can claim perfect objectivity or freedom from prejudice. We all labor under biases rooted in selfish desires and landmark experiences. But we can seek helpful biases and proper first principles that help us navigate difficult questions.

All evangelicals share a primary commitment to the personal God, the creator and redeemer, who has spoken to mankind in Scripture. But the Bible is a large, complex book. Good and skillful people disagree about its secondary teachings. Faced with complexity, we seek 1) passages that seem most foundational, and 2) methods that promise to organize the data. Both feminists and traditionalists trust fundamental texts and methods to guide them to sound conclusions.

BASIC TEXTS

For the sake of discussion, let us divide the Bible into two parts, narrative and discourse. Narrative is the account of biblical history. Discourse is everything else, including laws, prophecies, proverbs, prayers, psalms, speeches, and letters.

When egalitarians read biblical narrative, they see women such as Deborah, Huldah, and Priscilla teaching, leading, and prophesying. Clearly, they say, biblical narratives bless the teaching and leadership of women.

When egalitarians survey biblical discourse, they focus on texts that promote the spiritual equality of men and women. They see Joel 2:28-29: "I will pour out my spirit upon all flesh; your sons and your daughters shall prophesy . . . . Even on my servants, both men and women, I will pour out my Spirit in those days." They see Galatians 3:28, "There is neither Jew nor Greek, slave nor free, male nor female, for you are all one in Christ Jesus."

Egalitarians then interpret texts that seem to favor the traditional view so that these cohere with their guiding passages. For example, in Genesis 3:16 God tells Eve, the representative woman, "Your desire will be for your husband, and he will rule over you." But egalitarians interpret that as a description of the results of the Fall, not a prescription for marriage. If, they reason, women's subordination is part of the curse, then subordination should end wherever salvation reverses the curse.[9] Later, when Paul says, "I do not permit a woman to teach . . . ," feminists see it as a temporary injunction, suited to ancient churches where uneducated women sought to usurp leadership.

When complementarians read biblical narrative, they notice that God created Adam first and gave Adam the authority function of naming Eve. They see God appointing men to the vast majority of leadership positions in the Bible. Men are monarchs, priests, and apostles. They see no women in a public, solo leadership roles and conclude that Bible narratives bless male leadership.

When complementarians survey biblical discourse, they accent texts that describe a God-given order for the sexes. They stress that when Paul said women may not teach, he appealed to creation, not the Fall in 1 Timothy 2:13: "For Adam was formed first, then Eve." They cite Ephesians 5:22 (ESV), "Wives, submit to your own husbands," and observe that a woman cannot rule over her husband at church and submit to him at home.

Complementarians then interpret texts that seem to favor the egalitarian view so that these cohere with their guiding passages. For example, they know Galatians 3:28, "There is neither . . . male nor female, for you are all one in Christ Jesus." But, we believe, Galatians 3:28 describes the equality of all Christians in *salvation*, in union with Christ. It has implications for gender relations, but it does not eradicate male-female differences.[10]

METHODS

Evangelical scholars agree on the first principles of interpretation. We study passages in context, define key words, examine the logic of an argument, and allow for an author's literary style—all to discover a text's meaning and relevance. Still, each side has certain inclinations.

Egalitarians assert that key passages describing male-female differences must not be taken at face value.[11] Craig Keener says Paul stressed the submission of women in Ephesians 5 "because he was smart."[12] He had to show his Greco-Roman readers that Christianity upheld the social order.[13] But, Keener asserts, Paul "subordinates wives so weakly, and emphasizes mutuality so strongly, that it is difficult to believe that he is arguing for their transcultural subordination."[14] That is, Paul's instructions are a temporary measure, designed to make Christianity sound inoffensive. Keener continues, "Paul is responding to a specific cultural issue for the sake of the gospel, and *his words should not be taken at face value* in all cultures" (emphasis mine). Paul only asked women "in his day" to conform "to the gen-

eral social ideal without fighting it."[15] So, regardless of the words of
Ephesians 5, wives need not literally submit to their husbands.

Gordon Fee claims that when Paul says, "I do not permit a
woman to teach or to have authority over a man," these are "special
instructions" for a unique situation in which women "were advanc-
ing the errors . . . of the false teachers" who were misleading the
church in Ephesus.[16] Fee does not try to *prove* that Paul is merely correcting a temporary error. Indeed, it is hard to see how he could, since
the text of 1 Timothy 2 gives no sign that it is provisional (see chapter 6). Instead of offering evidence, Fee says that since the whole letter seeks to rescue women and the church from false teachers, it does
not apply to women who do not encounter false teaching. So it "cannot be demonstrated that Paul intended 1 Timothy 2:11-12 as a rule
in all churches at all times." Indeed it does not apply to all women,
for the Lord revealed his will for women when he gave them the Spirit
and his gifts.[17]

When Fee says 1 Timothy 2:11-12 is not a rule for the church
because it "cannot be demonstrated" that it is, he has reversed things.
The burden of proof should lie with those who *deny* that a passage
applies literally today.[18] But even if Paul does address a local problem,
why should his teaching not be taken at face value? Teachers answer
questions by appealing to their bedrock principles. We should assume
that answers to questions still apply widely.

Fee's reasoning reveals another tendency. Egalitarians tend to
focus on general principles and extrapolate from them. As almost
every feminist author does, Fee asserts that Paul cannot really mean
to ban women from teaching, seeing that the Spirit has given women
gifts for ministry. Thus the general principle—women have the Spirit
and his gifts—nullifies Paul's particular teachings. Another "general
principles" approach reasons this way:

Female subordination is a result of the Fall, not God's original
design.

We must work to reverse the effects of the Fall.

Therefore, we must work to end female subordination.

Aida Besançon Spencer follows this approach when she says
women and men were equal at creation. Therefore, now that "Christ's

redemption has lifted many of the effects of the Fall . . . all women are justified in trying to regain their relationship of equality . . ." in family and church.[19]

Keener, Fee, Spencer, and the others I cite are respected scholars whose methods are essential to typical evangelical feminism. One cannot take Ephesians 5, 1 Timothy 2, and 1 Corinthians 11 and 14 literally and be a feminist. Feminists *normally* argue that texts urging the quietness or submission of women are trumped by principles such as reversal of the curse, equality in Christ, and the gifting of women. They *must* argue that 1 Timothy 2 is temporary or unclear.[20] They regularly accentuate contrasts between principles and specific rulings.

Traditionalists take the texts we just noted at face value for two reasons. First, we think Paul's teaching rests on permanent principles, not temporary conditions. Second, we find consistency between the general principle that women have gifts (1 Cor. 12) and the particular command that women must not exercise authority over men (1 Tim. 2). We believe that general principles and specific rules explain or define each other well. To illustrate from another debate, the principle "You shall not kill" is defined by specific rules imposing the death penalty for murder.

Everyone has to decide when he should or should not take puzzling commands literally: "Greet one another with a holy kiss" (1 Cor. 16:20); "Praise [God] with tambourine and dancing . . . praise him with the clash of cymbals" (Ps. 150:4-5); "Do not go among the Gentiles" (Matt. 10:5). Egalitarians are slower to take a command at face value, at least on this issue. But it is better to assume that a command, especially from the New Testament era, remains in force than to assume that it does not. It is better to harmonize two commands that appear to be in tension rather than to declare one inoperative. When interpreting laws, traditionalists assume that the specific *rules* of Scripture incarnate, illustrate, and clarify its broad *principles*.[21]

Everyone agrees that women have gifts. Traditionalists believe that certain biblical rules specify *how* women should use their gifts. Paul clarifies his teaching that the Spirit distributes gifts to everyone (1 Cor. 12:7-11) when he says women should not exercise authority over a man (1 Tim. 2:12), when he says that males are responsible to "weigh" or evaluate what prophets say (1 Cor. 14:29-35), and when he says overseers must be *husbands* of one wife (1 Tim. 3:2).

Egalitarians and complementarians may disagree because they read the Bible differently. They may also disagree because each finds certain arguments more compelling.

BASIC ARGUMENTS FOR EGALITARIANS

Christian feminists' arguments fall into certain categories that I will call the "All Gifts" argument, the "Subjective Calling" argument, and the "Fullness of Time" argument. The *All Gifts* argument can be stated as a syllogism. Major premise: All who have gifts should be free to exercise them. Minor premise: Women have received the Spirit and his gifts. Therefore, women should be free to exercise every gift in every setting as leaders or followers. F. F. Bruce says, "If [the Spirit] manifestly withheld the gifts of teaching or leadership from Christian women, then we should accept that as evidence of his will (1 Cor. 12:11). But experience shows that he bestows these and other gifts with 'undistinguishing regard' on men and women alike."[22] Indeed, it is wicked to suppress the use of gifts, for Scripture forbids us to cover our light or bury our talents.[23]

Complementarians agree that women receive many spiritual gifts. But one can have a gift and exercise it privately. Huldah prophesied and Deborah judged, but they used their gifts privately.

The *Subjective Calling* argument begins with the fact that some women report that they experience a call from God to Christian ministry. The call may come to them unsought, during prayer or a dream, or when a woman sees a need no one else notices. The woman may be frightened by the call. But it comes—a mighty summons to perform a task for God.[24] When she serves, she reports, God blesses her labors. How, she asks, can anyone question her deeply felt and obviously fruitful call? Egalitarians believe that women must be free to act on a call to serve.[25] "The church educates children in sexless equality," but as little girls mature, the unqualified call to serve Christ evaporates. Women are told to "leave [their] talents at the door of the church." But deep within they know they should use their gifts in their Savior's house even if local churches offer no encouragement.[26] Careful scholars add that these women *feel* called subjectively because they *are* called objectively.[27] This argument implicitly challenges complementarians to prove them wrong. Only an overwhelming case against women in ministry could deny women the right to serve, and the very existence of the debate shows the case is not overwhelming.[28] Therefore, women may choose whatever path allows freedom in ministry.[29]

Complementarians reply that Scripture commands us to test all things, including our feelings (1 Thess. 5:21). If a man feels God has released him from an unhappy marriage, we must question that feeling. Sin deceives the emotions as well as the mind and body. Besides, the case for male leadership is not so unclear that we must let vague ideas such as "freedom in ministry" gain the right to arbitrate between competing interpretations of Scripture.[30]

The *Fullness of Time* argument first says the New Testament's limits on women's ministries were temporary concessions to their lack of education and social status in antiquity. The church liberated women as it could, but if Jesus had chosen female apostles and Paul had allowed female elders, it would have proved fatal for the church. Jesus and the apostles barred women from public leadership for the sake of the mission. But now the situation has reversed. When the church forbids women to lead, it alienates our broadly egalitarian society. "The church is slandered because it continues to insist on the submission of women."[31]

Today women increasingly lead in business, medicine, politics, and the media. Over half of all bachelors and masters degree recipients are female. In professional programs, female enrollment approaches the 50 percent mark so that ever more doctors, lawyers, and scientists are women. Men are learning, slowly, to make peace with women as their peers and even supervisors. It is becoming unthinkable to deny women the right to lead the church when they lead in every other sphere, except perhaps wrestling and monster truck driving.

Egalitarians say women used to circumvent the male-dominated power structures that barred their way. But now it is time to go through the front door.[32] When they do, some add, the church will profit, since it has not exactly thrived under all-male leadership. In 1888 Frances Willard declared that the female temperament must complement the male for the sake of the gospel. "Law and love will never balance" until a woman holds the scales. When women minister, the power of the gospel will double, for they are holy and have heart, and "religion is an affair of the heart."[33] More recently Stanley Grenz argued that women "tend to" understand the biblical pattern of servant-leadership better than men. They tend to practice consensual leadership, to empower the laity, to foster a caring and compassionate community, to encourage compassion, and "to confront social injustice and oppression more aggressively."[34]

An aggressive egalitarian might say the time for the gender debates is past. If men want to argue against women's ordination, let them. But let them also understand that women are ordained every day. Soon women will not need to *refute* traditional arguments; they will *ignore* them.

Complementarians know their position seems unpopular, but, they ask, since when are Christians led by polls? If someone says we must ordain women to avoid alienating society, that person is *assuming* the Bible and the church of the past only forbade female ordination for pragmatic reasons. But that is the very point in dispute!

When someone says we must ordain women to avoid alienating society, that person is adopting a consequentialist ethic, at least temporarily. Consequentialism says we should make decisions based on calculations of their consequences; whatever brings the greatest good is right. But our minds are too puny to judge accurately the consequences of our actions. To calculate all the consequences of an act, one must be omniscient, since a deed that initially seems beneficial may later have disastrous consequences. The initial evangelization of China is a case in point. Female missionaries far outnumbered males in the late nineteenth and early twentieth centuries, with single women outnumbering single men as much as six to one. It was hard to object since the field was so large, and women were willing to go. Their work bore fruit, especially with women, but some Chinese evangelicals believe the preponderance of female missionaries and female converts led to churches that are over 75 percent female in some areas.[35]

FROM EGALITARIANS TO TRADITIONALISTS

Feminists believe that three unassailable principles support their position: 1) Women are the spiritual equals of men, equally created in God's image, equally recreated by Christ. 2) Women receive all spiritual gifts. 3) Women must be free to exercise their gifts. But traditionalists agree with all three points. They simply believe women should use their gifts within an authority structure given by God to preserve order in the home and church.[36]

Unfortunately for traditionalists, arguments based on authority structures have limited appeal in the West. We value freedom more than order. But Christians in the past certainly understood the value of order for a good society. Today people want freedom to do what they wish as long as they harm no one. In this atmosphere, many think it strange that Christians debate whether women should be "free" to preach. Whatever limits freedom is suspect. But in other eras, whatever weakened order was suspect. People took 1 Timothy at face value because it provided order even if it limited freedom.

TWO KINDS OF TRADITIONALISTS

We can transition to the final chapter's comparison of views in church history by dividing traditionalists into two groups, which we will call the "Divine Decree" and "Congruent Creation" camps. *Divine Decree* traditionalists believe God simply decreed that men should lead. Men are no more fit to lead than women. They are no wiser, no more spiritual. No "masculine" traits—not a larger, stronger physique, not a tough, assertive disposition, not a rational and dispassionate mind— explain why God decided men should lead. God *chose* to govern his world through authorities. For reasons that please him, he chose men to lead the family and the church. We should neither look to male superiority nor to male traits to explain God's decree.

The *Congruent Creation* approach asserts that men and women are equal in value but different in nature. This view holds that men lead in home and church because God sovereignly chose to organize it through male headship, a headship granted without regard to the *merits* of men. Yet, it says, God etched traces of his sovereign decree into the nature of men and women. These traces of his decree lead men to seek headship and give women contentment as they follow male leaders. In the past, some theologians marked the strength or bearing of men. Today scholars explore the mental and relational styles of men and women. Some contemporary secular gender scholars agree with classical theologians Thomas Aquinas and John Calvin that men are more apt to make decisions based on rational calculation alone, whereas emotional and relational factors move women more. This view affirms that women and men have equal capacities but develop them differently, in ways suited to our social roles. Thus there is a congruence between the divine decree of male leadership and the nature of men and women.

We must distinguish Congruent Creation from the view, first stated by Aristotle, that men lead because women are intellectually and morally inferior. Certain traditional theologians have argued that women are more easily deceived.[37] But virtually no one asserts that women are globally inferior. Some say women are spiritually superior to men, and most say men and women are equal in virtue and ability even if they develop these differently.

CONCLUSION

Christians have gender debates because we favor different texts, methods, and arguments. But matters that are hotly debated in one place and time may enjoy almost complete consensus at others. Church history indicates that the women's issue was hardly debated for centuries. Perhaps a better understanding of the causes of our disagreement will help restore us to peace.

10

A History of
Women and Ministry

On the Use Of Church History

Humans are such creatures of habit and custom that whatever is, appears to be right. The mainstream of Western culture now accepts many tenets of commonsense feminism: Women should have the same rights as men—property rights, legal rights, marriage rights. They should have the same opportunities as men—the same educational opportunities, the same chance to excel. Commonsense feminists (or "equity feminists") "merely want for women what they want for everyone—a 'fair field and no favors.'"[1]

Biblical law pioneered the idea that women have the same legal and marital rights as men, and Jesus advocated the education of women. But the idea that women should not lead the church seems antiquated and unjust to many people. We know our age has not achieved the pinnacle of wisdom on all gender questions. Still, we struggle when we differ with the accepted views of our day. Francis Schaeffer said, "Tell me what the world is saying today, and I'll tell you what the church will be saying in seven years." So it is beneficial for us to collect the wisdom of the church's great theologians to see how they viewed gender issues, hoping their insights can illumine our debates.

Virtually without exception for nineteen centuries, orthodox Christian theologians shared the views of this book. They said women ought to learn quietly and submissively. Women could teach informally but not authoritatively. God fashioned men and women and ordained a structure for their relationships. He appointed males to

lead the church and home. Adam was the head of Eve from the beginning, but after the Fall, her subordination became subjugation, both
as a punishment for her sin and because men and women strive for
dominance, and men generally win.

Some egalitarians search for proto-feminists in ancient and
medieval church history. They want to show that their view is not
novel, not merely an echo of recent cultural developments. Still,
nearly everyone agrees that traditionalism really is the tradition of the
church. But feminists are not too impressed by a poll of heroes past.
Sophisticated feminists know the church long insisted on male leadership; they also know church leaders rarely gave sustained attention
to women's issues until the last century.

Discussions were not always highly enlightened. First, until the
sixteenth century, no leading theologian was married. Second, they
sometimes did little more than cite familiar texts and answer a few
recurring questions. (Pagan Greeks wondered if women had souls,
and for over a millennium Christians kept replying, "Yes, they do.")
Third, women long lagged so far behind men in education and experience that few could attain the qualifications for leadership.
Consequently, egalitarians might concede that orthodox theologians
barred women from positions of authority, but ask, "Since when do
polls of dead theologians determine truth?" Protestants remember
Luther's lonely stand against virtually the entire church. We also confess the authority of Scripture, not history, so we agree that polls of
heroes past cannot determine the truth.

Still, we profit by recovering the best thought of the church's best
minds. This means more than a mere collation of "who believed what
about female teachers." We hope to discover the reasoning of the theologians who engaged the issues and whose work stands the test of time.

The Ancient Church

By modern standards, ancient discussions of women's issues were rare
and unsophisticated. Whatever their reputations, ancient theologians
were not a band of misogynists. No major theologian advocated a
total ban on female teachers. All recognized that women do some
teaching in the Bible. They agreed that women may instruct their chil-

dren, may lead other women, and can instruct everyone by living nobly. Yet many centuries passed before any orthodox theologian granted women the right to hold formal teaching offices.

There are only isolated remarks about women in the most ancient sources. Cyprian (d. 258) cites 1 Corinthians 11:34-35 and 1 Timothy 2:11-14 and declares, "A woman ought to be silent in the church."[2]

Tertullian (d. 225) had reason to grant ministerial rights to women, for two female prophetesses, Priscilla and Maximilla, played major roles in the Montanist movement he joined later in life. Nonetheless, Tertullian insisted that women should be silent in the church, for "women should be under obedience." They may prophesy if covered with a veil, but, he says, women should not be too bold in their learning and must not be permitted to teach or administer the sacraments.[3] He reasons that women are not permitted even to *learn* with excess boldness; therefore, they certainly cannot have "the power of teaching and of baptizing!" Instead, women should "be silent . . . and at home consult with their own husbands."[4] All women should be veiled, according to Tertullian, because men have authority and deserve honor.[5]

Origen (ca. 185-250) rejected Montanism and the public prophecies of Priscilla and Maximilla. Origen believed that when Paul said, "The women should keep silent in the churches," he discredited female teachers. Of the Bible's female prophets, Origen finds that none spoke in public:

> If the daughters of Philip prophesied, at least they did not speak in the assemblies; for we do not find this fact in evidence in the Acts of the Apostles. Much less in the Old Testament. It is said that Deborah was a prophetess. . . . There is no evidence that Deborah delivered speeches to the people, as did Jeremias and Isaias. Huldah, who was a prophetess, did not speak to the people, but only to a man, who consulted her at home. The gospel itself mentions a prophetess Anna . . . but she did not speak publicly. Even if it is granted to a woman to . . . prophecy, she is nevertheless not permitted to speak in an assembly.[6]

Origen believes that Titus 2:3-4 confirms his position. There Paul commands "older women to be reverent in the way they live, not to be slanderers or addicted to much wine, but to teach what is good. Then they can train the younger women to love their husbands and children . . ." (Titus 2:3-4). Origen says that "men should not sit and listen to a woman . . . even if she says admirable things, or even saintly things, that is of little consequence, since they come from the mouth of a woman."[7] For Origen, it is enough that Paul says, "I permit no woman to teach or to have authority over men."[8] He never attempts to explain why women should not teach men. Yet he does permit women to be deacons, for "even women are instituted deacons in the church."[9]

The Apostolic Constitutions (late fourth century) even restricts private teaching by women. If someone should ask a widow about her faith, the widow should send the person to the church's governors since they have more learning.[10] The Constitutions say women may only "pray and hear those that teach." Why? "For our Master and Lord, Jesus himself, when he sent us the twelve to make disciples of the nations, did nowhere send out women to preach, although he did not want [lack] such. For there were with us the mother of our Lord and his sisters; also Mary Magdalene and Mary the mother of James, and Martha and Mary the sisters of Lazarus; Salome, and certain others." If Jesus had wanted women to teach, he would have appointed one of them. Further, the document continues, the ban on the ordination and teaching office of women is logical. "'If the head of the woman be the man,' it is not reasonable that the rest of the body should govern the head." If women did teach, it would abrogate the order of creation, for the man was created first.[11] The Constitutions did permit widows and female deacons to minister to women. As unordained servants of priests and bishops, they ranked far below presbyters and bishops.[12] So the Constitutions deny women the teaching office.

Tertullian, Origen, and the Constitutions all sharply restrict women's ecclesiastical roles. All agree that men must teach with authority and lead officially in the church. Yet they do allow women freedom to prophesy and to minister to women. Thus even strict traditionalists respected some impulses women have for ministry.

JEROME

Jerome (331-420) was initially reluctant to teach women, but when he did agree to teach a few noble women, their intellectual abilities amazed him. Of Paula, a widowed Roman aristocrat, Jerome said she was "slow to speak and swift to learn. . . . The holy Scriptures she knew by heart." When Paula studied Hebrew, she "succeeded so well that she could chant the Psalms in Hebrew and speak the language without a trace of the pronunciation peculiar to Latin."[13] Paula taught and led women, notably in a women's monastery she founded alongside Jerome's monastery for men in Bethlehem. She even taught men once. In Jerome's absence, a man taught heresy concerning eternal life, and Paula resisted both the error and its proponents, and "publicly proclaimed them as enemies of the Lord."[14]

Marcella, another noble Roman widow within Jerome's circle, taught yet more. Widowed months after her wedding, Marcella dedicated herself to chastity and asceticism. An older woman when Jerome arrived in Rome, she never met him without asking questions and entering long discussions about Scripture so that she would be prepared to answer similar questions herself.[15] This preparation allowed Marcella to do some teaching. After Jerome left Rome, Marcella was sometimes called in to settle disputes. When she spoke, she stressed that her opinion was not her own but came from Jerome or another teacher. Thus she admitted "that what she taught she had learned from others. For she knew that the apostle had said: 'I suffer not a woman to teach' and she would not seem to inflict a wrong upon the male sex many of whom . . . questioned her concerning obscure and doubtful points."[16]

She also took a more public role when a potent heresy "fouled the clear waters of the faith of Rome." When she saw that the faith was endangered, she "threw herself into the breach," publicly withstanding the heretics, "choosing to please God rather than men." By letter she challenged the heretics to appear to defend themselves, and when they refused to come, they were discredited.[17]

Jerome believed that Marcella's work did not violate Paul's rule that women must not teach men. As Jerome saw it, Marcella became his delegate in Rome, teaching other believers (including some priests) what she had learned from him. "All that I had gathered together by long study, and by constant meditation . . . , she first sipped, then learned, and finally took for her own."[18] Just as people had come to him when he was in Rome, so now people came to her because she had the fruits of his study.

Clearly, Jerome approved the teaching of Marcella as she filled the breach when heresy roiled the church. Yet it does not even occur to Jerome that Marcella should be ordained to teach. It seemed especially fitting that she teach privately and discreetly when others sought her, since she operated under the distant authority of a man, Jerome. Thus, Jerome limited women's ministry while yet training some women for ministry.

CHRYSOSTOM

Chrysostom (345-407) is renowned for his exposition of Scripture. Fortunately, his sermons on 1 Timothy and Ephesians 5 have survived to this day. Commenting on 1 Timothy 2:8-12, Chrysostom asserts that women are "naturally somewhat talkative" and can disrupt the church with their clamor on "unprofitable topics."[19] Therefore, women should be silent in the church so they can learn something.

Further, women should be silent because Adam was created first, and Eve was deceived. Chrysostom anticipates an objection: "What does the creation and subsequent sin of Adam and Eve have to do with women of the present?" First, the law that made women subject to men rests on creation. By forming man first, God "shows their superiority." God created Adam first to show that "the male sex enjoyed the higher honor" and "had preeminence in every way."[20] Second, the Fall sealed woman's subordinate status. "For the woman taught the man once, and made him guilty of disobedience, and wrought our ruin. Because she made bad use of her relational powers, God made her subject to her husband." Third, she was a poor teacher because she was "deceived by . . . an inferior and subordinate animal" and "captivated by appetite." Eve's sin was typical, for her sex "is weak and fickle . . . collectively."[21]

Such comments rightly elicit a reaction. Yet Chrysostom's homily on Romans 16 generously lauds the women whose ministry Paul blesses there. He acclaims women such as Mary, Tryphena, and

Nereus's sister.[22] Chrysostom takes the individual named Junia or Junias in 16:7 to be a woman. That decision is important because Paul calls her his fellow prisoner and an "apostle" (16:7). But Chrysostom does not read "apostle" as an equal to the twelve who laid the foundation for the church in doctrine and evangelism. He interprets "apostle" in the sense of someone commissioned by the church for a task (Acts 13:2-3; 14:14).

Chrysostom's comments about Mary, a woman whom Paul praised in 16:6, are consistent with his view of Junia. Like some other women, Mary puts men "to shame" by leaving them "far behind" as she carries on "the race apostles and evangelists ran."[23] But how, Chrysostom asks, can this comport with Paul's dictum, "I suffer not a woman to teach"? He replies that Paul hinders women from speaking publicly (1 Cor. 14:35) and from taking the seat of the clergy. But he does not silence women completely. Women may admonish their children and husbands. He approves "private conversing for their own advantage," but disapproves public instruction by women "before all . . . in the public assembly." Hence, Chrysostom praises women who perform "all other ministries," but not public teaching.[24] Similarly, Chrysostom's commentary on Priscilla in Acts 18 never imagines that her instruction of Apollos indicates that women can regularly teach men doctrine. He stresses her willingness to minister, to show hospitality, and to teach privately.[25]

Chrysostom does belittle women at times, charging that they are weaker beings who are "easily carried away and light minded." So they are subject to their husbands "for the benefit of both."[26] Nonetheless, he enunciated several enduring arguments for male leadership in the church: 1) Man was created first and thereby destined to preeminence by God. 2) The woman abused her initial equality with man by leading him into sin and was punished for it. 3) Women are less rational than men, somehow weaker and less honorable, and therefore less suited to lead.

THE MIDDLE AGES

Medieval commentary on gender roles in the church is rare and incidental until Hildegard arrives in the twelfth century (1099-1179). A

Benedictine abbess, visionary, and healer, she dispensed counsel, sought and unsought, to four popes, two emperors, and the patriarch of Jerusalem. She reached monks, abbots, dukes, ecclesiastical officials, and humble folk. She denounced the sins of the church and called it to look to Christ rather than to priests for salvation.[27] Her authority came from her visions. "From my infancy my soul has always beheld this light," she asserted. Wide awake, without trances or dreams, she perceived spiritual matters in her soul.[28]

In her forty-third year, she saw a vision and heard a voice commanding her to speak and write. "A flashing fire of light . . . transfused my brain, my heart," and at once she understood the full meaning of all Scripture.[29] Hildegard began to write. Framed as visions, her books and letters are artless but orthodox.[30] She never sought an office and soothed male sensibilities by calling herself an unlearned woman who simply wrote down what she received as a vessel for divine truth.[31]

The discussion of women's ordination begins roughly when Hildegard began to publish her visions. Perhaps with Hildegard in mind, Thomas Aquinas (1225-1274) asked whether "the charism of wisdom in speech and knowledge pertains to women" as well as men. It appears so, says Aquinas, because "prophecy is granted to women," and the "grace of prophecy is greater than that of speech." Further, all have received gifts, and women cannot administer the grace of wisdom and knowledge unless they speak. On the other hand, Aquinas counters, "St. Paul says . . . 'I permit no woman to teach or to have authority over men.'"[32]

Aquinas eventually decides that women may not teach publicly in the church. He distinguishes private speech, which "becomes a woman," and public speech before "the whole church," which does not. Public speech "is not conceded to women" because they "must be subject to man, according to Genesis. But to teach and persuade publicly in the church is not the task of subjects but of prelates."[33] The subjection of women has two aspects. Woman's penalty for her role in the Fall requires that she "bear with . . . her husband's will against her own." This subjection is accidental, pertaining to woman's history but not her nature. The second subordination is permanent and essential to woman "since even before the Fall the man was the head of the woman."[34]

Why would woman be subject even without the Fall? Women "generally speaking are not perfected in wisdom" and so should not minister publicly, Aquinas contends.[35] They "seldom keep a firm grip on things." Some individual women are most reasonable, and yet women generally lack "in firm rational judgment. . . . their conduct is not based on solid reason, but easily swayed by feeling." They do "not pursue what reason has counseled."[36] However this sounds to us, Thomas meant to be subtle. He intended to evaluate the inclinations of women, not just their capacities. He says women *seldom* keep a firm grip, that they are *easily* swayed, that they do not *pursue* the counsels of reason. That is, he intended to affirm that many women defy these generalizations.

Thomas bans women from office for several reasons. Female priests might incite men to lust.[37] Tonsure, which is required for ordination, is impossible for women (1 Cor. 11). Above all, women cannot receive ordination because of their subjection to men. Women are not inferior to men; their creation is part of God's good plan for humanity. Still, subjection is woman's natural state.[38] Her subjection promotes order, for the human family should be governed by the wise, and "the power of rational discernment is by nature stronger in man."[39]

Thomas does not believe in a global moral and intellectual inferiority of women.[40] Many women are virtuous, and husband and wife can delight in each other's virtue and in their marriage.[41] Further, Thomas never denies that some women are governed by reason, though he does think that feeling guides women more than men.

Duns Scotus (ca. 1266-1308) agrees that women should not be ordained but denies that there is any ground for this prohibition; it is simply the will of God. "The church would not have presumed to deprive the entire sex of women, without any fault of their own, of an act which would licitly have been theirs, and which might have been ordained for the salvation of women and others in the church through her. . . ." Scotus, foreseeing pastoral benefits that might accrue from the ordination of women, concludes that the ban rests on the pure will of Christ, not on the good of the church, not on the inability of woman to bear the image of Christ (as Bonaventure had argued earlier), and not on a nature suited to subjection (as Aquinas argued). Yet Scotus adds that the will of Christ is just somehow. Further, women may at least be deaconesses and "official" widows, but their offices would entail neither ordination nor authority.[42]

Women's Ministry in the Middle Ages

A tiny number of medieval women taught men by letter or by private audience. More often women taught fellow women. There were some all-female monasteries, and abbesses could wield considerable power over the sisters in them.[43] A few abbesses may have rivaled the authority of local bishops, but such outcomes depended on local conditions and personalities.

If medieval women became teachers, they did so by circumventing ordinary channels. None exercised authority through the regular paths to church office.[44] They did not attend universities, let alone teach at them. They did not receive ordination or celebrate the Mass. Female mystics claimed divine illumination and often denigrated their skills and status. Though a learned woman, Julian of Norwich (fourteenth century) called herself a "simple, unlettered creature . . . lewd, feeble and frail," who felt she had to publish her visions of the goodness of God.[45] Yet, because "all is according to Scripture," her readers cannot accept one vision and reject another.[46] We wonder if Julian was truly self-effacing or if she posed to gain acceptance in a male-dominated world. Still, if one has received a vision, formal authority seems superfluous.[47]

Around the same time, the German nun and playwright Hroswitha admitted she was "capable of learning . . . divinely gifted with abilities" with "moderate knowledge" of philosophy, though she also confessed she was limited by "my woman's understanding."[48] Gertrude of Helfta (thirteenth century) was less prone to question her capacity and confidently accepted authority.[49] Like Julian, she claimed she received visions that instructed her and granted her powers like those of a priest. "Behold, I give my words into your mouth," she claimed Christ said to her, commanding her to teach, advise, counsel, and preach.[50]

Medieval female teachers such as Hildegard, Hroswitha, Gertrude, and Julian were all single nuns. Catherine of Siena, famed for mystical visions and for a crusade for reform, never married either. Brigitta, another reformer, began her career after her husband died. Margery Kempe is the exception that proves the rule. A wife and mother of fourteen children, she began her public work as a visionary and itinerant evangelist after she convinced her husband to join her in a pact of chastity and separation—a virtual divorce—sworn before a bishop.[51] In short, if a woman wanted to teach in the Middle Ages, the pattern was to have a vision, but not a husband. To lead, women had to be free from the authority of a husband or father. Their visions granted them "direct authorization to act as mediators to others."[52] Thus they circumvented the strictures that the official church used to deny them ordination.

The history of medieval sects corroborates this view. Sometimes persecuted by the church for nothing more heretical than their critique of its excessive authority, medieval sects often allowed women to minister publicly. The Waldensians promoted the popular use of Scripture and the rights of laymen. They let women proclaim the Word, too. If someone cited Paul's words about the silence of women, they replied that the women were teaching rather than formally preaching, and counter-quoted Titus 2:3.[53] The Hussites also admitted the laity, including women, to the preaching office.[54]

So the ancient and medieval church consistently opposed the ordination of women to formal offices of teaching and authority. If women taught men, they justified it by claiming God had directly commissioned them. The church allowed women to teach privately, to teach other women, and to publish their visions. Tertullian and Aquinas even permitted women to prophesy; yet they denied that such prophecy gave women official status. The church's position rested on a plain reading of texts such as 1 Timothy 2 and 1 Corinthians 11. The explanations of the ban varied.[55] Some believed women were intellectually inferior, hence prone to deception. Others held that women were as capable but had less interest in reason. Some believed a sensual nature dominated women.[56] Thus, most theologians doubted that women had the moral or intellectual capacity to lead the church. All came to the same conclusion, but the reasons were diverse.

THE REFORMATION

If the Reformation was a theological earthquake, justification by faith alone, salvation by grace alone, and the authority of Scripture alone stood at the epicenter. But its shock waves reached women and the family. With the Reformation, praise for marriage supplanted praise of celibacy, and support for marriage replaced its vilification. As the status of marriage rose, so did that of women, and theologians began to rethink their views of women and their role in the church.

Luther

Luther (1483-1546) revered women as wives, mothers, and household managers. He embraced marriage as God's ordinary will for mankind. The bustling house is God's school of character. In it, Luther said, woman is "much weaker" than man, with less "glory and prestige," as the moon's glory is less than the sun's. Yet woman is "similar to Adam so far as the image of God is concerned, that is, in justice, wisdom, and happiness." Women "may not be excluded from any glory of the human creature," although they are "inferior to the male sex," weak, often foolish, and prone to chaotic talk.[57] Yet God created women so that if she had not sinned, "she would have been the equal of man in all respects." Before the Fall, Eve was Adam's equal in body and mind. After the Fall, man still cannot get along without woman.[58]

Luther believed that 1 Timothy 2 instructed women in their behavior in the public assembly of the church and stressed modest dress and silence.[59] In the assembly, "a woman must be completely quiet . . . a hearer and not . . . a teacher. . . . She should refrain from teaching" or even praying in public. She can speak at home. "This passage makes a woman subject. It takes from her all public office and authority."[60]

Luther conceded that sacred literature has examples of women who "have been very good at management." Why then does Paul deprive women of the administration of the Word? "Where men and women have been joined together, there the men, not the women, ought to have authority." Luther believed women did not have the voice, eloquence, and memory necessary for skill at preaching.[61] Women who "are without husband, like Huldah and Deborah" are exceptions, for they are not teaching contrary to a man or his authority. "Where there is no man, Paul has allowed that they can do this."[62]

Luther justifies the ban on women in authority in two ways. First, Paul wants to preserve God's order "that a man be the head of the woman, as 1 Corinthians 11:3 tells us." There is a disturbance when women argue against a doctrine that is taught by a man. If a woman thinks she is wise, "let her argue with her husband at home." Second, "where a man teaches there is a well-rounded argument."[63] So men ought to teach both to maintain order in the church and, Luther thinks, because men are more capable and logical teachers.

Luther denies that male authority includes "physical domination" by men. But woman should not "have the last word" or appear wiser in the home or church. Man deserves authority because "God himself has ordained that man be created first—first in time and first in authority." Adam has the right of primogeniture. But man also rules because of merit. "Not only has God's wisdom ordained this, but there was more wisdom and courage in Adam. . . . Experience has been witness of this. . . . It was not Adam who went astray. Therefore there was greater wisdom in Adam than in the woman."[64] Luther ponders Satan's strategy, stressing that "Satan did not attack Adam." He avoided "the fearless person [Adam] and attacked the weaker one." Sin entered the world "by her fault." Thus, woman's position is also a punishment, "a memorial of [her] transgression. . . ."[65] For Luther, then, men lead because God ordained it, because they are stronger, wiser, and more courageous, and because women deserve to be punished for Eve's role in the Fall.

Calvin

Calvin (1509-1564) declares that by "the ordinary law of God" women are "formed to obey." Thus, government by women "has always been regarded by all wise persons as a monstrous thing." They must be quiet, for "to teach implies the rank of power and authority."[66]

Women may instruct their families, but Paul "excludes them from the office of teaching, which God has committed to men only." If anyone adduces Deborah, Philip's daughters, Abigail, and other female prophets and teachers, Calvin replies that they never held "the office to speak in the assembly."[67] Further, their cases are extraordinary and "do not overturn the ordinary rules of government," which bind us. God "is above all law" and can do such things.[68] If a woman should teach or govern for a season, we should conclude not that women may hold authority, but that God wants to shame men by causing "women and little children to reign."[69] But such acts of God set no precedent for human government.[70]

Calvin says Paul "assigns two reasons why women ought to be subject to men." First, God enacted a law from the beginning. Women have never been received to public office because "nature" imprints the knowledge that it is "unseemly . . . to have women govern men."[71] When Paul says Adam was created first, he reflects on the nature, not just the timing, of creation. Woman was created as "a kind of appendage to the man." She was "at hand to render obedience to him" as "an inferior aid."[72]

Second, God inflicted subjection "as a punishment on the woman" for her sin. Both Eve and Adam were entangled in deceit, but she was the source of their sin and more at fault. Because she gave "fatal advice, it was right that she should learn that she was under the power . . . of another." Thus woman's subordination was "natural from the beginning," but after Eve's disobedience, "the subjection was now less voluntary and agreeable." Because she exalted herself against her Creator and her husband, her subjection now has a "note of ignominy and shame."[73]

Why are women subject to men? Sounding like Aquinas, Calvin says God "appointed a certain kind of policy and order . . . to provide for the weaker sort."[74] Yet women were the first witnesses to Jesus' resurrection. God allowed this to happen as a "gentle chastisement" to the Twelve. If someone objects that the women "are not less carnal and stupid" than the apostles, Calvin almost agrees. "It does not belong to us to estimate the difference between the Apostles and the women."[75] If Jesus wants to appear to women first, or if God wants to appoint Deborah a judge, that is his prerogative. He is free to bypass his laws on occasion—perhaps "to condemn the supineness of men"—since "all laws proceed from his will."[76]

Calvin claimed women were, in an undefined way, created for subordination and service. Yet the Scotist line never disappears. God established a male-governed order because it pleased him. "We can allege no desert why God preferred us before women." Yet even if men have no greater worth, women have no right to murmur against the divine order. Let them remember they bear God's image and rule the lower creation.[77] Thus Calvin is unsettled, sometimes affirming a kind of inferiority for women and sometimes affirming the intrinsic equality of men and women.[78]

THE PURITANS

The Puritans produced the first sustained treatment of marriage and gender in Christendom.[79] They believed that God structured human society by ordaining "degrees of superiority and inferiority, of authority and subjection."[80] He governs the world through magistrates and subjects, ministers and churches, husbands and wives, parents and children, masters and servants. In each relationship, superiors obtain authority through their position, not their virtue, though they must uphold their position virtuously.

In marriage "the husband is made the head of his wife, though the husband were, before the marriage, a very beggar, and of mean parentage, and the wife very wealthy and of a noble flock."[81] The subjection of woman is "against the law of nature as it was before the fall, but against the law of corrupted nature it is not." A servant is inwardly "equal to his master"; yet in the outward civil order, "the master is above the servant and the servant . . . must be subject."[82]

What if the husband is an impious, lewd drunkard, and the wife is a "sober, religious matron"? Must she still "account him her superior, and worthy of an husband's honor"? Certainly, for his evil disposition does not deprive him of the "civil honor" that God bestowed on "his place and office."[83] The best wife always retains her inward reverence. She may disobey her husband only if his commands contradict God's Word.[84]

These remarks restrict women but also liberate them in several ways. First, the Puritans addressed women directly as no one else had. Second, they assumed women had the competence to evaluate their husbands' directives and the courage to resist orders when necessary. Third, they respected woman's conscience. Before executing major decisions, husbands must gently persuade wives of their wisdom, letting them deliberate, too.[85] Moreover, if she cannot agree with him, despite patient instruction, he must not enforce his will lest he damage her conscience.[86]

William Gouge said a wife's words should be "few, reverent and meek" in the home and the church since Paul commands women to be silent.[87] A wife may speak a little, Gouge explains, for complete silence suggests stubbornness as much as loquacity implies disrespect. "Silence" means a wife listens and learns from her husband and speaks to him sparingly and reverently.[88] Yet Gouge says women may teach. As joint governor of the family, she rightly teaches children and all servants in her husband's absence. This does not conflict with 1 Timothy 2, Gouge explains, for that passage considers "public assemblies, and churches, in which she may not teach, but not to private families, in which she may." Husbands have the chief responsibility for household worship; yet wives may pray, read, and teach if their husbands are away or neglect their duties.[89]

Still, women must yield to their husbands and pastors.[90] Some Puritans believed that men lead because of their superiority. Robert Bolton said men lead because they are superior in mind and body. The husband has a "more manly body, tempered with a natural fitness of the soul." Therefore, he "ought to exceed the wife in understanding, and dexterity to manage business." But the wife's soul is "something damped by the frailty of that weaker body."[91] William Whately agreed that "nature hath framed the lineaments" of the male's body "to his superiority, and set the print of government in his very face."[92] John Winthrop, governor of Massachusetts Bay Colony, said another governor's wife went insane because she meddled in the affairs of men, "whose minds are stronger."[93]

But most Puritans explained that men lead because of the need for order. As William Perkins put it, "there must be orders of men" for family, church, and commonwealth to stand.[94] Gouge said God commands all men to submit to one another "because everyone is set in his place by God . . . for the good of others."[95] Thomas Gataker said husbands must lead because "the man was first created . . . and therefore the man hath the birthright (1 Tim. 2:13)." Nature proves the same thing, for "the woman was made for the man. . . ." She is the "image and glory of the man, as the man is the image and the glory of God" (1 Cor. 11:7). And historically, Eve sinned first and drew Adam into sin with her.[96]

The Puritans refined the complementarian position. They did not abandon the idea that men are more fit to lead, but their principal rationale for male leadership is the need for order in society. Further, the Protestant principle of the priesthood of believers made them respect woman's conscience. Since they affirmed woman's capacity, the Puritans granted women substantial freedom. Some turned their finances over to their wives.[97] Gouge even permitted wives to lead family worship in some circumstances.[98]

The Reformers recognized the mental and spiritual capacities of women. But if women are as capable and spiritual as men, why are they barred from office and leadership? That question came soon enough. In England women became active in the religious sects that emerged during the Civil War. In 1666 Margaret Fell, the second wife and co-laborer of George Fox, published a proto-feminist tract, "Women's Speaking Justified, Proved, and Allowed by the Scriptures." More a protest than a treatise, it asserts that "those that speak against the Woman's speaking, speak against the Church of Christ."[99]

NINETEENTH-CENTURY FEMINISTS AND TRADITIONALISTS

In the nineteenth century, women began to teach in church schools, write hymns, battle social ills, speak at revivals, and work on mission fields. As more women participated in revivals, some began to sense a call from God to preach. Some reported that they resisted God before succumbing to the summons.[100] As the missions movement expanded, women began to teach, train, and preach abroad. Women typically worked with women. But the harvest was plentiful and the workers few; so they inevitably spoke to men on occasion. Charlotte

Moon worked first with women and children, but she came to believe she had to reach men if she wanted results. Hudson Taylor said no offense is given if men in China listen to the Bible lessons of a missionary sister.[101] Soon new practices led to new publications.

Early feminist writers such as Catherine Booth (of the Salvation Army), Frances Willard, and Katherine Bushnell sounded many themes found in contemporary feminist Christian writings. In *Female Ministry, or Woman's Right to Preach the Gospel*, Catherine Booth (1829-1890) says women are fit to preach, for God has given them "a graceful form and attitude, winning manners, persuasive speech, and . . . a finely-toned emotional nature," all of which qualify them for public speaking."[102] Scripture also permits women to preach, Booth argues. She cites Joel 2:28, Acts 2:17, and 1 Corinthians 11:4-5 and equates women's prayer and prophecy with preaching. When women prophesy, it is "not the foretelling of events, but the preaching to the world at large the glad tidings of salvation by Jesus Christ." If women prophesied, they preached, too. In Booth's view, when Deborah, Huldah, Miriam, and Anna ministered beside men, they also preached.[103] Junia, Philip's daughters, and Phoebe the deacon (Rom. 16:1) were all fruitful preachers, Booth claims. Phoebe "traveled much and propagated the gospel in foreign countries."[104] Booth believed that 1 Timothy 2:11-12 barred women from domineering at home but said nothing to the church.[105]

Women in the Pulpit, by Frances Willard (1839-1898), is also more a protest than a theological treatise.[106] Willard claimed that the call for women's silence in the church "grows out of the one-sided male interpretation of the Bible." Male theologians explain away uncomfortable passages, such as 1 Corinthians 7, on celibacy, but take passages on the subjection of women literally.[107] "Personal predilection" and a desire to control women lies behind literal interpretation of one text and "fast and loose" explanations of the next, she asserts.[108] The root problem is male pride. Ministers think, *Does a woman think to rank with me . . . in the most sacred of all callings?* But Willard believes women are *more* suited to pulpit ministry because of their moral superiority. "Woman's holiness and . . . pure heart, specially authorize her to be a minister of God."

It is *men* who have . . . lighted inquisitorial fires, and made the
Prince of Peace a mighty man of war. It is men who have taken the
simple, loving, tender Gospel . . . and translated it into . . . the dead
letter rather than the living Gospel. The mother-heart of God will
never be known to the world until translated into terms of speech
by mother-hearted women. . . . Men preach a creed, women will
declare a life. Men have always tithed mint and rue and cumin . . .'
while the world's heart has cried out for compassion, forgiveness,
and sympathy.[109]

Willard believed that the female temperament must complement
the male if the world is to hear the whole message of Christianity.
"Love and law will never balance in the realm of grace until a woman's
hand shall hold the scales." Religion is an affair of the heart, and
woman has heart.[110]

God's Word to Women, by Katherine Bushnell (1856-1925), con-
cedes that Paul says women must not teach or exercise authority
over men (1 Tim. 2:12), but 1 Timothy is only a "personal epistle."
Paul "merely states . . . his own practice in times of fierce persecution and a fierce attack upon the moral reputation of Christians—
under those conditions he did not allow women to teach men."[111]
Bushnell says that when the church faced no persecution, Paul
allowed women to pray and prophesy and made "no distinctions
as regards sex in the Christian body."[112] During persecution
men should bear the danger and take the lead, especially since men
have denied women opportunities to gain the leadership experience necessary to ply rough seas.[113] But Paul's teaching is merely
his wish and advice, which Christians may disregard "with
impunity."[114]

Some points from Booth, Willard, and Bushnell have become
mainstays of Christian egalitarian thinking:
- Temporary social conditions led Paul to ban women from
  teaching.
- The ban contradicts other Scriptures.
- Men read Scriptures selectively in order to keep women in a
  subordinate position.
- The distinction between public and private teaching is denied,

so that private teaching and prophesying by women negates Paul's ban on public teaching and preaching.

Patrick Fairbairn, Abraham Kuyper, and Charles Hodge represent traditionalist exegesis in roughly the same era. Fairbairn and Kuyper enter the Thomist camp by stressing the differences between men and women, while Hodge sounds more Scotist, stressing their essential equality.

According to Fairbairn (1838-1912), both the constitution and vocation of women require men to lead. Adam's "precedence in time" implies "superiority in place and power." The inversion of this order overthrew paradise.[115] Fairbairn confesses that the invocation of Eve's deception as a ground of male leadership (1 Tim. 2:14) "has often been deemed strange." Still, the Fall is a

> mournful example . . . of the evil sure to arise if . . . woman should quit her proper position as the handmaid of man, and man should concede to her the ascendancy. She [lacks], by the very constitution of nature, the qualities necessary for such a task—in particular the equability of temper, the practical shrewdness and discernment, the firm, independent, regulative judgment which are required to carry . . . leaders . . . above first impressions and outside appearances, to resist solicitations, and amid subtle entanglements and fierce conflicts to cleave unswervingly to the right. Her very excellencies in other respects— . . . the finer sensibilities and stronger impulses of her emotional and loving nature—tend in a measure to disqualify her here. With man . . . the balance . . . between the intellectual and the emotional inclines as a rule in the opposite direction.[116]

Eve is deceived by "impressions" derived from the subtle serpent. Her failure is "a beacon to future generations," warning women not to assume functions they are not qualified or called to fill.[117] Like Aquinas, Fairbairn says woman's emotional nature only tends to disqualify her; men are not always more rational. Similarly, Kuyper claims women are no less holy or believing than men, but they are more susceptible to some temptations. "Her sensibilities are more alert to impression of the concrete and the attractive." It is harder for her to resist sensory beauty.[118]

Charles Hodge (1797-1878) explains that woman's subordination rests on the idea that "order and subordination pervade the whole universe, and are essential to its being."[119] But subordination does not entail inferiority. Since the Son is subordinate to the Father, though equal with him in nature, "the subordination of the woman to the man" is "perfectly consistent with their identity as to nature."[120] Women must not be public teachers, Hodge says, but they should learn. Further, since women have the same spiritual capacity as men, they may "exercise the gift of prophecy." Yet "the refinement and delicacy" of woman and the need for order require that women neither speak nor prophesy in public in the church.[121]

Fairbairn stresses the differences between men and women, while Hodge emphasizes their essential equality. But Fairbairn thinks men and women have different inclinations. For Hodge, male leadership says more about the plan of God than about the nature of mankind.

THE DEBATE TODAY

The main schools of thought on gender have been clear for a couple of decades. Critics are almost monolithically feminist. They dismiss complementarian texts several ways:

1. Ephesians and 1 Timothy are pious forgeries, and not part of Paul's authentic teaching.

2. If Paul did write Timothy and Ephesians, they contradict Galatians 3 and 1 Corinthians 12, where Paul declares male and female to be one in salvation and giftedness. Ephesians and Timothy contradict Paul's earlier, nobler sentiments.

3. Paul's teaching on male leadership applies only to local, temporary circumstances that troubled the church around A.D. 60 to 90. They are passé today.

4. The Bible is a patriarchal book and a product of its patriarchal times. Some of its authors realized that their faith leads to greater freedom for women. We must seize the Bible's liberating messages and promote justice for women through them.

Evangelical feminists argue that women must be free to use their gifts in every calling. A few evangelicals adopt some of the critical strategies just listed, playing texts where women lead or teach against others that restrict women. But the great majority of evangelical egalitarians claim that the whole Bible is egalitarian. Thus they assign themselves the task of refuting all biblical evidence for male leadership. They must show that God's choice of male monarchs, priests, and apostles is not normative and that Ephesians 5 and 1 Timothy 2 do not hold, at face value, today.

In a way there is no trajectory for traditionalists. We reaffirm longstanding interpretations of Scripture and ways of life. Still, traditional writings have changed. We gather biblical data to reaffirm what was once accepted without question. We are also quicker to affirm the gifts and ministries of women.

The unresolved question touches the nature of mankind, male and female. How different are we? Are men and women identical except for biological structures and the effects of a culture that trains boys to play with guns and trucks and trains girls to play with tea sets and dolls? Do men and women differ in their patterns of thought, communication, and relationship? If so, are the differences large or small, innate or enculturated, good or bad?

Sometimes it seems that secular people are more willing to discuss gender differences than evangelicals are. Secular scholars pour out streams of research and popular literature on male-female differences.[122] The "Men Are from Mars, Women Are from Venus" series has sold millions of copies. But theologians hesitate to ponder how the bodies and minds of men and women differ and how those differences affect gender roles. Perhaps they fear that analysis of male-female differences, linked to male leadership, will sound like an investigation of male superiority, even if we affirm the equal value of men and women. If so, our hesitation stems from a laudable desire to avert controversy. Yet investigate we must. Otherwise, whether we intend it or not, our refusal will place us in the position of Duns Scotus (above), in the Divine Decree camp (chapter 9). We will seem to say men lead because God simply decreed it. In a profound sense this is true. God is the Sovereign. With his own wisdom and counsel, he formed creation (Isa. 40:13-14; Rom. 11:34). Yet God calls the wise man and the scientist to investigate his creation, to discern his wisdom (Isa. 44:24). Has God simply issued a decree, "Men shall lead"?

Or has he woven his decree into creation, designing men and women to flourish when they follow his decree?

One argument, the "Family Order" argument, takes the Divine Decree approach one step farther. It says that God ordained that husbands and fathers lead marriages and households.[123] In marriage, someone must bear final responsibility to make decisions and chart a course, should the two disagree. God has ordained that the husband is that leader. But if husbands lead at home, they must also lead at church. Otherwise, a husband could set a course at home that his wife might contradict at church if she has ecclesiastical authority.

If someone believes husbands should lead the home, this argument effectively promotes male leadership at church. But it only works for those who affirm male leadership at home. It will hardly convince skeptics or feminists, who doubt the premises of the argument. For them, the Family Order argument is just another appeal to God's decree. Meanwhile, feminists and champions of self-esteem whisper that women should aspire to whatever they choose.

The Family Order argument also bypasses single women and the church—no trivial matter given the millions of single women in Western society. Scarcely anyone *argues* that the church should give single women special ministerial prerogatives, but we sometimes function that way.[124] Certain early churches apparently recognized an order of widows, above sixty years in age, who performed limited diaconal functions. Medieval abbesses, writers, and visionaries were almost always single. Among Protestants the mission field became an outlet for single women who longed to minister. Lottie Moon declined a marriage proposal while in China, partly to preserve her freedom for ministry.[125] For centuries strong female leaders have tended to be single or widowed. The exceptions prove the rule. The Montanists' Maximilla and Priscilla, the visionary Margery Kempe, the evangelists Aimee Semple McPherson and Kathryn Kuhlman were all married women who left their husbands when they started to lead the church.[126]

The larger point, however, is that the Divine Decree approach, including the Family Order argument, will not persuade egalitarians. Most evangelicals are hesitant, but I believe we must explore reasons for male leadership. We certainly seek reasons for other unpopular teachings. For example, when we tell young adults to remain pure until marriage, we explain how they will flourish if they heed God's command. We should do the same with male leadership.

Moses asked Israel, "What does the LORD your God ask of you but to fear the LORD your God, to walk in all his ways, to love him . . . and to observe the LORD's commands and decrees that I am giving you today for your own good?" (Deut. 10:12-13). Conversely, when we reject God's ways, sin ensnares and traps us (Prov. 5:21-23; 11:3; Ps. 34:21; 1 Tim. 6:9). These statements invite us to investigate *why* it is good to walk in God's ways, including the way of male leadership. Such investigations prepare us to answer when little girls and mature women ask why men lead. We need to say more than "God decreed this at creation, and his will remains in effect." An appeal to God's decree may stiffen the resolve of evangelical traditionalists, but it will hardly convince evangelical feminists, who think the evidence is on their side. And it will never satisfy secular people. If we believe male leadership is good for men and women, we must explore how this is so. Did God weave traces of his decree into the hearts of men and women, to prepare them to thrive in God's appointed order? Are there subtle differences between men and women that echo his decree? The topic is immense, but let us at least propose ideas that others can evaluate.

Let us admit the dangers in such a study. We may exaggerate the differences between men and women. We may endorse pseudo-science because it supports our prejudices. We may promote questionable exegesis. This peril especially applies to 1 Timothy 2:13-14, which explains that men must teach because Adam was formed first and because Eve was deceived, not Adam.[127]

Those two verses have led some theologians to say that women are prone to deception. This interpretation rests in part on historical factors. The vastly influential Greek philosophers Plato and Aristotle were convinced of female inferiority; they even wondered if women had souls. Further, for centuries few women received the education or gained the experience that promote wisdom.

But the view that women are prone to deception also has theological factors. Paul never says women suffer deception more than men, but he twice says that Eve, the first woman and mother of all women, was deceived (1 Tim. 2:14; 2 Cor. 11:3).[128] In fact, Paul sometimes puts his references to historical Old Testament figures to typological use. Thus Abraham, David, Jacob, and Esau are both individuals and representative types. Abraham is the good man who is justified by faith. David is the man whose sins are forgiven. Jacob is the elect and Esau the nonelect man.[129] So it seems that Paul might intend to describe woman's nature when he cites the sin of Eve, the first woman. First Timothy 2:13-14 certainly states why Paul entrusted the care of doctrine to men.[130]

But Paul cannot believe that women are generically irrational or gullible. Otherwise, why would he let them teach other women and children (Titus 2:3-5)? Why would he let them join his ministry teams? If women lack discernment, they should not teach anyone. But Paul does urge women to teach other women and children, and so Eve apparently does not function typologically this time.

But if 1 Timothy 2 does not mean that women are prone to deception, what does it mean? Here those who argue against the gullibility of women falter. Divine Decree complementarians maintain that Paul's comment about Eve illustrates what happens when men abdicate and women usurp leadership. They say the race fell into sin because Adam stood by while Eve took the lead in responding to the serpent's challenge. If Ephesian women repeat Eve's mistake and seek to lead, they will "bring similar disaster on themselves and the church."[131] But why should "similar disasters" occur if Eve's failure in no way typifies women?[132] If women have no more propensity to doctrinal error than men, why should the church expect disaster if roles reverse? Does disaster occur purely because the wrong person leads? Do women possess sound judgment until they usurp leadership, and then it suddenly flees? James Hurley has explained that Adam, as the first-formed, was trained by God to be the spiritual leader of the family. Eve was not deceived due to a fragile or gullible mind, but because God had not appointed or prepared her to encounter Satan's temptation. She fell, therefore, because she was tricked into taking Adam's role as leader and defender of the faith.[133] This view is attractive, but a comparison of Genesis 2:16-17, 3:2-3, and 3:11 shows that Eve had at least the essential knowledge about the tree of knowledge when the serpent tempted her.

However we resolve these difficulties, today's complementarians typically avoid arguments for headship that appeal to male and female traits.[134] The archetypal Divine Decree advocate argues that men lead because we need social order, and God willed this order, period. Men are no more fit to lead than women. No "masculine" traits—not physical strength, not mental makeup—shed light on God's decree.[135]

The alternative to the Divine Decree position is the Congruent Creation approach. It agrees that God summoned men to lead apart from any merit. Yet, it says, God designed men and women to delight in his decision and to prosper within it. He formed men to lead, protect, and serve, and he formed women to receive loving leadership. God etched traces of his sovereign decision into the nature of male and female. In centuries past, when men earned bread and fought battles with their hands, it seemed obvious that the physical size and strength of men prepared them to lead. Today we have more interest in mental and relational styles. Christians should explore God's designs for men and women, even as secular scientists explore the similarities and differences between male and female.

For example, Mary Stewart Van Leeuwen, a Christian egalitarian, believes that women recognize the emotional and relational aspects of God and the social nature of the faith more readily than men.[136] She concludes the church should have female leaders to enrich its community and to promote compassion. Yet she admits that woman's sociability becomes a liability when it leads to enmeshment—that is, the preservation of relationships at all costs even when these have become abusive. The misuse of sociability leads women to preserve relationships and avoid the exercise of "accountable dominion."[137]

Social scientists also note the male tendency toward competition and disputation and the female tendency toward relatively more cooperation and affiliation.[138] They observe that women's tendency to enmeshment makes them unwilling to recognize and confront flaws in loved ones. Carol Gilligan, a secular feminist, said girls and women tend to emphasize relational factors, whereas boys tend toward detached analysis when making ethical decisions. Deborah

Tannen, a secular communication expert, found that men use speech more to establish their independence and status, whereas women speak more to build community and offer support. Martin van Creveld, a historian of war, argues that whatever ancient myths and modern ideologies say, and however much women may support war efforts, "very few women have ever fought" in combat, and almost none are suited to do so.[139]

Many secular thinkers agree on these points. I propose that these qualities are traces of God's creation plan that he wove into the nature of man and woman. Are women prone to enmeshment? Are men prone to detached, critical assessment? Detached critique is what defenders of doctrine need to detect and root out heresy. But woman's relational nature could limit her willingness to uproot error if promulgated by a friend. This does not mean men are more doctrinally astute than women, but perhaps men can more easily set aside the fact that the heretic before them is a friend when they guard doctrine. Men's greater willingness to disagree on intellectual points, while no intrinsic virtue, does suit them to defend the faith.

With no desire to belittle women or men, I ask that we at least investigate whether God has engraved reflections of his sovereign decree into human nature. Our *inclinations* can differ while our capacities are equal. Further, all such inclinations must be partial; no one thinks that all men are more rational and all women more relational. Many women outdo their male friends in logical analysis and disputation. Still, perhaps God has etched traces of his plan of male leadership into human nature so that men tend to seek leadership in the home and the church and women look for godly male leaders. God's decree rests upon his will, not male superiority. Nonetheless, he can press reflections of his will into the fabric of human nature.

CONCLUSION

Our survey of church history showed that women find ways to use their gifts even in the company of staunch complementarians. Today, egalitarians insist on woman's freedom to perform every ministry from every office. Complementarians affirm that women should be trained to use all their gifts; yet we do reserve some tasks for male elders. This chapter has shown that the church has generally seen the issue of women and ministry as our earlier chapters have: Women may do all sorts of things but not everything. As kings, priests, prophets, and apostles bore responsibility in the past, so male elders bear final responsibility to proclaim and defend the church's teaching. May we recognize the callings of men and the gifts of women, that we may serve him in unity.

APPENDIX 1:
WORD STUDIES FOR
1 TIMOTHY 2:12

IN 1 TIMOTHY 2:12 ESV Paul says, "I do not permit a woman to teach or to exercise authority over a man." His word choice and grammar show that he is restricting the teaching of doctrine, not all teaching. Scholars on both sides of the debate know they must not rely too heavily on word studies, since most words have a range of possible meanings, and context must guide us to the right one. To illustrate, the noun *stand* has about twenty meanings, including 1) a final line of defense (an army's "last stand"), 2) a strongly held position on a debated issue (a "stand" on abortion), 3) an open-air structure for a small retail operation (a hot-dog stand), and 4) a group of plants growing together (a stand of aspen trees). Only the context can tell us the intended meaning. The case is the same with the key words "teach" and "exercise authority." In our passage, "teach" and "exercise authority" have only a few possible meanings. Yet the context must still guide us to the right choice.

The Greek word for "teach" (*didaskō*—διδάσκω) ordinarily means just that, to teach or instruct. But in Paul's letters, what is taught is usually the gospel fundamentals. For example, as Paul gives his last instructions to Timothy, he says, "And the things you have heard me say in the presence of many witnesses entrust to reliable men who will also be qualified to *teach* others" (2 Tim. 2:2). Similarly, in 1 Timothy 4:10, Paul declares that men should put their hope in God the Savior and then adds (v. 11), "Command and *teach* these things." Since the passage preceding ours discusses conduct at worship and since the next passage explains the duties of elders and deacons, it is all but certain that Paul has the teaching of doctrine in mind.

This definition agrees with Paul's most common use of "teach." By my estimate, of the fifteen verses that use the verb "teach," five certainly refer to basic doctrine (1 Cor. 4:17; Gal. 1:12; 2 Thess. 2:15; 2 Tim. 2:2; 1 Tim. 4:11), and seven probably or almost certainly do (Rom. 12:7; Eph. 4:21; Col. 1:28; 2:7; 3:16; 1 Tim. 2:12; 1 Tim. 6:2), leaving three that refer to other teaching (Rom. 2:21 [where "teach" appears twice]; 1 Cor. 11:14; Titus 1:11). Given that the context of 1 Timothy 2:12 is worship, it seems all the more likely that Paul has formal instruction in mind.[1]

The cognate nouns for "teaching," *didachē* (διδαχή) and *didaskalia* (διδασκαλία), are similar. The first word, *didachē*, refers to Christian doctrine in four of its six uses in the New Testament—in Rom. 6:17; 16:17; 2 Tim. 4:2 and Titus 1:9, but not in 1 Cor. 14:6, 26. The second word, *didaskalia*, refers to false teaching five times (Matt. 15:9; Mark 7:7; Eph. 4:14; Col. 2:22; 1 Tim. 4:1). But in all other uses, including fourteen uses in Timothy and Titus, the "teaching" is sound and commendable doctrine (1 Tim. 1:10). The "teachings" are the apostolic message, the essential content of the faith, carefully handed down by spoken words and letters (Gal. 1:6-12; 2 Thess. 2:14-15). Especially in Timothy and Titus, the "teachings" are usually the foundations of the faith. Paul says an elder must "hold firm to the trustworthy word as taught, so that he may be able to give instruction in sound doctrine and also to rebuke those who contradict it" (Titus 1:9 ESV). The phrase "sound doctrine" is literally "sound teaching" (*didaskalia*—διδασκαλία). Paul uses the phrase "sound teaching" several times (1 Tim. 1:10; 2 Tim. 4:3; Titus 1:9; 2:1). He declares there is an authentic doctrine that Christian leaders must know and hold as a standard to measure other teaching. Authentic doctrine shows false teaching to be heretical (1 Tim. 1:3-10; 6:3; Titus 1:13—2:2), sick (1 Tim. 6:3-4), even demonic (1 Tim. 4:1, 6). It brings envy and strife (1 Tim. 6:4-5). But good teaching leads to good character (2 Tim. 3:10) and good works (3:16).

So, when Paul says, "I do not permit a woman to teach," he

means men must present the gospel truths that are the heart of the faith. Elders must proclaim, guard, and defend the deposit of gospel truth. Paul says, "The things you have heard me say in the presence of many witnesses entrust to reliable men who will also be qualified to teach others" (2 Tim. 2:2). The point is not that "men must do all the teaching" or that "a woman must never teach anything to a man." Rather, those who regularly teach the foundations of the faith must be men who are tested, approved, and consecrated by the church for the task.

Paul also says men must "exercise authority." The Greek word *authenteō* (αὐθεντέω) is difficult because it is rare (appearing about 100 times overall in ancient Greek texts and just once in the New Testament) and sometimes has negative connotations. Most scholars think "rule" or "exercise authority" is the best definition, but some propose definitions such as "domineer," "instigate violence," or even "murder."[2] David Huttar has shown that the meaning "murder" is "not attested in any living, natural Greek used in ordinary discourse."[3] But it is discouraging to learn that the two most thorough studies of the word (both examining virtually every use of the term in antiquity) come to opposite conclusions. Scott Baldwin asserts that it has the positive sense "rule" or "exercise authority," and Leland Wilshire decides for the negative "instigate violence."[4] Given the heat of the gender debates, both scholars have faced criticism. Baldwin looks better in the end for two reasons: 1) Wilshire's essay fails to distinguish the members of the *authent* (αὐθέντ) word group from one another, so that he wrongly assumes the verb shares the meaning of the noun *authentēs* (αὐθέντης), which *can* sometimes mean murderer, as well as author or master. 2) Wilshire's first essay so lacked a clear conclusion that certain scholars thought he was arguing for Baldwin's view—"exercise authority."[5] Still, Baldwin admits that *authenteō* (αὐθεντέω) means tyrannize at least once and can occasionally mean "usurp authority."[6] Since "usurp authority" is at least a possibility, we must see if the context allows it.

In fact, structural and grammatical elements suggest that the definition "exercise authority" is correct. First, 2:11 and 2:12 balance one another antithetically so that "all submissiveness" is the antonym of "exercise authority."[7]

POSITIVELY	NEGATIVELY
A woman should learn in quietness (11a).	I do not permit a woman to teach (12a).
A women should learn in quietness and all submissiveness (11b).	I do not permit a woman to teach or to exercise authority over a man (12b).

Second, the grammatical structure points to "exercise authority." Grammatically, the terms "teach" (*didaskō*—διδάσκω) and "exercise authority" (*authenteō*—αὐθεντέω) are joined by the Greek conjunction *oude* (οὐδέ). It may mean the following: "and not," "nor," "neither," "not even." But Andreas Kostenberger has demonstrated that *oude* (οὐδέ) has a telling grammatical feature.[8] When it links two verbs, it either links two concepts that are bad in themselves or two that are good in themselves, but not one that is positive and one that is negative. To illustrate, suppose I take a group of children into a museum. If they are budding delinquents, I may say, "I do not permit you to steal or break anything here." "Steal" and "break" are both negative in themselves; the Greek would join them with *oude* (οὐδέ). If the children are little angels, I may still say, "Do not pick up or even touch anything in the museum." Both "pick up" and "touch" are positive in themselves but forbidden in the museum. Again, Greek would join them with *oude* (οὐδέ). So in the New Testament *oude* (οὐδέ) joins two verbs that have the same value; both are either negative in themselves and forbidden, or both are positive in themselves but forbidden or denied due to the context.

But if someone wants to negate two activities, one positive and one negative in themselves, Greek uses a different construction, *kai mē* (καὶ μή). At the museum, if I say, "I don't want anyone to run or crash into things," we see that "run" is positive in itself, but "crash" is negative. Greek would join them with *kai mē* (καὶ μή). Here are a few examples from the New Testament:

Two activities are positive in themselves, but denied due to circumstances, joined by *oude* (οὐδέ).

Matt. 6:28	Flowers neither toil nor (*oude*—οὐδέ) spin.
Gal. 1:16-17	Paul neither consulted nor (*oude*—οὐδέ) went up to Jerusalem.
Col. 2:21	Legalists say neither handle nor (*oude*—οὐδέ) taste nor (*oude*—οὐδέ) touch.

Two activities are negative in themselves, hence to be denied or avoided, joined by *oude* (οὐδέ).

Matt. 6:20	Store up treasure in heaven where thieves neither break in nor (*oude*—οὐδέ) steal.
2 Thess. 2:2	Believers should neither become unsettled nor (*oude*—οὐδέ) alarmed.
Rev. 7:16	In heaven we will neither hunger nor (*oude*—οὐδέ) thirst.

Two activities, one positive in itself, one negative in itself, are joined by *kai mē* (καὶ μή) ("and not").

Matt. 17:7	Rise and (*kai mē*—καὶ μή) do not be afraid.
John 20:27	Put your hand in my side and (*kai mē*—καὶ μή) do not doubt.
Rom. 12:14	Bless and (*kai mē*—καὶ μή) do not curse.
1 Tim. 5:16	Families ought to support their widows and not (*kai mē*—καὶ μή) let the church be burdened.[9]

In our passage, when Paul forbids women to teach or exercise authority, he joins them with *oude* (οὐδέ). This means that either both are positive, or both are negative in themselves. Now "teach" is clearly positive for Paul in the Pastoral Epistles (1 Tim. 4:11; 6:2; 2 Tim. 2:2). Indeed he uses a rare, distinctive word to describe heretical teaching in 1 Timothy 1:3; 6:3 (*heterodidaskaleō*—ἑτεροδιδάσκαλέω). Since "teach" is positive for Paul, *authenteō* (αὐθεντέω) must have the positive meaning "exercise authority," not the negative meaning "domineer."[10] The traditional translation of 1 Timothy 2:12 seems correct, therefore: "I do not permit a woman to teach or to exercise authority over a man." That is, a woman may not teach doctrine to a man publicly. Further, she may not exercise authority over him. Teaching doctrine is itself an authoritative action, but there are other ways to exercise authority, and these are not granted to women in the church either.

Appendix 2:
Wives or Deaconesses in
1 Timothy 3:11

In 1 Timothy 3:8-13, Paul describes the qualifications for deacons. In the middle of the discussion, he writes one verse, one sentence, about women who are either deaconesses or the wives of deacons (3:11). Here is the text in context.

> *8Deacons, likewise, are to be men worthy of respect, sincere, not indulging in much wine, and not pursuing dishonest gain. 9They must keep hold of the deep truths of the faith with a clear conscience. 10They must first be tested; and then if there is nothing against them, let them serve as deacons. 11In the same way, their wives are to be women worthy of respect, not malicious talkers but temperate and trustworthy in everything. 12A deacon must be the husband of but one wife and must manage his children and his household well. 13Those who have served well gain an excellent standing and great assurance in their faith in Christ Jesus.*

Deacons, like elders, are set apart to lead the church. Elders especially care for the ministry of the Word, and deacons oversee the ministry of deeds. Fittingly, Paul says deacons must *adhere* to the "deep truths" of the faith, but he does not say they must *teach* them. The work of deacons is grounded in the truth, but they are men of action. They may speak to explain what they are doing, but they are not teachers.

Like elders, deacons are "the husband of but one wife" in 3:12. But what shall we make of verse 11? The NIV and ESV make it seem easier than it is, rendering it as a series of qualifications for "their wives." But other translations translate it "the women." The root of this uncertainty is the Greek word *gynē* (γυνή), which can mean either "woman" or "wife" (the comparable masculine noun can mean either "man" or "husband"). Thus we are unsure if 3:11 addresses deaconesses or deacon's wives.

To translate literally, 3:11 says, "women likewise" or "wives likewise" must be respectable, not slanderers, and so on. The phrase may mean one of four things:

First, the women may be part of the general order of deacons. But this is unlikely since they are set apart from deacons by the term *likewise* (hōsautōs—ὡσαύτως) and by a distinct list of qualities.

Second, the women are female deacons or deaconesses who correspond somehow to the male deacons. This is unlikely for two reasons. First, while the term *likewise* does introduce deacons and differentiate them from elders in 3:8, the statement about the wives or women is embedded in a larger section that describes the duties of male deacons. If deaconesses are a distinct group, why is their charter (3:11) sandwiched between three verses that describe the qualities of deacons (3:8-10) and two that comment on deacons' deeds and reputation (3:12-13)? Second, outside this passage we have no clear reference to an office of deaconess. In Romans 16:1 Phoebe *may* be a deaconess, but we cannot be sure she had an office, since Romans 16 does not focus on church order and since the word *diakonos* (διάκονος) is often nontechnical in the New Testament. The following texts call Christian leaders "deacons" in this looser sense: Romans 15:8 (used of Christ); 1 Corinthians 3:5 (of Paul and Apollos); 2 Corinthians 3:6, 6:4 (of Paul); Ephesians 6:21 (of Tychicus); Colossians 1:7 (of Epaphras); Colossians 1:23 and 25 (of Paul).

On the other hand, there are three reasons to believe a separate office is in view. First, *likewise* marked a new category in 3:8; so it could do the same here. Second, the Greek does not have a possessive pronoun—"their wives"—or even a definite article—the wives; this suggests that the women are a separate group, not simply deacons' wives. Third, why should deacons' wives be singled out for a separate list of qualities when no qualities are required for the wives of elders?

The third option is that women are assistants to deacons, perhaps taking on duties that especially pertain to ministry to women. This is plausible for two reasons. First, some women's needs could be handled more appropriately by women than by men. Second, there may be a hint that women have special, recognized tasks elsewhere in the Pastoral Epistles. For example, Paul takes note of exemplary widows in 1 Timothy 5:9-10 and blesses older women who train younger women in Titus 2:3-5. If option three is correct, then churches might rightly have women's advisory committees that regularly work with the deacon as consultants on policy and serving the needy.

The fourth option is that the women are indeed the wives of deacons. Despite the points for other views, there are several arguments for option four. First, given that gynē (γυνή) can mean woman or wife, we note that the term means "wife" twice in this context, in 3:2 and 3:12. Second, Paul's failure to mention this person's marital status, prominent as marriage was with elders and deacons, indicates that it refers to deacons' wives. (The absence of the possessive pronoun or definite article, mentioned above, is not so forceful because Paul often omits the definite article when referring to people in this section.) Third, if the women are wives, it would explain why 3:11 is embedded in the section on deacons: One requirement for deacons is that their wives be apt to assist them. More tentatively, Paul's strong concern for sexual purity and irreproachable behavior could indicate that wives are in view, since a mixed group of male and female officers would be morally suspect.

In my judgment, options three and four are more probable than options one and two, and number four is most likely of all. But whichever view is correct, Paul anticipates that women will have a hand in diaconal work. (And even if deaconesses are not mentioned here, Phoebe may still prove that the church had deaconesses.) It certainly makes sense that deacon's wives or deaconesses be respectable and free from slander, since they need to help the needy without telling tales.

Whatever view of 1 Timothy is correct, all four views agree that women should be involved in diaconal work. As long as we do not see deacons as authorities on a par with elders, there is little to quarrel over. Deacons lead, but they lead from alongside, not from above. They lead the way most leadership occurs—by service and example, by experience and persuasion. If we view deacons this way, as leaders in service, it matters little precisely how we label the women who work hard at diaconal ministry, as long as they stay involved. Calvin bent his thought to this issue when he distinguished two types of deacon. One would be more administrative and financial; men served there by "administering the affairs of the poor." But women could take as a "public office of the church" the task of "caring for the poor themselves."[1]

As chapter 8 said, the church will live well, even if we cannot finally resolve the proper interpretation of 1 Timothy 3:11, if we keep women deeply involved in diaconal work. We may label women deacons or deaconesses, deacons' assistants or deacons' advisors. The main thing is that women whom God calls to care for the needy do the work and help others do the same.

NOTES

CHAPTER 1:
INTRODUCTION TO THE CALLINGS OF WOMEN

1. Michael Gurian, *The Wonder of Girls* (New York: Pocket Books, 2002), 26-96; Michael Gurian, *The Wonder of Boys* (New York: Putnam, 1996); Beth Bailey, *From Front Porch to Back Seat: Courtship in Twentieth-Century America* (Baltimore: Johns Hopkins, 1988); Wendy Shalit, *Return to Modesty* (New York: Free Press, 1999).
2. See the many references to Anna in Joseph Frank, *Dostoyevsky: The Miraculous Years, 1865-71* and *The Mantle of the Prophet, 1871-81* (Princeton: Princeton University Press, 1995, 2002).
3. Christina Hoff Sommers contrasts commonsense or "equity feminists" and radical or "gender feminists" in *Who Stole Feminism?* (New York: Simon and Schuster, 1994), 22-49. Commonsense feminists stressed equality in education, equality before the law, and the right to vote, own property, marry and divorce, and live as freely as men.
4. Christopher J. H. Wright, *Walking in the Ways of the Lord* (Downers Grove, IL: InterVarsity Press, 1995), 24-34; Christopher J. H. Wright, *An Eye for an Eye* (Downers Grove, IL: InterVarsity Press, 1983), 40-5, passim.
5. Kevin Vanhoozer, *Is There a Meaning in This Text?* (Grand Rapids: Zondervan), 367-78.

CHAPTER 2:
THE MINISTRIES OF WOMEN IN BIBLICAL HISTORY: A SURVEY

1. Many feminists, critical and evangelical, avoid this chapter's argument by viewing male leadership ("patriarchy") in the Old Testament as an evil God tolerated. I answer that objection at the end of the chapter.
2. The phrase "the book of the law" is almost a technical term for Deuteronomy in much of the Old Testament.
3. It is conceivable that Paul is referring to a practice of which he does not approve, rather like the odd Corinthian custom of baptism for the dead (15:29). But there are no overt signs that he disapproves here.
4. On social status, James Jeffers, *The Greco-Roman World* (Downers Grove, IL: InterVarsity Press, 1999), 195.
5. The Greek term *diakonos* (διάκονος) can be translated "servant" or "deacon."
6. Since there is a feminine form of the noun, the fact that the masculine is here applied to a woman might indicate that an official position is in view. For more on deaconesses, see chapter 8 and appendix 2. See also C. E. B. Cranfield, *A Critical and Exegetical Commentary on the Epistle to the Romans* (Edinburgh: T & T Clark, 1975-1979), 2:780-83; Douglas Moo, *The Epistle to the Romans* (Grand Rapids: Eerdmans, 1996), 913-14; Thomas Schreiner, *Romans* (Grand Rapids: Baker, 1998), 786-87.
7. The Greek preposition *en* (ἐν) may be used either way.
8. Hebrew *shaphat* is traditionally translated "judge," but it can mean "lead" as well.
9. Esther's speech to Xerxes in Esther 7 and Nehemiah's plea to Artaxerxes in Nehemiah 1 are very similar. Confessions of faith can also become Scripture. See Matthew 15:27 and John 20:28.
10. On the primacy of priests over prophets as regular teaching authorities, see chapter 5 also.
11. Aaron is also rebuked, although more mildly, for questioning Moses' authority. For Miriam, the issue is both her gender and her refusal to accept God's ordained leader.
12. Elizabeth Schussler Fiorenza, *In Memory of Her, A Feminist Theological Reconstruction of Christian Origins* (New York: Crossroad, 1983), 49-56, 82-92.
13. Some sources for the New Testament include Herman Ridderbos, *Redemptive History and the New Testament Scriptures,* 2nd rev. ed. (Philipsburg, NJ: Presbyterian and Reformed, 1988); Craig Blomberg, *The Historical Reliability of the Gospels* (Downers Grove, IL: InterVarsity Press, 1987); D. A. Carson, Douglas Moo, and Leon Morris, *An Introduction to*

the *New Testament* (Grand Rapids: Zondervan, 1992; Darrell Bock, *Studying the Historical Jesus* (Grand Rapids: Baker, 2002); John Wenham, *Redating Matthew, Mark and Luke* (Downers Grove, IL: InterVarsity Press, 1992).

14. William J. Webb, *Slaves, Women & Homosexuals: Exploring the Hermeneutics of Cultural Analysis* (Downers Grove, IL: InterVarsity Press, 2001), 73-91.

15. Craig Keener, *Paul, Women and Wives* (Peabody, MA: Hendrickson, 1992), 144-47.

16. Guenther Haas, "Patriarchy as an Evil That God Tolerated: Analysis and Implications for the Authority of Scripture," *Journal of the Evangelical Theological Society* 38 (1995): 326-29, 332-36. Of course, difficult Mosaic laws remain. They must be studied one by one.

17. Christopher J. H. Wright, *Walking in the Ways of the Lord* (Downers Grove, IL: InterVarsity Press, 1995), 24-34; Wright, *An Eye for an Eye* (Downers Grove, IL: InterVarsity Press, 1983), 40-45, passim.

18. Bible scholars, including biblical feminists such as Gordon Fee, sometimes say a narrative pattern is normative only if the principle is explicitly taught elsewhere. See Gordon Fee and Douglas Stuart, *How to Read the Bible for All Its Worth* (Grand Rapids: Zondervan, 1982), 97-102. I question the sufficiency of this view and propose a modification in *Putting the Truth to Work,* 189-210 and 51-54. But Fee correctly says a narrative pattern is authoritative when verified by explicit law.

19. C. E. B. Cranfield, *The Epistle to the Romans* (Edinburgh: T & T Clark, 1975), 1:224ff.; Leonhard Goppelt, *Typos: The Typological Interpretation of the Old Testament in the New,* trans. Donald H. Madvig (Grand Rapids: Eerdmans, 1982), 136ff.

CHAPTER 3:
THE ROLES OF WOMEN IN THE MINISTRY OF JESUS

1. Philo, "The Special Laws," in *The Works of Philo,* trans. F. H. Colson (Cambridge, MA: Harvard University Press, 1937), 7:581-83.

2. Jose ben Johanon, in *The Mishnah,* trans. Herbert Danby (New York: Oxford University Press, 1933), 1946. The quotation is from Aboth 1:5. Aboth contains landmark statements by revered teachers who often lived well before Christ, but the final editing of the *Mishnah* occurred in A.D. 150 or later.

3. See Aida Besançon Spencer, *Beyond the Curse: Women Called to Ministry* (Peabody, MA: Hendrickson, 1985, 1997), 46-57.

4. James Hurley, *Man and Woman in Biblical Perspective* (Grand Rapids: Zondervan, 1981), 82-83.

5. On women in the ministry of Jesus, I recommend, from a complementarian perspective, Hurley, *Man and Woman in Biblical Perspective* and James Borland, "Women in the Life and Teaching of Jesus," in *Recovering Biblical Manhood and Womanhood,* John Piper and Wayne Grudem, eds. (Wheaton, IL: Crossway, 1991), 113-23. From an egalitarian perspective, Spencer, *Beyond the Curse,* 46-63; Mary Evans, *Woman in the Bible* (Downers Grove, IL: InterVarsity Press, 1983), 44-57; Ben Witherington, *Women in the Ministry of Jesus* (Cambridge: Cambridge University Press, 1984).

6. See note 10 below.

7. There are variants in the Greek text. Witherington sorts them out in *Women in the Ministry of Jesus,* 102-3.

8. The Twelve were with Jesus, but others joined his entourage at times.

9. By custom "to sit at someone's feet" is to be that person's disciple. See Acts 22:3; Luke 8:35.

10. The Greek literally reads, "She [Mary] was listening to his word." There are two nuances: 1) She "was listening" implies she stayed awhile; 2) The singular "his word" is probably a technical term since in Luke and Acts "the word of God" or "the word" often means the essential gospel message. See Luke 5:1; 8:11-15; 11:28; Acts 4:4, 29, 31; 6:4.

11. When Luke says Martha was *distracted* by her service, it implies that she wanted to listen to Jesus, but let herself be drawn away by her preparation of an elaborate meal. Joseph Fitzmyer, *Luke 10—24* (New York: Doubleday, 1985), 2:893-94.

12. Despite appearances, the phrase "Tell her to help me" need not mean that she is *commanding* Jesus to remand Mary to her side. In Greek the imperative is often used for requests made of superiors. See Luke 11:1; 15:6.

13. The Greek literally says, "Mary has chosen the good portion" (see ESV). But most translators and commentators render it "better" since the "positive" adjective is often used with a comparative sense. See Nigel Turner, *Syntax,* vol. 3 of *A Grammar of New Testament Greek,* ed. J. H. Moulton (Edinburgh: T. & T. Clark, 1963), 31-32.

14. Witherington, *Women in the Ministry of Jesus*, 101.
15. To sample some translations—NASB: "workers at home," NRSV: "good managers of the household," CEV: "good homemaker[s]," NCV: "good workers at home."
16. The KJV preserves a more literal, more surprising translation "Blessed is the womb that bare thee, and the paps which thou hast sucked."
17. But Jesus both accepts and corrects her compliment. Darrell Bock in *Luke 9:51—24:53* (Grand Rapids: Baker, 1996), 1095, rightly says, "The woman's remark is correct, but not exhaustive." He is with Robert Stein, *Luke* (Nashville: Broadman, 1992), 333-34, and Fitzmyer, *Luke 10—24*, 2:927-28, but against G. B. Caird, who says Jesus dismissed her compliment "as sheer sentimentality" in *Luke* (London: Black, 1964), 156.
18. Margaret Thrall demonstrates that the sometimes ambiguous Greek particle *menoun* (μενοῦν) means "Yes, but rather," not "No, rather" in *Greek Particles in the New Testament* (Grand Rapids: Eerdmans, 1962), 35.
19. Fitzmyer, *Luke 10—24*, 2:927.
20. Witherington summarizes a great deal of data in *Women in the Ministry of Jesus*, 49-52, 77-79.
21. On Jesus choosing and training foundational eyewitnesses, see Herman Ridderbos, *Redemptive History and the New Testament Scriptures*, 2nd rev. ed. (Philipsburg, NJ: Presbyterian and Reformed, 1988), 12-24.
22. Non-evangelical Christian feminists do deny the veracity of the gospel accounts. They allege that there were many female leaders in the early church and that a male-dominated hierarchical church later suppressed information about early female leadership. See chapter 9 for more on non-evangelical feminists.
23. On finding precedents in Scripture, see chapter 2, "A Note on Method."
24. This summarizes published arguments and conversations with feminists. See Rebecca Groothuis, *Good News for Women* (Grand Rapids: Baker, 1997), 109-11; Paul K. Jewett, *The Ordination of Women* (Grand Rapids: Eerdmans, 1980), 58-60; Stanley Grenz, *Women in the Church: A Biblical Theology of Women in the Ministry* (Downers Grove, IL: InterVarsity Press, 1995), 211-12. For a rejoinder, see James Borland, "Women in the Life and Teachings of Jesus," 120.
25. Borland, "Women in the Life and Teachings of Jesus," 120-23.
26. Spencer, *Beyond the Curse*, 45, note 5.
27. Most men found in New Testament leadership lists have Gentile names. In Colossians 4:11-14, Paul records several and then adds that Barnabas and Jesus-Justus are "the only Jews among my fellow workers."

CHAPTER 4:
FOUNDATIONS FOR MALE-FEMALE ROLES: GENESIS 1 AND EPHESIANS 5

1. Some doubt that Paul refers to Genesis 1 when he declares "the Law says" women should be submissive (1 Cor. 14:34). But leading feminists (Craig Keener, *Paul, Women and Wives* [Peabody, MA: Hendrickson, 1992], 86-7) and traditionalists (James Hurley, *Man and Woman in Biblical Perspective* [Grand Rapids: Zondervan, 1981], 192) agree that he does.
2. J. M. Wilson, "Birthright," in *International Standard Bible Encyclopedia* (Grand Rapids: Eerdmans, 1979), 1:515-6; I. H. Marshall, *New Bible Dictionary*, 2nd ed. (Wheaton, IL: Tyndale, 1982), 377ff.; Roland de Vaux, *Ancient Israel* (New York: McGraw Hill, 1965), 1:41-42.
3. Primogeniture also illumines the promises of Psalm 89:19-29, especially 89:27. It explains Elisha's request for a double portion of Elijah's spirit; he is asking for the full inheritance of the firstborn.
4. Feminists object that in Genesis 1, the last creation—mankind—is the apex. On that principle, Eve, the last formed in Genesis 2, would be supreme. (Feminists jibe that God was practicing with Adam and reached perfection with Eve.) But that reasoning conflates the accounts of Genesis 1 and 2, denying each passage its own voice. Genesis 1 builds to a climax; mankind, male and female, is fashioned last and rules all. Genesis 2 works differently, building to a climax that focuses on relationship, not rule, in 2:23-25.
5. These paragraphs are adapted from my *The Life of a God-Made Man* (Wheaton, IL: Crossway, 2002), 54-57.
6. Susan T. Foh, "What Is the Woman's Desire?" *Westminster Theological Journal*, 37, Spring 1975, 376-83; James Boice, *Genesis: An Expositional Commentary, Volume 1: Genesis 1:1—11:32* (Grand Rapids: Zondervan, 1982), 178-80; Gordon Wenham, *Word Biblical Commentary: Genesis 1—15* (Waco, TX: Word, 1987), 80-82. I am also indebted to my colleague Jack Collins.

7. Susan T. Foh, "What Is the Woman's Desire?" 381-82.
8. The Hebrew *mashal* means "to rule," not dominate or subdue. It is usually a positive word, although it has a wide enough lexical range that we cannot tell, from the word alone, if man's rule will be benevolent or tyrannical.
9. Mary Stewart Van Leeuwen, *Gender and Grace* (Downers Grove, IL: InterVarsity Press, 1990), 44-45; Gilbert Bilezikian, *Beyond Sex Roles* (Grand Rapids: Baker, 1985), 55, 229.
10. Hurley, *Man and Woman*, 139-41; Wayne Grudem, Editor's Note to "Husbands and Wives as Analogues of Christ and the Church," in *Recovering Biblical Manhood and Womanhood*, John Piper and Wayne Grudem, eds. (Wheaton, IL: Crossway, 1991), 493, note 6.
11. On the meaning of "head," see chapter 5, note 23.

CHAPTER 5:
WOMEN, MEN, AND MINISTRY IN CORINTH

1. Bruce Winter, *After Paul Left Corinth* (Grand Rapids: Eerdmans, 2001).
2. When Rome re-founded Corinth in 46 B.C., prostitution dwindled but did not disappear. Ibid., 76-120, 215-40.
3. Ben Witherington, *The Paul Quest* (Downers Grove, IL: InterVarsity Press, 1998), 186-94.
4. Winter, *After Paul Left Corinth*, 81-93, 226-29, cf. 191.
5. Ibid., 110-13, 122-23; Albert Bell, *A Guide to the New Testament World* (Scottsdale, PA: Herald Press, 1994), 234-37; Richard Horsley, "Slavery in the Greco-Roman World," *Semeia* 84 (2001), 44-45. Winter notes two limits: 1) social disapproval of excess, and 2) disapproval of some homosexual acts.
6. Demosthenes, *Orations: Against Neara*, trans. A. T. Murray, 7 vols. (Cambridge, MA: Harvard University Press, 1939), 6:445-46, paragraph 122.
7. Winter, *After Paul Left Corinth*, 228-29. Plutarch, "Advice to Bride and Groom," in *Moralia*, trans. Frank Babbitt, 15 vols. (Cambridge, MA: Harvard University Press, 1928), 2:309, paragraph 140.
8. Archibald Robertson and Alfred Plummer, *The First Epistle of St. Paul to the Corinthians* (Edinburgh: T & T Clark, 1911, 1994), 134.
9. "Unmarried" (*agamois*—ἀγάμοις) means "widowed." See Gordon Fee, *The First Epistle to the Corinthians* (Grand Rapids: Eerdmans, 1987), 287-88, and Anthony Thiselton, *The First Epistle to the Corinthians: A Commentary on the Greek Text* (Grand Rapids: Eerdmans, 2000), 515-16.
10. The Greek is *diakrino*—διακρίνω. Here it means to sift, to use discernment, to use judgment.
11. The context seems to be a gathering for worship. 1) Paul discusses the Lord's Supper and the use of gifts to edify the church in the following passages (11:17—12:31. 2) God gave the prophetic gift to edify the whole church (14:1-12).
12. A few say that Paul advocated veiling, but their evidence is weak. James Hurley, *Man and Woman in Biblical Perspective* (Grand Rapids: Zondervan, 1981), 254-71.
13. Cynthia Thompson, "Hairstyles, Head-coverings, and St. Paul: Portraits from Roman Corinth," *Biblical Archaeologist* 51 (1988): 99-115; David Gill, "The Importance of Roman Portraiture for Head Coverings in 1 Corinthians 11:2-16," *Tyndale Bulletin* 41.2 (1990): 244-60; Hurley, *Man and Woman in Biblical Perspective*, 66-68, 168-71, 254-71; Craig Keener, *Paul, Women and Wives: Marriage and Women's Ministry in the Letters of Paul* (Peabody, MA: Hendrickson, 1990), 22-30; Ben Witherington, *Women in the Earliest Churches* (Cambridge: Cambridge University Press, 1988), 81-83; Jerome Murphy O'Connor, "Sex and Logic in 1 Corinthians 11:2-16," *Catholic Biblical Quarterly* 42 (1980): 482-500; Jerome Murphy O'Connor, "1 Corinthians 11:2-16 Once Again," *Catholic Biblical Quarterly* 50 (1988): 265-74.
14. See photographs in Thompson, "Hairstyles, Head-coverings," 101-11; Winter, *After Paul Left Corinth*, xviii-xx.
15. Gill, "The Importance of Roman Portraiture," 252-54.
16. Witherington, *Women in the Earliest Churches*, 82.
17. Gill, "Roman Portraiture," 254-56.
18. Keener, *Paul, Women and Wives*, 30; Winter, *After Paul Left Corinth*, 123-26.
19. Murphy O'Connor, "1 Corinthians 11:2-16 Once Again," 265-66.
20. R. E. Oster, "Use, Misuse and Neglect of Archaeological Evidence in Some Modern Works on 1 Corinthians," *Zeitschrift für die neutestamentliche Wissenschaft* 83 (1992): 68; Gill, "Roman Portraiture," 246-51.
21. Gill, "Roman Portraiture," 250-51.

22. Women also loosened their hair in the cult of Dionysus, which was often connected with moral scandal and social disruption. Paul wanted no one to think Christians were part of that cult.

23. For "authoritative headship," see Wayne Grudem, "Does *Kephalē* ('Head') Mean 'Source' or 'Authority Over' in Greek Literature? A Survey of 2,336 Examples," *Trinity Journal* 6 (1985): 38-59; Wayne Grudem, "The Meaning of *Kephalē* ('Head'): A Response to Recent Studies" in *Recovering Biblical Manhood and Womanhood*, John Piper and Wayne Grudem, eds. (Wheaton, IL: Crossway, 1991), 425-68, 534-41; Joseph Fitzmyer, "*Kephalē* in 1 Corinthians 11:3," *Interpretation* 47 (1993): 52-59.

24. A. C. Perriman, "The Head of a Woman: The Meaning of κεφαλή in 1 Corinthians 11:3," *Journal of Theological Studies* 45 (1994), 602-22, especially 618; Gregory Dawes, *The Body in Question: Metaphor and Meaning in the Interpretation of Ephesians 5:21-33* (Leiden: Brill, 1998), 122-49; Thiselton, *1 Corinthians*, 812-23.

25. See "Jesus, Subordination and Equality," chapter 4, page 59.

26. Greek uses one word (ἀνήρ—*anēr*) to denote both "man" and "husband" and one word (γυνή—*gynē*) to denote both "woman" and "wife." Since most adults were married, the meaning of the terms is fluid.

27. Thiselton, *1 Corinthians*, 818-19, based on Chrysostom, *Homilies on First and Second Corinthians*, trans. Talbot Chambers, in *The Nicene and Post-Nicene Fathers*, 1:12, ed. Philip Schaff (Grand Rapids: Eerdmans, 1848, 1983), 150 (Homily 26:3).

28. The interest in visible representations of respect could suggest that the setting is public, but tokens of respect are always appropriate.

29. Hurley, *Man and Woman in Biblical Perspective*, 172-73.

30. Karl Barth, *Church Dogmatics*, vol. 3/4 (Edinburgh: T & T Clark, 1961), 149-50; Thiselton, *1 Corinthians*, 835-36. Similarly, Paul says the glory of believers is complete when each uses his or her gifts for the other.

31. Two other proposals: 1) "The angels" are evil. Women should dress modestly lest they arouse the desire of evil angels. 2) "The angels" are good. They guard human order, and we should not offend them by our disorder.

32. Winter, *After Paul Left Corinth*, 133-38.

33. Epictetus, *Discourses*, trans. W. A. Oldfather, 2 vols. (Cambridge, MA: Harvard University Press, 1928), 2.15-19 (Book 3.1.27-37).

34. "Life Along the Catwalk," *Time*, 14 August 1995, 66. Author not listed.

35. Daniel Doriani, *Getting the Message* (Philipsburg, NJ: Presbyterian and Reformed, 1996), 122-54; Daniel Doriani, *Putting the Truth to Work* (Philipsburg, NJ: Presbyterian and Reformed, 2001), 240-78; Jack Kuhatschek, *Taking the Guesswork Out of Applying the Bible* (Downers Grove, IL: InterVarsity Press, 1990); William Klein, Craig Blomberg, and Robert Hubbard, *Introduction to Biblical Interpretation* (Waco, TX: Word, 1993), 401-26.

36. Paul makes this statement to the "brothers," but "brothers" includes male and female Christians in his epistles.

37. There are four unlikely ways to resolve Paul's apparent contradiction: 1) Paul did contradict himself, saying one thing in 11:5 and another in 14:34. 2) Paul never permitted women to speak in 1 Corinthians 11:5. He merely entertained the possibility; *if* they spoke and did so without a head covering, it would be a disgrace. 3) First Corinthians 14:34-35 is not from Paul; this is an explanatory note added by an early copyist (Fee, *1 Corinthians*, 699-705). 4) First Corinthians 11:5 is a general principle for all churches; First Corinthians 14:34-35 is temporary counsel for Corinth where women were quite uneducated or unruly. The problems with some of these explanations are obvious. For a detailed critique of these views, see the exhaustive work of D. A. Carson, "Silent in the Churches: On the Role of Women in 1 Corinthians 14:33b-36," in *Recovering Biblical Manhood and Womanhood,* ed. John Piper and Wayne Grudem (Wheaton, IL: Crossway, 1991), 140-51, and Thiselton, *1 Corinthians*, 1150-58.

38. For this formulation I am indebted to Dr. Robert Yarbrough of Trinity Evangelical Divinity School.

39. Someone might object that option one requires "prophecy" to have one sense in 11:5—informal sharing—and another in 14:26—formal instruction. But the term "prophecy" had a wide range of meanings in Greek and biblical literature; so it could well have two different meanings when used several chapters apart.

40. Hurley, *Man and Woman in Biblical Perspective*, 188-89; Carson, "Silent in the Churches," 151-53; Thiselton, *1 Corinthians*, 1158; Witherington, *Women in the Earliest Churches*, 101-2.

41. In Timothy, the term is "overseer," but "overseer" and "elder" are interchangeable. See Acts 20:17, 28; Titus 1:5, 7.
42. I follow Hurley, *Man and Woman in Biblical Perspective*, 188-89.
43. See footnote 15, chapter 6.
44. Some, like Elijah, came and went rapidly. Others, like Jeremiah and Amos, were rejected by Israel's leaders.
45. Wayne Grudem, *The Gift of Prophecy in the New Testament and Today* (Wheaton, IL: Crossway, 1988), 17-114; D. A. Carson, *Showing the Spirit* (Grand Rapids: Baker, 1987), 94-100.
46. For more evidence that prophets have limited authority: 1) First Corinthians 14 assumes the words of even recognized prophets must be tested. 2) Prophecy cuts such a low profile that Paul must tell the Thessalonians not to hold it in contempt (1 Thess. 5:20). 3) Church leaders such as Tertullian, Origen, Aquinas, and Calvin agreed that prophecy must be tested.
47. Carson, *Showing the Spirit*, 120; Grudem, *Gift of Prophecy*, 70-74.
48. Argued at length in Grudem, *The Gift of Prophecy,* and Carson, *Showing the Spirit.*
49. On the connection between priests and elders, see John E. Johnson, "The Old Testament Offices as Paradigm for Pastoral Identity," *Bibliotheca Sacra* 152 (April-June 1995): 193-96; Peter Leithart, "Attendants of Yahweh's House: Priesthood in the Old Testament," *Journal for the Study of the Old Testament* 85 (1999): 3-24, especially 22-3; Robert S. Rayburn, "Three Offices: Minister, Elder, Deacon," *Presbyterion* 12 (1986): 108-110; Paul Schrieber, "Priests Among Priests," *Concordia Journal* 14:3 (July 1988): 215-27; Raymond Brown, *Priest and Bishop* (New York: Paulist Press, 1970), 10-20.

CHAPTER 6:
1 TIMOTHY 2

1. The first Greek word in 2:1 is *oun* (οὖν). It usually marks a strong connection with whatever precedes: "therefore."
2. Gordon Fee, *1 and 2 Timothy, Titus* (Peabody, MA: Hendrickson, 1988), 61-65. See 1-31 for more background to the epistle.
3. The rationale: 1) The topic and mode of prayer fit worship. They pray for authorities and "lift holy hands" (2:1-4, 8). 2) First Timothy 2:8 (ESV) says that men should pray (literally) "in every place." "In every place" means "place of worship" in 1 Corinthians 1:2, 2 Corinthians 2:14, and 1 Thessalonians 1:8. "The place" is also a circumlocution for God's temple in the Gospels (Matt. 24:15; John 4:20; 11:48). 3) Paul says *males* should pray, not using the word for mankind (*anthrōpos*—ἄνθρωπος), but the one for adult males (*anēr*—ἀνήρ), and we know men normally led in prayer in Jewish worship (J. N. D. Kelly, *The Pastoral Epistles* [London: Adam and Charles Black, 1963], 65; Craig Keener, *Paul, Women and Wives: Marriage and Women's Ministry in the Letters of Paul* [Peabody, MA: Hendrickson, 1990], 126, note 67). 4) The modest apparel of women fits worship since prominent Greco-Roman women displayed their social status with costly clothes and elaborate coiffures. 5) The command that women learn in silence fits worship since women may speak at home or in private meetings (1 Cor. 14:34).
4. Strong feminist interpretations of our passage include Keener, *Paul, Women and Wives*, 101-32 and I. H. Marshall, *The Pastoral Epistles* (Edinburgh: T & T Clark, 1999), 436-71. Among traditionalists, see Douglas Moo, "What Does It Mean Not to Teach or Have Authority Over Men: 1 Timothy 2:11-15," in *Recovering Biblical Manhood and Womanhood,* ed. John Piper and Wayne Grudem (Wheaton, IL: Crossway, 1991), 179-93; William D. Mounce, *Pastoral Epistles* (Nashville: Thomas Nelson, 2000), 94-149; Thomas R. Schreiner, "An Interpretation of 1 Timothy 2:9-15: A Dialogue with Scholarship," in *Women in the Church: A Fresh Analysis of 1 Timothy 2:9-15,* ed. Andreas Kostenberger, Thomas R. Schreiner, and H. Scott Baldwin (Grand Rapids: Baker, 1995), 105-54.
5. A few scholars believe the Greek term γύνη (*gynē*), rendered "women" in almost all English translations, should be translated "wives." Gordon Hugenberger, "Women in Church Office: Hermeneutics or Exegesis? A Survey of Approaches to 1 Timothy 2:8-15," *Journal of the Evangelical Theological Society* 35 (1992): 341-60. Greek does use the same word for women and wives, but "women" seems right since 1) when Paul wants γύνη (*gynē*) to indicate a wife, he mentions marriage or their husbands in the context; 2) Paul would hardly forbid wives to dress ostentatiously but permit single women to do so. See Schreiner, "An Interpretation of 1 Timothy 2:9-15," 115-17.
6. "I want" indicates Paul's command, not his mere desire. The Greek means "I counsel," not

"I wish." One may call it stereotyping, but Paul warns *men* about anger (2:1) and warns *women* about ostentation.

7. After a long complaint about the jewels, makeup, perfumes, and luxuries of women, Juvenal adds, "Meantime she pays no attention to her husband." See Juvenal, "Satire 6" in *Juvenal and Persius*, trans. C. G. Ramsey (Cambridge, MA: Harvard University Press, 1965), 121-25.

8. David Scholer, "Women's Adornment: Some Historical and Hermeneutical Observations on the New Testament Passages," *Daughters of Sarah* 6 (1, 1980): 5.

9. Paul does not ban all hair styling as if tangles signified godliness. Hair braids could be simple. The problem is elaborate, expensive hairstyles. See James Hurley, *Man and Woman in Biblical Perspective* (Grand Rapids: Zondervan, 1981), 198-99, 257-59; Keener, *Paul, Women and Wives*, 104-5.

10. The Greek verb is imperative.

11. See Philo, "On the Creation" and "The Special Laws," in *The Works of Philo*, trans. F. H. Colson (Cambridge, MA: Harvard University Press, 1929 and 1937), 1:131 and 7:581-83 respectively.

12. The term *hēsychia* (ἡσυχία) can mean total silence but more often describes a quiet attitude. All the terms for silence and quietness overlap with each other somewhat, but the family of *siōpaō, sigē*, and *sigaō* (σιωπάω, σιγή, σιγάω) is more likely to denote speechlessness, perhaps by choice (Luke 9:36; Acts 15:13). The term *phimoō* (φιμόω) can mean to be silenced by an order (Mark 1:25; 4:39), by being ashamed (Matt. 22:12), or by a refutation (Matt. 22:34). *Epistomizō* (ἐπιστομίζω) means to keep someone from speaking (Titus 1:11). We must not exaggerate the differences among these words, but our term seems apt to describe the relative silence that is a virtue for students. See Aida Besançon Spencer, *Beyond the Curse: Women Called to Ministry* (Peabody, MA: Hendrickson, 1985, 1997), 75-81.

13. Ibid., 84-6; Keener, *Paul, Women and Wives*, 109-13; Gilbert Bilezikian, *Beyond Sex Roles* (Grand Rapids: Baker, 1985), 179.

14. Stephen Baugh, "A Foreign World: Ephesus in the First Century" in *Women in the Church*, 45-47.

15. Paul uses the verb for "permit," ἐπιτρέπω (*epitrepō*), just two other times. Neither one records mere preferences (1 Cor. 14:34; 16:7). Feminists suggest that since Paul does not use an imperative, he is not actually commanding anything. But Greek has many ways to register commands; the imperative mood is but one of them. Further, Paul uses the first singular present indicative mood for universal, authoritative instruction in many texts: Romans 12:1, 3; 1 Corinthians 4:16; 2 Corinthians 5:20; Galatians 5:2, 3; Ephesians 4:1; 1 Timothy 2:1, 8. See George Knight, *Commentary on the Pastoral Epistles* (Grand Rapids: Eerdmans, 1992), 140.

16. By my estimate, in the fifteen verses that use the verb *teach*, three certainly refer to basic doctrine (1 Cor. 4:17; Gal. 1:12; 2 Thess. 2:15), and six almost certainly do (Rom. 12:7; Eph. 4:21; Col. 1:28; 2:7; 1 Tim. 2:12; 4:11), leaving six that refer to other teaching. There are two cognate nouns for teaching—*didachē* (διδαχή) and *didaskalia* (διδασκαλία). The first word, *didachē*, refers to Christian doctrine in four of its six uses in the New Testament (Rom. 6:17; 16:17; 2 Tim. 4:2; Titus 1:9, but not 1 Cor. 14:6, 26). The second word typically refers to false teaching (Matt. 15:9; Mark 7:7; Eph. 4:14; Col. 2:22, but not Rom. 15:4) until we get to the Pastoral Epistles. There Paul specifies if something is sound doctrine or not (1 Tim. 1:10). See also Knight, *Pastoral Epistles*, 88-89, 140-41; Kelly, *Pastoral Epistles*, 50; Schreiner, "An Interpretation of 1 Timothy 2," 127-28.

17. For "exercise authority" see H. Scott Baldwin, "A Difficult Word: ΑΥΘΕΝΤΕΩ in 1 Timothy 2:12" and "Appendix 2: ΑΥΘΕΝΤΕΩ in Ancient Greek Literature" in *Women in the Church*, 65-80, 269-305. For alternate proposals, see Leland E. Wilshire, "The TLG Computer and Further Reference to ΑΥΘΕΝΤΕΩ in 1 Timothy 2:12," *New Testament Studies*, 34 (1988), 120-34; and "1 Timothy 2:12 Revisited: A Reply to Paul W. Barnett and Timothy J. Harris," *Evangelical Quarterly* 65 (1993): 54. Wilshire's first article is amenable to Baldwin's view; his second is not.

18. See John Chrysostom, *Sermons in Genesis*, cited in Greek and English in Baldwin, "ΑΥΘΕΝΤΕΩ in 1 Timothy 2:12," 73-74, 283.

19. Andreas Kostenberger, "A Complex Sentence Structure in 1 Timothy 2:12," in *Women in the Church*, 84-104.

20. Paul uses a distinct word for false teaching (*heterodidaskaleō*—ἑτεροδιδασκαλέω) in 1 Timothy 1:3 and 6:3.

21. F. F. Bruce, "Women in the Church: A Biblical Survey," in *A Mind for What Matters* (Grand Rapids: Eerdmans, 1990), 263; Mary Evans, *Woman in the Bible* (Downers Grove, IL:

InterVarsity Press, 1983), 103-4; Keener, *Paul, Women and Wives*, 113-16. Keener admits "it is easy to see why many readers take" 1 Timothy 2:12-13 to appeal to "God's ideal plan."

22. Luke Johnson says Paul writes "out of patriarchal reflex," "cultural conservatism," and poor logic to reach conclusions that are flawed enough in tone and substance that the only option is "to engage the words of Paul in a dialectical process of criticism within the public discourse of the church, both academic and liturgical." Johnson, *The First and Second Letters to Timothy* (New York: Doubleday, 2001), 205-11.

23. Paul even links Jesus' supremacy to his status as the firstborn over creation (Col. 1:15).

24. Richard Longenecker, *New Testament Social Ethics for Today* (Grand Rapids: Eerdmans, 1984), 84-92.

25. Stanley Grenz, "Anticipating God's New Community: Theological Foundations for Women in Ministry," *Journal of the Evangelical Theological Society* 38 (1995): 601-2, 604. Richard Hove replies in *Equality in Christ?: Galatians 3:28 and the Gender Dispute* (Wheaton, IL: Crossway, 1999), 100-104.

26. Hove, *Equality in Christ?*, 107-24.

27. William J. Webb, *Slaves, Women and Homosexuals: Exploring the Hermeneutics of Cultural Analysis* (Downers Grove, IL: InterVarsity Press, 2001), 263-68.

28. Faith Martin, *Call Me Blessed* (Grand Rapids: Eerdmans, 1988), 153.

29. To be precise, the Greek term "for" (*gar*—γάρ) appears only in verse 13.

30. Paul usually uses the word *save* (*sōzō*—σώζω) for eternal salvation. But the meaning "preserve, keep safe" is common in the Gospels and everyday Greek. Because "childbearing" has a definite article in the Greek, some believe Paul is teaching that women are saved through "*the* childbearing," that is, the birth of Christ. But this proposal is unlikely. First, the context is discussing gender roles, not the Incarnation. Second, "the childbearing" is a most obscure way of referring to Jesus' birth. Third, the Incarnation does not save; the cross does. Fourth, the rules for the Greek definite article are so complex and obscure we should not make too much of one definite article; it may not refer to any particular childbirth. See Schreiner, "An Interpretation of 1 Timothy 2:9-15," 147-49.

31. The Greek is *oikourgous agathas* (οἰκουργοὺς ἀγαθάς).

32. Daniel Doriani, *The Life of a God-Made Man* (Wheaton, IL: Crossway, 2002), 39-42.

CHAPTER 7:
THE GIFTS OF THE SPIRIT AND THE ROLES OF WOMEN

1. The lists seem to be partial for three reasons: 1) No two lists are even nearly identical; even short lists have terms missing from long ones. 2) Some terms are listed as independent gifts in one place and as the result of a gift in others: Encouraging is a gift in Romans 12:8, but a result of the gift of prophecy in 1 Corinthians 14:3. Knowledge is independent in 1 Corinthians 12:8 and a result of prophesy in 1 Corinthians 14:6. 3) Some unlisted skills appear to be gifts. Music appears with the gifts of teaching, tongues, and interpretation in 1 Corinthians 14:26. God gave Bezalel and Oholiab artistic skill to construct the tabernacle (Exod. 31:2; 35:30; 36:1-2). Hospitality may also be a gift, since it is mentioned near two gift lists (Rom. 12:13; 1 Peter 4:9) and clearly aids church life (Rom. 16:23; 1 Tim. 5:10; 3 John 8).

2. The phrase "spiritual gifts" appears in many translations but never occurs in the Greek.

3. The ordinary words are *dōrea* (δωρεά) and *dōma* (δῶμα) (Eph. 4:7-8). The word is usually plural, though Paul does exhort Timothy to stir up the *gift* given to him with prophecy (1 Tim. 4:14; 2 Tim. 1:6; cf. 1 Peter 4:10).

4. Some gifts are listed but neither defined nor described; so our knowledge is limited.

5. Scripture neither defines the relation between natural gifts and spiritual gifts, nor describes the role of preparation. Certainly sometimes there may be a link. Jesus prepared the Twelve for apostleship by teaching them and setting an example for ministry. Paul's rabbinic training, Roman citizenship, and intellectual ability all prepared him to be the apostle to the Gentiles.

6. We can prepare to pray for a healing, but healing comes "straight from heaven" in a way sermons do not.

7. We have only limited information about some gifts. For example, the gift of knowledge is never defined in Scripture. Is it ordinary knowledge, hence much like wisdom? Or is it supernatural knowledge, given when normal sources fail, as many Charismatics think?

8 For example, prophets such as Moses, Jeremiah, and the apostle John sometimes wrote what they heard and saw, directly from God; so their word was purely supernatural. But they sometimes spoke in response to events they witnessed (or endured) and remembered, so that the natural element enters.

9 There are exceptions to this principle. For example, miracles and speaking in tongues are all or nothing.

CHAPTER 8:
MINISTRIES OF WOMEN IN THE CHURCH: TRADITIONAL IDEAS AND FRESH PROPOSALS

1. This passage illustrates the non-doctrinal teaching described in chapter 6. The Greek term is *sōphronizō* (σωφρονίζω), not *didaskō* (διδάσκω), the term for authoritative teaching found in 1 Timothy 2:12.
2. I have observed this pattern innumerable times as a speaker. It holds in all North American cultures and, it seems, in the European and Asian nations I have visited.
3. I share this position with many others, including Luther and Calvin, cited in chapter 9.
4. First Thessalonians 5:12 and Hebrews 13:7, 17 also mention church leaders without specifying the gender. Yet in context the writers probably assumed male leadership.
5. See Malcolm Gladwell, *The Tipping Point* (Boston: Little, Brown and Company, 2002), 182-92.
6. Kenny Moore, "Track and Field's Master Teacher," *Sports Illustrated*, 24 January, 2000, 41-43.

CHAPTER 9:
EGALITARIANS AND COMPLEMENTARIANS: A COMPARATIVE STUDY

1. For a longer comparison of the views of egalitarians and complementarians, see Craig Keener, Linda Belleville, Thomas Schreiner, Ann Bowman, and James Beck, *Two Views on Women in Ministry*, James Beck and Craig Blomberg, eds. (Grand Rapids: Zondervan, 2001).
2. On the distinction between patriarchal and patricentric, see D. I. Block, *Judges, Ruth* (Nashville: Broadman, 1999), 94 (fn. 68), 378-79.
3. Jane Schaberg, "Luke," in *Women's Bible Commentary*, Carol A. Newsom and Sharon H. Ringe, eds. (Louisville, KY: Westminster Press, 1998), 363.
4. Elizabeth Schussler Fiorenza, *In Memory of Her: A Feminist Theological Reconstruction of Christian Origins* (New York: Crossroad, 1983), 13-19; Elizabeth Schussler Fiorenza, *Bread Not Stone: The Challenge of Biblical Feminist Interpretation* (Boston: Beacon, 1984), 14, 88. Rosemary Ruether says, "the promotion of full humanity of women" is the "critical principle for feminist theology." See Ruether, *Sexism and God-Talk: Toward a Feminist Theology* (Boston: Beacon, 1983), 18-19.
5. For this discussion, I define a critic as someone who is willing to say, "The Bible says 'x,'" and the Bible is wrong."
6. Rudolf Bultmann, "New Testament and Mythology," in *Kerygma and Myth: A Theological Debate*, Hans Werner Bartsch, ed., R. M. Fuller, trans. (New York: Harper & Row, 1961), 1-44; John MacQuarrie, *Jesus Christ in Modern Thought* (Philadelphia: Trinity Press International, 1990), 70, and many others.
7. Fiorenza, *Bread Not Stone*, 269.
8. Luke Timothy Johnson, *The First and Second Letters to Timothy* (New York: Doubleday, 2001), 206, 209-11.
9. Rebecca Groothuis, *Good News for Women: A Biblical Picture of Gender Equality* (Grand Rapids: Baker, 1997), 139-44. Richard Longenecker, *New Testament Social Ethics for Today* (Grand Rapids: Eerdmans, 1984), 84, 92. Longenecker says Paul's emphasis on redemption indicates that "what God has done in Christ transcends what is true simply because of creation" (92).
10. Richard Hove, *Equality in Christ?: Galatians 3:28 and the Gender Dispute* (Wheaton, IL: Crossway, 1999).
11. The second sentence in Rebecca Groothuis's analysis of 1 Timothy 2 and 1 Corinthians 14 begins, "Neither of these texts can be taken at face value as a direct statement of universal principle. . . ." Groothuis, *Good News for Women*, 209.
12. Craig Keener, *Paul, Women and Wives* (Peabody, MA: Hendrickson, 1992), 139.
13. Ibid., 144-47.
14. Ibid., 169-70.
15. Ibid., 171. Keener believes Paul's summons to mutual submission rules out male leadership. For more analysis of Keener, see Daniel Doriani, "The Historical Novelty of Egalitarian Interpretations of Ephesians 5," in *Biblical Foundations for Building Strong Families in Your Church*, ed. Wayne Grudem (Wheaton, IL: Crossway, 2002).
16. Gordon Fee, *1 and 2 Timothy and Titus* (Peabody, MA: Hendrickson, 1984, 1988), 72-76.

17. Gordon Fee, "Issues in Evangelical Hermeneutics, Part III: The Great Watershed—Intentionality and Particularity/Eternality: 1 Timothy 2:8-15 as a Test Case," *Crux* 26 (1990): 34-6.

18. Bruce Waltke, "1 Timothy 2:8-15: Unique or Normative?" *Crux* 28 (1992): 22-27.

19. Aida Besançon Spencer, *Beyond the Curse: Women Called to Ministry* (Peabody, MA: Hendrickson, 1985, 1997), 17-42, especially 41-42. For a sophisticated expression of this argument, see William J. Webb, *Slaves, Women and Homosexuals: Exploring the Hermeneutics of Cultural Analysis* (Downers Grove, IL: InterVarsity Press, 2001), 76-81, 110-20.

20. Pleading that uncertainty vitiates key texts, Sanford Hull ("Exegetical Difficulties in the 'Hard Passages'" in Gretchen Hull's *Equal to Serve* [Tarrytown, NY: Revell, 1987], 251-66) lists every conceivable uncertainty in the interpretation of 1 Corinthians 11:2-16, 1 Corinthians 14:33-36, and 1 Timothy 2:8-15, and then reasons that these uncertainties make it impossible to use the texts to construct a view of gender roles. He should know that the same ploy could be used with his favored texts and that his method shares deconstruction's pessimism about communication.

21. Daniel Doriani, *Putting the Truth to Work: The Theory and Practice of Biblical Application* (Philipsburg, NJ: Presbyterian and Reformed, 2001), 82-84, 240-59, especially 245-49.

22. F. F. Bruce, "Women in the Church: A Biblical Survey," in *A Mind for What Matters* (Grand Rapids: Eerdmans, 1990), 263-64. See also Spencer, *Beyond the Curse*, 99-100; Mary Stewart Van Leeuwen, *Gender and Grace* (Downers Grove, IL: InterVarsity Press, 1989), 34-37, 231-50; Gretchen Hull, *Equal to Serve*, passim; Clarence Boomsma, *Male and Female, One in Christ: New Testament Teaching on Women in Office* (Grand Rapids: Baker, 1993), 23-29, 103-5; Stanley Grenz, *Women in the Church: A Biblical Theology of Women in the Ministry* (Downers Grove, IL: InterVarsity Press, 1995), 215.

23. The "All Gifts" argument appeared already in the text and introductory letters to Frances E. Willard's *Women in the Pulpit* (Boston: D. Lothrop Co., 1888). In his letter on page 13, Joseph Cook declares that women have all natural, spiritual, intellectual, and social endowments necessary for ministry and then asks, "What Scriptural authority can be quoted of greater weight than the divine command not to keep a light under a bushel, or talents in a napkin?"

24. This reasoning was prominent in the Middle Ages. Completely banned from official avenues to ministry, women reported that God called them, irresistibly, in visions. Only by "direct authorization" did ministry roles open to them. See Caroline Bynum, *Jesus as Mother: Studies in the Spirituality of the High Middle Ages* (Berkeley: University of California Press, 1982), 184ff. Frances Willard also urged younger women "who feel a call" to pursue their "wistful purpose of entering upon that blessed gospel ministry" where their "strong yet gentle" ministry may comfort the wounded (Willard, *Women in the Pulpit*, 62). See also Daniel Doriani, "A History of the Interpretation of 1 Timothy 2," in *Women in the Church: A Fresh Analysis of 1 Timothy 2:9-15*, Andreas Kostenberger, Thomas Schreiner, and Scott Baldwin, eds. (Grand Rapids: Baker, 1995), 229-35.

25. Patricia Gundry, *Neither Slave nor Free* (New York: Harper & Row, 1990), v-vi.

26. Faith Martin, *Call Me Blessed* (Grand Rapids: Eerdmans, 1988), 3-11; E. Margaret Howe, *Women and Church Leadership* (Grand Rapids: Zondervan, 1982), 162-68.

27. Grenz, *Women in the Church*, 13-51 (*passim*).

28. Bruce, "Women in the Church," 264; Keener, *Paul, Women and Wives*, 227-28; Groothuis, *Good News for Women*, 238-41.

29. Bruce says, "Whatever in Paul's teaching promotes true freedom is of universal and permanent validity; whatever seems to impose restrictions on true freedom has regard to local and temporary conditions" ("Women in the Church," 263).

30. Robert Yarbrough, "The Hermeneutics of 1 Timothy 2:9-15," in *Women in the Church: A Fresh Analysis of 1 Timothy 2:9-15*, Andreas Kostenberger, Thomas Schreiner, and Scott Baldwin, eds. (Grand Rapids: Baker, 1995), 182-84; Doriani, "History of the Interpretation of 1 Timothy 2," 216-18.

31. Alan Padgett, "The Pauline Rationale for Submission: Biblical Feminism and the *hina* Clauses of Titus 2:1-10," *Evangelical Quarterly* 59 (1987): 51-2; Keener, *Paul, Women and Wives*, 230-34; Letha Scanzoni and Nancy Hardesty, *All We're Meant to Be* (Waco, TX: Word, 1974), 202.

32. Grenz, *Women in the Church*, 33-39; Patricia Gundry, *Neither Slave nor Free*, vi-viii (the front-door analogy is mine).

33. Willard, *Women in the Pulpit*, 45-50. On page 39, Willard says, "If the purest should be

called" to ministry, then women "outrank" men "in actual fitness for the pulpit," as
woman's holiness especially authorizes her "to be a minister of God."
34. Grenz, *Women in the Church*, 25-26, 218, 222-30. Similarly, Mary Stewart van Leeuwen
commends women for favoring social policies that oppose wars and "protect consumers,
citizens and the environment." See *After Eden* (Grand Rapids: Eerdmans, 1993), 442-43,
584-86.
35. Jane Hunter, *The Gospel of Gentility: American Women Missionaries in Turn-of-the Century
China* (New Haven: Yale University Press, 1984), 11-38, 52, 174-204; Irwin T. Hyatt, *Our
Ordered Lives Confess* (Cambridge, MA: Harvard University Press, 1976), 65-92. The statis-
tic is from private conversation with Dr. Sam Ling, a Christian leader from mainland China
and the director of China Horizon.
36. Some traditionalists have questioned the spiritual equality of women, but others have
asserted that women are spiritually superior to men.
37. Webb, *Slaves, Women and Homosexuals*, 263-68. Note that his most recent citation is from
1963.

CHAPTER 10:
A HISTORY OF WOMEN AND MINISTRY

1. Christina Hoff Sommers, *Who Stole Feminism?* (New York: Simon and Schuster, 1994), 51.
2. Cyprian, "The Treatises of Cyprian," trans. Earnest Wallis, in *AnteNicene Fathers*, ed.
Alexander Roberts and James Donaldson, 9 vols. (Grand Rapids: Eerdmans, 1979-1985),
5:546. The absence of argumentation is common. He "proves" most precepts simply by
quoting proof texts. Subsequent references will cite the *AnteNicene Fathers* as ANF.
3. Tertullian, "Against Marcion," trans. Peter Holmes, ANF, 3:446.
4. Tertullian, "On Baptism," trans. S. Thelwall, ANF, 3:677.
5. Tertullian, "On the Apparel of Women," trans. S. Thelwall, ANF, 4:33.
6. Origen, "Fragments on 1 Corinthians," in Roger Gryson, *The Ministry of Women in the
Early Church*, trans. Jean Laporte and Mary Louise Hall (Collegeville, MN: The Liturgical
Press), 28.
7. Ibid., 28-29.
8. Origen, "Homilies on Isaiah [Homily 6]," in Gryson, *Ministry of Women*, 27.
9. Ibid., 31, from Rom. 16:1-2.
10. "The Constitutions of the Holy Apostles," trans. J. Whiston and Irah Chase, ANF, 7:427.
The anonymous Constitutions claim to be written by the twelve apostles.
11. Ibid., 427-28, 394.
12. Ibid., 430-31, 492.
13. Jerome, "To Eustochium" (Letter 108), trans. W. H. Freemantle, in *Nicene and Post Nicene
Fathers*, 28 vols. in two series, ed. Philip Schaff (Grand Rapids: Eerdmans, 1952-1956),
Second Series, 6:209-10. Subsequent references will cite the *Nicene and Post Nicene Fathers*
as NPNF.
14. Ibid., 207-9.
15. Jerome, "To Principia" (Letter 127), in *Select Letters of St. Jerome*, trans. F. A. Wright
(Cambridge, MA: Harvard University Press, 1954), 453.
16. Ibid., 455. Jerome, writing in Latin, slips into Greek for just the two words cited in the
Greek.
17. Ibid., 457-61.
18. Ibid., 455.
19. Chrysostom, "Homilies on Timothy" (*Homilies* VIII, IX), trans. Philip Schaff, NPNF, First
Series, 13:432-35.
20. Ibid., 435.
21. Ibid., 435-36.
22. Chrysostom, "Homilies on Romans, Homily 31," trans. George B. Simcox, NPNF, First
Series, 11:553-56.
23. Ibid., 554-55.
24. Ibid., 554.
25. Chrysostom, "Homilies on Romans, Homily 30," NPNF, First Series, 11:550-52.
26. Chrysostom, "Homilies on 1 Corinthians, Homily 37," trans. T. W. Chambers, NPNF, First
Series, 12: 222.
27. David S. Schaff, *The Middle Ages: From Gregory 7, 1049, to Boniface 8, 1294*, vol. 5 of *History
of the Christian Church*, Philip Schaff, ed. and principal author, 9 vols. (Grand Rapids:

Eerdmans, 1953-1957), 5:371-3; Henry Osborn Taylor, *The Medieval Mind* (Cambridge, MA: Harvard University Press, 1949), 462-75.

28. Taylor, *Medieval Mind*, 465-66.

29. Ibid., 466-67.

30. Ibid., 466, 470-75. But Hildegard's work betrays familiarity with Augustine, Boethius, and contemporary science, according to Frances and Joseph Gies, *Women in the Middle Ages* (New York: Harper and Row, 1978), 76-85.

31. Taylor, *Medieval Mind*, 466-68.

32. Thomas Aquinas, *Prophecy and Other Charisms*, trans. Roland Potter, in *Summa Theologica*, ed. Thomas Gilby and T. C. Gilby, 60 vols. (New York: McGraw Hill, 1963-1974), 45:133.

33. Ibid.

34. Thomas Aquinas, *Well-Tempered Passion*, trans. Thomas Gilby, in *Summa Theologica*, 44:177.

35. Ibid., 45:133.

36. Ibid., 44:21.

37. Ibid., 45:133.

38. Ibid., *Man Made to God's Image*, trans. Edmund Hill, *Summa Theologica*, 13:35-39.

39. Ibid., 13:36-39.

40. Aquinas is sometimes accused of misogyny (Ruth Tucker and Walter Liefeld, *Daughters of the Church* [Grand Rapids: Academie, 1987], 164-65), but the sources are very complex. Aquinas considers, then rejects (less resoundingly than we might like) Aristotle's notion that women are inferior. See Daniel Doriani, "A History of the Interpretation of 1 Timothy 2," in *Women in the Church: A Fresh Analysis of 1 Timothy 2:9-15*, Andreas Kostenberger, Thomas Schreiner, and Scott Baldwin, eds. (Grand Rapids: Baker, 1995), 231-32.

41. Aquinas believes a "delightful" friendship can develop between a husband and a wife through pleasure in the "generative act," by providing for "mutual needs" for the common good, and by the "virtue proper to . . . husband and wife." Thomas Aquinas, *Commentary on the Nicomachean Ethics*, trans. C. I. Litzinger, 2 vols. (Chicago: Regnery, 1964), 2:766-68.

42. Francis Cardman, "The Medieval Question of Women and Orders," *The Thomist* 42 (1978): 590-92.

43. Gies, *Women in the Middle Ages*, 66.

44. For the view that the church has deliberately suppressed the truth that women held ordained office in the Middle Ages, see Joan Morris, *The Lady Was a Bishop: The Hidden History of Women with Clerical Ordination and the Jurisdiction of Bishops* (New York: Macmillan, 1973).

45. Edmund College and James Walsh, "Editing Julian of Norwich's Revelations: A Progress Report," *Medieval Studies* 38 (1976): 410-16, 420-23.

46. Julian of Norwich, *Revelations of Divine Love* in *Women and Religion: A Feminine Sourcebook of Christian Thought*, Elizabeth Clark and Herbert Richardson, eds. (New York: Harper and Row, 1977), 104; Julian of Norwich, *Revelations of Divine Love*, trans. Clifton Walters (New York: Penguin, 1966), 213.

47. College and Walsh, "Editing Julian," 406, 410, 421-23; See Julian, *Revelations of Divine Love*, 75, 139, passim.

48. Lina Eckenstein, *Women Under Monasticism* (New York: Russell and Russell, 1896), 180-82. The quotation is from a letter to patrons of her plays.

49. Caroline Bynum, *Jesus as Mother: Studies in the Spirituality of the High Middle Ages* (Berkeley: University of California Press, 1982), 207-8.

50. Ibid., 184-87, 196-202.

51. Clark and Richardson, *Women and Religion*, 105-7.

52. Bynum, *Spirituality*, 184.

53. Schaff, *History of the Christian Church*, 5:503-4.

54. Philip Schaff, *The Middle Ages: From Boniface 8, 1294, to the Protestant Reformation, 1517*, vol. 6 of *History of the Christian Church*, 6:393.

55. Rosemary Ruether, "Misogynism and Virginal Feminism in the Fathers," in *Religion and Sexism: Images of Women in Jewish and Christian Tradition* (New York: Simon and Schuster, 1974), 150, 157-64, 179.

56. Gies, *Women in the Middle Ages*, 41-52. Dominican Humbert de Romans was one of the rare men who argued that women are superior to men, possessing more grace and more glory; Ibid., 37-41.

57. Martin Luther, *Lectures on Genesis: Chapters 1-5*, trans. George V. Schick, vol. 1 of *Luther's*

Works, ed. Jaroslav Pelikan and Walther T. Lehman (St. Louis: Concordia, 1955-1972), 1:68-69, for the quotation. For the rest, *Table Talk*, trans. and ed. Theodore G. Tappert, vol. 54 of *Luther's Works*, 54:221, 183, 428.

58. Luther, *Works*, *Genesis*, 1:115; *Table Talk*, 54:160-61. See also 54:171, 223.
59. Martin Luther, *Lectures on 1 Timothy*, trans. Richard Dinda, vol. 28 of *Luther's Works*, 28:270-76.
60. Ibid., 276.
61. Ibid., and *Word and Sacrament II*, trans. Frederick Ahrens, vol. 36 of *Luther's Works*, 36:151-52.
62. Ibid., 276-77 and *Works*, 36:152. Luther takes "woman" to mean wife and "man" to mean husband. But the decision concerning *gynē* (γυνή) and *anēr* (ἀνήρ) had no apparent influence on his interpretation.
63. Ibid., 277.
64. Ibid., 277-78.
65. Ibid., 278-79.
66. John Calvin, *Commentaries on the Epistles to Timothy, Titus, and Philemon* (Grand Rapids: Eerdmans, 1948), 68.
67. Ibid., 67; John Calvin, *Sermons on Timothy and Titus* (Oxford: Banner of Truth Trust, 1983), 226. Facsimile of a 1579 London edition printed by G. Bishop.
68. Calvin, *Commentaries*, 67.
69. Calvin, *Sermons*, 227.
70. Ibid., 225. We hear the Scotist in Calvin saying, "we must make a difference between the common order which God will have to be observed among men for a rule" and his unusual work. "For we may not make God subject to a law, because all laws proceed from his will."
71. Ibid., 212.
72. Calvin, *Commentaries*, 68-69. The term "inferior" ordinarily referred to social rank at the time of the Reformation and does not necessarily imply incapacity.
73. Ibid., 69-70; *Sermons*, 209 (209 is the printed page number; it is erroneous and should be 213).
74. Calvin, *Sermons*, 223.
75. Calvin's references to the weakness of women are very rare and always seem to allude to either 1 Corinthians 1:27 or 1 Peter 3:7. Nonetheless they earn him feminist ire. (See Tucker and Liefeld, *Daughters*, 176-77). John Calvin, *Commentary on the Gospel According to John*, trans. John Pringle (Grand Rapids: Baker, 1981), 247-48, 260-61.
76. Calvin, *Sermons*, 225; with John Calvin, "Letter to William Cecil" in *Letters of John Calvin: Selected from the Bonnet Edition* (Edinburgh: Banner of Truth Trust, 1980), 211-13.
77. Ibid., 214-12 (215). Calvin's commentaries on Genesis, John, and Corinthians sound similar. The last especially insists on the spiritual equality of men and women, that the differences flow from "civil order and honorary distinctions, which cannot be dispensed with in ordinary life." See John Calvin, *Commentary on the Epistles of Paul the Apostle to the Corinthians*, trans. John Pringle (Grand Rapids: Baker, 1981), 353-55.
78. Almost all scholars agree that Calvin is a traditionalist on gender roles. Jane Douglass claims Calvin was open to female church leaders but knew his society would never accept them as pastors. For my reply, see, "A History of the Interpretation of 1 Timothy 2," 241-43.
79. William Gouge wrote a 700-page tome, *Of Domesticall Duties*, Daniel Rogers wrote a 400-page book, *Matrimoniall Honour* (London, 1642), and John Dod, Robert Cleaver, Thomas Gataker, William Whately, Paul Baynes, and Nicholas Byfield all wrote substantially on marriage, family, and gender.
80. William Gouge, *Of Domesticall Duties* (London, 1622), 591.
81. Ibid., 272-73.
82. William Perkins, *Works* (London, 1616-18), 3:698.
83. Gouge, *Duties*, 272-73.
84. Ibid., 654.
85. William Whately, *A Bride Bush* (London, 1617), 21-29. Whately urged husbands to conceal their use of authority rather than insisting on it, as speakers conceal their use of rhetoric.
86. Rogers, *Honour*, 264-65; Gouge, *Duties*, 378; Whately, *Bride*, 33-34.
87. Gouge, *Duties*, 281-82. Regarding the translation of *authentein* (αὐθεντεῖν) as "usurp authority," Gouge does not *argue* for his translation; he is merely quoting the King James translation. I have discovered no debate of the meaning of *authentein* until the modern era.

88. Ibid., 282.
89. Ibid., 256-60; quotations from 258, 260.
90. Ibid., 337-38.
91. Robert Bolton, *Some General Directions for a Comfortable Walking with God* (London, 1625), 245.
92. William Whately, *Directions for Married Persons*, ed. John Wesley, *A Christian Library in Thirty Volumes* (London: T. Cordeux, 1821), 12:299.
93. John Winthrop, *History of New England, 1630-1649*, ed. James Kendall Hosmer, 2 vols. (New York: Barnes and Noble, 1908, 1966), 2:225.
94. Perkins, *Works*, 3:511.
95. Gouge, *Duties*, 5-7. He comments on Ephesians 5:21.
96. Thomas Gataker, *Certaine Sermons* (London, 1635), 2:188-89.
97. Edmund Morgan, *Puritan Family: Religion and Domestic Relations in Seventeenth-Century New England* (New York: Harper & Row, 1966), 43.
98. Gouge, *Duties*, 256-60.
99. Margaret Fell, *Women's Speaking Justified, Proved, and Allowed by the Scriptures* (London, 1666), 3-12; reprinted by Mosher Book and Tract Committee of the New England Yearly Meeting of Friends, Amherst, MA, 1980.
100. Tucker and Liefeld, *Daughters*, 259-63, passim.
101. Irwin Hyatt, *Our Ordered Lives Confess: Three Nineteenth-Century American Missionaries in East Shantung* (Cambridge, MA: Harvard, 1976), 104, 109-11; *Missionary Review of the World* 11 (November 1898), 874; See Tucker and Liefeld, *Daughters*, 303-18.
102. Catherine Booth, *Female Ministry, or Woman's Right to Preach the Gospel* (New York: The Salvation Army, 1859, reprinted 1975), 5-6.
103. Ibid., 6-17.
104. Ibid., 15-19.
105. Ibid., 12-13; but see page 17 for the charge of prejudiced mishandling of Scripture.
106. Frances Willard, *Women in the Pulpit* (Boston: D. Lothrop Co., 1888). Pages 17 to 62 are Willard's own work, but her chief ideas all appear in pages 17 to 50. Pages 63-112 consist primarily of testimonies by dozens of men and women to the efficacy of women in the ministry. The last sixty pages contain a critique and counter-critique of Willard's views by two male theologians.
107. Ibid., 37, 17-20.
108. Ibid., 21-22, 39-40, 45. In the beginning, Willard compares women's rights and liberation to slave's rights and liberation, 22.
109. Ibid., 46-47, emphasis hers. These remarks, she briefly notes at the end, apply only to the "intolerant sacerdotal element" of the church, not to all. But the disclaimer follows pages of general remarks about men.
110. Ibid., 47-50.
111. Katherine C. Bushnell, *God's Word to Women: One Hundred Bible Studies on the Place of Women in the Divine Economy*, repr., 1919 ed. (North Collins, NY: Ray B. Munson, 1976), paragraphs 334-37. (No pagination; paragraphs average about three-fifths of a page.)
112. Ibid., paragraphs 310-26, especially 325-26.
113. Ibid., paragraphs 338, 341-42.
114. Ibid., paragraphs 306-9.
115. Patrick Fairbairn, *Commentary on the Pastoral Epistles* (Grand Rapids: Zondervan, 1874, repr. 1974), 128.
116. Ibid., 129.
117. Ibid., 130.
118. Abraham Kuyper, *Women of the Old Testament*, trans. Henry Zylstra (Grand Rapids: Zondervan, 1933), 5-8.
119. Charles Hodge, *An Exposition of the First Epistle to the Corinthians* (Grand Rapids: Eerdmans, 1950), 206, 211.
120. Ibid., 205-7. Incidentally, Hodge's view that equality and subordination are perfectly consistent is no novelty but was the consensus view of the church until this century, which suddenly "views distinctions of class and rank as evil per se." E. E. Ellis, *Pauline Theology: Ministry and Society* (Grand Rapids: Eerdmans, 1989), 57.
121. Ibid., 304-5.
122. There is a stream of research on the differences between the male and the female brain, between male and female speech and reasoning. Secular books that effectively popularize

these studies include Michael Gurian, *The Wonder of Girls* (New York: Simon and Schuster, 2002); Michael Gurian, *The Wonder of Boys* (New York: Putnam, 1996); Christina Hoff Sommers, *The War Against Boys: How Misguided Feminism Is Harming Our Young Men* (New York: Simon and Schuster, 2000); Carol Gilligan, *In a Different Voice: Psychological Theory and Women's Development* (Cambridge, MA: Harvard University Press, 1982); and Deborah Tannen, *You Just Don't Understand: Men and Women in Conversation* (New York: Ballantine Books, 1990). Naturally, these books have been sharply criticized from some quarters.

123. Vern Poythress, "The Church as Family," 238-42 and D. A. Carson, "Silent in the Churches: On the Role of Women in 1 Corinthians 14:33b-36," both in *Recovering Biblical Manhood and Womanhood*, eds. John Piper and Wayne Grudem (Wheaton, IL: Crossway, 1991), 152-53.

124. Ellis, *Pauline Theology*, 75, does note that single women might form a special case.

125. Irwin T. Hyatt, *Our Ordered Lives Confess* (Cambridge, MA: Harvard University Press, 1976), 98-99.

126. It is long alleged but not quite certain that Maximilla and Prisca left their husbands. McPherson's husband briefly rejoined her and their children four years after she separated from him to start her ministry. See Tucker and Liefeld, *Daughters*, 100, 364-65, 392. For Kempe, at footnote 72 above.

127. See the conjunction *gar* (γάρ), which Paul tends to use to give reasons for immediately preceding remarks.

128. Paul uses the terms *apataō* (ἀπατάω), *apatē* (ἀπάτη), *exapataō* (ἐξαπατάω) to describe who deceives—sin, evil, riches—and to warn his readers not to be deceived. He is not describing who is deceived. Paul's use of the *planaō* (πλανάω) family is similar.

129. Romans 4:1-25; 9:10-18. See 1 Corinthians 10:1-6, regarding Israel in the wilderness, Galatians 3:6-9 regarding Abraham, Galatians 4:21-31 regarding Sarah and Hagar. Paul, like other Jewish and Christian exegetes, "regards Adam and Eve as historical persons, but also as archetypes of the human race." J. N. D. Kelly, *The Pastoral Epistles* (London: Adam and Charles Black, 1963), 68. See Leonhard Goppelt, *Typos: The Typological Interpretation of the Old Testament in the New*, trans. Donald H. Madvig (Grand Rapids: Eerdmans, 1982), 136-37.

130. The Greek word *gar* (γάρ) (found in verse 13 but carrying over to 14) typically gives a reason for an immediately preceding remark.

131. Douglas Moo, "What Does It Mean Not to Teach or Have Authority Over Men? 1 Timothy 2:11-15," in *Recovering Biblical Manhood*, 190.

132. Ben Witherington, in *Women in the Earliest Churches* (Cambridge: Cambridge University Press, 1988), 122, tries to split the difference, suggesting that "not all women, but only weak and guilty women are . . . susceptible to being led astray." This sounds attractive initially, but we do not explain much when we say, "Weak women are prone to deception." Surely weak men are too.

133. Hurley, *Man and Woman in Biblical Perspective*, 206-16.

134. But four contributors to *Recovering Biblical Manhood and Womanhood*, the anthology where Moo's work appears, explore ontological differences between men and women. See John Piper, "A Vision of Biblical Complementarity," 35-52; Vern Poythress, "The Church as Family: Why Leadership in the Family Requires Male Leadership in the Church," 239; David Ayers, "The Inevitability of Failure: The Assumptions and Implementations of Modern Feminism," 312-31; Gregg Johnson, "The Biological Basis for Gender-Specific Behavior," 280-93.

135. In prior centuries some traditionalists may not have explained their view because there was no debate.

136. Van Leeuwen, *Gender and Grace*, 39-41.

137. Ibid., 45-46. Popular books on codependency decry the tendency toward enmeshment. See, for example, Robin Norwood, *Women Who Love Too Much* (Los Angeles: Jeremy Tarcher, 1985); Susan Forward and Joan Torres, *Men Who Hate Women and the Women Who Love Them* (New York: Bantam, 1986).

138. See Walter Ong, *Fighting for Life: Contest, Sexuality and Consciousness* (Ithaca, NY: Cornell University Press, 1982), and Tannen, *You Just Don't Understand*, 149-87.

139. Martin van Creveld, *Men, Women & War* (London: Cassell and Co., 2001). On women fighting, see 49-80, 99-148. On women instigating war, see 13-26. On women unsuited for combat, see 149-237.

APPENDIX 1:
WORD STUDIES FOR 1 TIMOTHY 2:12

1. See J. N. D. Kelly, *The Pastoral Epistles* (London: Adam and Charles Black, 1963), 50; George Knight, *Commentary on the Pastoral Epistles* (Grand Rapids: Eerdmans, 1992), 88-89, 140-41; I. H. Marshall, *The Pastoral Epistles* (Edinburgh: T & T Clark, 1999), 455; Thomas R. Schreiner, "An Interpretation of 1 Timothy 2:9-15: A Dialogue with Scholarship," in *Women in the Church: A Fresh Analysis of 1 Timothy 2:9-15*, ed. Andreas Kostenberger, Thomas R. Schreiner, and H. Scott Baldwin (Grand Rapids: Baker, 1995), 127-28; K. Wegenast, "Teach," in *The New International Dictionary of New Testament Theology* [NIDNTT] (Grand Rapids: Zondervan, 1971), 3:759-771.

2. See literature surveys in Marshall, *Pastoral Epistles*, 475-76 and H. Scott Baldwin, "A Difficult Word: ΑΥθΕΝΤΕΩ in 1 Timothy 2:12" and Appendix 2: "ΑΥθΕΝΤΕΩ in Ancient Greek Literature," in *Women in the Church*, 66-69.

3. David Huttar, "ΑΥθΕΝΤΕΙΝ in the Aeschylus Scholium," *Journal of the Evangelical Theological Society* 44 (2001): 625. He admits that there is one use, "but only in the ingenuity of an etymologizing hypothesis on the part of some comparatively late [thirteenth-century] Byzantine scholar" (625).

4. See Baldwin, "ΑΥθΕΝΤΕΩ in 1 Timothy 2:12," 72-80 and 269-305; and Leland E. Wilshire, "The TLG Computer and Further Reference to ΑΥθΕΝΤΕΩ in 1 Timothy 2:12," *New Testament Studies* 34 (1988): 120-34; and "1 Timothy 2:12 Revisited: A Reply to Paul W. Barnett and Timothy J. Harris," *Evangelical Quarterly* 65 (1993): 54.

5. Schreiner, "An Interpretation of 1 Timothy 2:9-15," 131, especially note 116.

6. Baldwin, "ΑΥθΕΝΤΕΩ in 1 Timothy 2:12," 75.

7. George Knight, "ΑΥθΕΝΤΕΩ in Reference to Women in 1 Timothy 2:12," *New Testament Studies* 30 (1984): 143-57.

8. Andreas Kostenberger, "A Complex Sentence Structure in 1 Timothy 2:12," in *Women in the Church*, 84-104.

9. See also Matthew 21:21; John 12:48; Romans 15:1; 1 Corinthians 15:34; Hebrews 13:17. But *kai mē* (καὶ μή) occasionally links two positives, as in Matthew 13:19 and Romans 12:2.

10. Feminist scholars sometimes say *autheteō* (αὐθεντέω) must mean "domineer" rather than "exercise authority," since Paul would have used a more common verb for exercising authority, such as *exousiazō* (ἐξουσιάζω) or *kyrieuō* (κυριεύω) if he wanted to discuss its positive use. It is reasonable to wonder why a rare word is used; *autheteō* (αὐθεντέω) appears just once in the New Testament. But the alternative words are hardly common. He uses *exousiazō* (ἐξουσιάζω) just three times and *kyrieuō* (κυριεύω) just six.

APPENDIX 2:
WIVES OR DEACONESSES IN 1 TIMOTHY 3:11

1. John Calvin, *Institutes of the Christian Religion*, trans. Ford Lewis Battles (Philadelphia: Westminster Press, 1960): 2:1061 (4.3.9).

INDEX

SCRIPTURE INDEX